To Laurence
with best wishes
Francis Hartman

Don't
Park
Your
Brain
Outside

Don't Park Your Brain Outside

A Practical Guide to Improving Shareholder Value with SMART Management

Francis T. Hartman

Project Management Institute

Library of Congress Cataloging-in-Publication Data

Hartman, Francis T., 1950–
    Don't park your brain outside : a practical guide to improving
shareholder value with SMART management / Francis T. Hartman.
        p.   cm.
    Includes bibliographical references and index.
    ISBN: 1-880410-48-6 (pbk. : alk. paper)
    1. Industrial project management.   I. Title.
HD69.P75H373   1999
658.4'04 – – dc21   99–41752
                                                                       CIP

ISBN: 1-880410-48-6

Published by: Project Management Institute, Inc.
                Four Campus Boulevard
                Newtown Square, Pennsylvania 19073-3299 USA
                Phone: 610-356-4600 or Visit our website: www.pmi.org

10 9 8 7 6 5 4 3 2 1

Contents

Figures

Tables

Foreword

Some years ago, in the wee hours of the morning, as I was pouring over schedules, project plans, and budgets for a client, I had a moment of clarity. Quite simply: *There has to be a better way to manage projects.* Whether updating clients on current status, forecasting a completion date, or planning the next series of project activities, traditional project management methods were proving to be too reactive and too time consuming.

I was convinced that there must be a set of project management techniques that would ensure that both my clients and I had the project information that we needed—when we needed it—and that would allow me to anticipate issues before they became crises. More than a rigid set of project management steps, we needed a whole new framework—a new philosophy—that would facilitate clear communication among all project team members and project stakeholders.

Since that night long ago, I've managed hundreds of client engagements, and as chief knowledge officer for KPMG Consulting, LLC, I have found the *better way*—the SMART way.

At KPMG Consulting, we've used SMART on a number of critical projects, and I've experienced the transformational change that Dr. Hartman's SMART philosophy can inspire among organizations and individuals. Whether managing a multi-million dollar global client engagement; an internal project, or simply managing day-to-day activities, SMART offers a refreshingly simple set of concepts and principles that generate dramatic improvements in productivity, quality, and cost effectiveness.

In this book, Dr. Hartman describes the SMART tools, processes, and competencies that combine to improve communication, to better assess and mitigate risk, and to build more effective teams. He addresses many of the issues that project managers and professionals wrestle with every day:

- Striking and maintaining a balance among business objectives, technical delivery issues, and social concerns
- Achieving stakeholder alignment and explicit agreement on project expectations

- Mitigating risk in a way that has a visible and tangible impact on the project schedule and cost
- Building better project teams
- Recognizing that single-point estimates are misleading and potentially dangerous to the success of a project
- Identifying clearly what will be delivered, when, and by whom
- Taking a "less is more" approach to reporting by focusing squarely on management's key information needs.

Whether you're an overworked project manager staring at the Gantt charts that have begun to substitute for office wallpaper, or a project team member trying to maximize your project effectiveness, there is a better way: SMART Project Management™.

Kevin L. Martin
Chief Knowledge Officer
KPMG Consulting, LLC
McLean, VA
www.kpmgconsulting.com

Acknowledgments and Thanks

This book took a lot of hard work and *my* kind of research: stealing good ideas from more than three places. Many people have contributed to this book. Most of them did so without realizing it and even without me realizing it, as I was influenced by their ideas and, more so, by their practices. While many contributed ideas, a few gave more in the way of encouragement, help, inspiration, and coffee.

Margaret: Thank you for staying my friend and wife through the production of this book and for your faith in my ability to get this project done. Especially, thanks for being so patient with my frail temper as technology tried to beat me.

Tamsin, Richard, Christopher, and Kirsten: thanks for being so patient and generous in giving up your dad to this work for so long.

To my friends and colleagues at KPMG, who helped with ideas, teased progress out of me, and helped develop the ideas into powerful working tools:

- Tom Gosse: advisor and chief cattle prodder.
- Mike O'Neil: one of the most creative thinkers—must be the Irish in you. Who else would emphasize the importance of signing *on* to a project plan, rather than signing *off*? Mike also added several other neat and essential ideas to the product, including identifying the need for a project lexicon.
- Ken Hanley: a practitioner who knows how to make things happen with SMART Management™, and who has helped others do so, too.
- Kevin Martin: thank you for the leadership role you played in getting SMART into the workplace.

To my colleagues, associates, and students at the University of Calgary, where I have the privilege of holding the Chair in Project Management, who all contributed time and ideas:

- George Jergeas, Associate Professor and contracts whiz.
- Janice Thomas, Assistant Professor and critical thinker.
- Elke Romahn, Research Associate and hardworking, organized, and enthusiastic collaborator.
- Doctoral candidates: Connie Guss, Greg Skulmoski, Keith Pedwell, Dean Sheppard—thank you for tolerating my distractions, listening to my ideas, and contributing your advice and suggestions.

- Masters' students and others who have graduated from the project management program at the University of Calgary: you probably will never realize how much you contributed as you shared your ideas and patiently listened and reacted to mine.

Industry and government sponsors who always gave much more than money to the program. Thank you for the opportunity to use your projects to try out my ideas, for your contributions in the classroom—from which I stole the best—and for your continued advice on what is important to your businesses in terms of teaching good management practices and in the research that was important to you. Because there are too many of you, please forgive me for just including those of you who are currently on the Advisory Board of the Organization for Project Advancement and Leadership (OPAL), an industry organization based at the University of Calgary, Alberta, Canada:

- Dick Balfour, President Richard Balfour Engineer Construct and Fellow of PMI
- Ardean Braun, Vice President TransCanada International (Chair of Research Taskforce)
- Larry Brocklebank, Vice President, ATCO Structures
- Tom Brown, Head, Civil Engineering, University of Calgary
- Raleigh Dehaney, VP Education of PMI, SAC, Telus Mobility
- Howie Dingle, Vice President, Imperial Oil Resources (Past Chair)
- Jim Frideres, Office of VP Research, University of Calgary
- Pete Garrett, Vice President, Nortel Networks (Chair)
- Jim Goodwin, Partner, Cohos Evamy & Partners
- Tom Gosse, Partner, KPMG
- Ken Hanley, KPMG
- Ken Harris, Senior Project Manager, SNC Lavalin Engineers & Constructors Inc.
- Doug Harrison, Vice President, Reid Crowther & Partners
- Kevin Hogan, Vice President, Shell Canada Limited, (Past Chair)
- Peter Jeffrey, Vice President, Computing Devices Canada
- George Jergeas, Professor, Project Management Specialization
- Jennifer Krahn, Project Manager, OPAL
- Conrad Loban, President, Conrad Loban Consulting
- Ben Magnusson, Shell Canada
- Mike Maher, Dean, Faculty of Management, University of Calgary
- Roger Mapp, Vice President, Bantrel Inc.
- Greg McAvoy, Nortel Networks
- Gordon Moore, Head, Chemical Engineering, University of Calgary
- Bob Peterson, President, R. C. Peterson Ltd.
- Dave Phillips, Engineering Manager, Optima Engineers & Constructors (Chair Curriculum Taskforce)
- Murray Propp, Vice President, Tiger Resources
- Gerry Protti, President, PanCanadian Resources Limited

- Zuhair Shlah, Executive, SHL Systemhouse Inc.
- Allan Side, Director, Mutual Life of Canada
- Peggy Simons, Engineering Internship Program, University of Calgary
- Dave Stuart, VP and General Manager, VECO Engineering Ltd.
- Ron Tibbatts, PMI Representative, Imperial Oil Resources
- S. Chan Wirasinghe, Dean, Faculty of Engineering, University of Calgary.

To all of you, thanks for the support.

Thanks to the many colleagues and friends in the research and academic world and to wise folks all over, whose ideas have influenced me. It would take pages to name you all, so please consider yourselves thanked, even if I have not included you here:

> Chimay Anumba, Karlos Artto, Andrew Baldwin, Al Cahoon, Davidson Frame, Frank Harris, Ralph Levene, Rolf Lundin, Ronald McCaffer, Christoph Midler, Roger Midler, Peter Morris, Dick Neale, Joseph Paradi, Jeffrey Pinto, Asbjorn Rolstados, Nigel Shrive, Ed Silver, Rodney Turner, Stephen Wearne.

The work that I do at the University of Calgary is supported in large part by the Natural Sciences and Engineering Research Council of Canada and the Social Sciences and Humanities Research Council of Canada. These research-funding agencies support a program of Chairs across Canada focused on management of technological change. To them and my Chair colleagues across Canada, also a thanks—you have been another wellspring of ideas, inspiration, and support.

Last, but not least, thanks to the team at PMI® who helped turn my manuscript into a real book: Toni Knott, who edited the book and provided all sorts of help and advice while making it a much better project; Michelle Owen, who made the graphics work; and Lisa Fisher, who made sure we had all fixed the inevitable little mistakes.

Finally, thank *you* for buying this book. If you have suggestions, stories, or ideas, please let me know. I can be reached at: smartmanager@hotmail.com. You can fax me at (403) 282-7026, call me at (403) 220-7178, or write to me at:

Project Management Specialization
The University of Calgary
Room ENF 230
2500 University Drive NW
Calgary, Alberta, Canada
T392A3

A Personal Note

From the desk of Francis Hartman, Ph.D., P.Eng., PMP
e-mail: fhartman@UCalgary.ca or smartmanager@hotmail.com

Dear Reader:

First, let me thank and congratulate you on acquiring this book. I hope that you enjoy reading it, and that it leads to better projects for you.

Do not be surprised if I have written about things that you already do or know. I hope that you will find enough that is fresh and new to enable you to have better projects in the future, regardless of how good they are today.

If nothing in this book is new—then give it to a client or a supplier or two. At least they will know why you are successful and why you do things the way that you do!

SMART Management has its roots in both project and organizational management. It builds on the strengths of both and helps to bridge the critical gap between the two.

SMART Management builds on the wisdom, knowledge, and talent of numerous practitioners from around the world. Although I have added my own ideas, my primary contribution is in its assembly. It works as a *balanced*, *cohesive*, *aware*, and *effective* way to deliver projects, programs, and organizational promises.

I wish you every success and would be proud to make even a small contribution.

Best wishes,

Francis Hartman

Francis Hartman
Calgary, 2000

GETTING STARTED

It says: "You are here!"

Chapter 1

INTRODUCTION TO SMART MANAGEMENT

Everything we do of any significance today is probably a project; making every project a winner is what SMART Management™ is all about. Not winning with a project happens often, because the odds are against us from the outset. This book includes the gleanings of years as a practitioner and researcher, one who has had the advantage of working with many of the best in the business. Being SMART about what we do requires a balance of business, technical, and social issues. We need to maintain balance on our team, and we have to balance tools, processes, and competencies.

SMART Management is a cohesive collection of ideas taken from the best habits of exceptional managers. You will recognize much of what you see in this book as things that you already do. What makes SMART smart is the use of all of these habits at the same time. Flying a plane really well is totally useless if you cannot land or navigate.

SMART is a balanced approach to managing finite work. It is a risk-aware and stakeholder-sensitive way of managing projects, programs, and businesses—both in the public and private sectors—in a fast-changing environment. As you read through this book, I hope you will enjoy the experience, and that it will get you thinking about how you can make your workplace even more successful.

SMART Management is a culmination of many years of theoretical and practical research followed by tests on what are now hundreds of projects and businesses. To understand and use SMART Management at a basic level and reap the rewards, you will need to know what SMART is (Section A), its principles and theory (Section B), and then how to apply it (Section C). To test where you are and identify areas for improvement, you will need to do some self-evaluation and problem solving (Section D). For further reading, consult the bibliography, which tells you where I stole ideas.

1.1   Accelerating Change Is Here to Stay!

Many of us are faced with challenges at work, regardless of our roles; many of these challenges are driven by change. Our organizations, the business world in which we work, technology, and society have all been knocked off balance by changes. As we search for ways to deal with them, many of us cling to the management processes that previously worked, which is natural. Why change that too when we can barely cope with all the rest of what is going on around us?

What we see in the way of changes that affect us is becoming so complex that we struggle to understand them, let alone deal with them. To make matters worse, we see real or apparent inconsistencies or contradictions. More and more, we end up in situations where our bosses and our customers or clients seem irrational or just plain stupid. To make matters worse, the systems and tools we have in place to bring some structure and order into our businesses seem to be increasingly ineffective. What is going on (apart from the obvious and ubiquitous changes) that is making life so difficult? If we look for patterns rather than details, we are in effect stepping back from the mess that we see, and, as we step back, the patterns become clearer. Think of being lost in a strange town. As the traffic gets busier and there are more street signs, traffic signals, and pedestrians trying to rush across the street, it becomes harder to figure the correct route to take. If we could hover a few hundred feet in the air, we would see the pattern of the streets, and it would be much easier to find our way.

By the same token, if we hover over our business environment, and look for patterns, we can see a pattern and an easier way to work. This book is about learning to effectively rise above the details of our everyday problems and taking advantage of this new skill to make us more effective.

 Do not get bogged down in detail. Understanding the big picture—what is going on around us—helps us see how to deal with situations more effectively.

1.2   The Start of SMART Management

What got things started on the path to SMART Project Management™ was partly serendipity. A senior vice president of a large multinational company offered me some advice on how we should develop our research program at the University of Calgary. He told me:

> We are darned good at delivering our projects on time, within budget, and to customer expectations. The only little fly in the ointment is that we deliver the wrong projects! Help us find a way to solve our front-end problem, and you will do something very useful.

A few days later, another advisor—this time, one of the retired principals of a large engineering company, who was partly responsible for its growth into a hugely successful global business—suggested that enough had changed in the world that we should probably be looking for a "new model for project management." I took this to mean a distillation of the best practices that we could find. With both pieces of advice ringing in my head, I set about the task with a series of pilot studies that eventually helped us piece together SMART Project Management. It led to an interesting approach to research, heavily influenced by years as a practitioner in industry. My definition of research is that if you take ideas from one place, it is theft; from two places, it becomes plagiarism. But if you take ideas from three or more places, well, that has got to be research! So we stole from lots of places, and we could, because the ideas were already there; they were public knowledge or were used with permission of the source. The result was a view from a few hundred feet above, revealing a pattern of management tricks, behaviors, practices, and processes that were simple, cohesive, and potentially very effective. This set of tools and ways of doing things are what eventually became what we now call SMART Management. In this book, I focus on the critically important part that delivers or sustains shareholder value: SMART Project Management.

 The first step in managing projects well is to pick the right project. No matter how well you manage it, if it is the wrong project, it is bound to fail.

 The second step in managing projects well is to keep its management process relevant to what you are doing and as simple as possible.

1.3 SMART Management of Projects

Managing projects in a way that is relevant to the project and yet as simple as possible requires attention to a number of factors. These factors, put together, give a holistic view of the project. First, we need to ensure that we keep the project in tune with the organization for which we work. Any project undertaken by any organization needs to pass a simple test: Can we identify what the project does to add value? How does it help the organization achieve its strategic objective? If we cannot do this, no matter how big or small the project is, we should not be doing it.

The second item to consider is what we need to do to minimize the waste of effort associated with so many projects. Wasted effort manifests itself in a number of ways. We see it as redundant work; effort spent meeting unjustified deadlines; doing the wrong thing and having to go back and fix it later; waiting for information, materials, or tools; dealing with items that have just become critical and thus necessitate a sudden change in plans and priorities; and much more.

The third item we need to address is having an effective team working for or with us on the project. This is made tough by a number of factors. First, we do not get to pick our team most of the time. We usually have to make do with a group of people who have not necessarily worked together, may not want to work together, or already have a lot of things to do for their regular jobs. They may be asked to work on our project in addition to one or even several other projects, which usually seem to have higher priority! Therefore, we need to have an effective way to manage our project teams so that they will *want* to work on our projects.

The fourth element in a holistic approach is the ability to keep an eye on the world around us. It will not keep still while we try to make our project work. Not only that, but the chances are good that our project will affect this world in some way. Typically, the larger the project, the greater the impact, although this is not necessarily true. What does it mean? Two things in particular: 1) we are managing something that will change, and 2) what we are managing will happen in a changing world. We are working with transition.

The word SMART is an acronym. It represents the four points that we have just reviewed.

- SM = Strategically Managed
- A = Aligned
- R = Regenerative work environment
- T = Transitional management.

To deliver successful projects, we need to take a holistic and balanced approach that reflects the need to address being strategically managed and aligned, working with an effective and regenerative team, and recognizing that what we manage is transitional.

The significance of these four elements is discussed in this chapter, together with how they provide a framework to address the apparent contradictions in the management of increasingly complex projects and the higher uncertainty that characterizes many of today's business needs.

1.4   What Exactly Is SMART Project Management?

The objective of SMART Project Management is to deliver projects significantly more efficiently than *classical* or *modern* project management techniques. Traditional project management is based on many principles and assumptions that date back to the 1950s and 1960s. Just as generals had for many years fought the previous war when a new one broke out—look at the Magniot Line in France at the outset of World War II and how we tried to fight in Vietnam—so we are managing today's projects with yesterday's ideas. And has not everything significantly changed? Today's projects may be described as both more uncertain and more complex than those from previous decades. (This is explored further later in the book.) Dealing with increased uncertainty and complexity does require quite different skills in the management of projects. These skills may be summarized as follows:

- We need to be more aware of the business environment and the drivers that set the ground rules for success of our projects. In other words, we need to know how to manage our projects in the context of the business strategy of the company or organization that wants the results toward which we will be working. This is particularly important when the results are not fully understood or declared at the outset of the project—an increasingly common phenomenon!
- We need to understand the technical implications of the project. Are we headed into high- or low-risk technology? How stable is it? How sustainable? The answers to these questions will help us understand the significance of the decisions that we make in terms of technology. An example of how these are often not fully or

carefully thought through is in the growing use of data warehouse software, the large and completely integrated data management systems for corporations. Currently, they are so expensive to purchase and install that only the larger corporations can afford them. Also, what happens when a system is outgrown or becomes obsolete? Will these companies have a problem on their hands that will make the Year 2000 issue seem trivial in comparison?

- Finally, we need to understand the societal issues around the projects we undertake. They are potentially huge. Two current examples are 1) the link between tobacco and cancer and 2) the link between greenhouse gasses (carbon dioxide and methane, for example) and the rising temperatures of our home planet. New issues will relate to the jobs that are destroyed (and the hopes and aspirations of whole sections of our global society), as we introduce new technologies. The full impact of information and telecommunication technologies probably has not been completely understood yet. The potential impact may be seen in a few obvious examples: distribution of pornography on the Internet, electronic fraud, and invasion of privacy. Less-obvious examples include the growing gap between those who have access to information technology and those who do not. We are rapidly disenfranchising a whole segment of society, as wealth distribution becomes more polarized, and with it the tendency toward a tiered society develops. Historically, tiered societies have led to political instability.

Managers need to stay in tune at all times with these three primary sets of issues: 1) business, 2) technology, and 3) societal (the larger environment). Staying in tune and fully understanding are not the same thing. There is far too much information around for us to absorb even a small portion of the whole. What is important is to maintain a balanced and (as far as practical) an objective view. This balance is a thread throughout SMART Management.

 Successful projects are based on a balanced scorecard that considers business, technical, and societal needs.

1.5 A Bird's-Eye View of Our Product

The need to maintain this balance is founded on our need to develop the bird's-eye view of our business and projects. We must pay attention to detail while never losing the big picture. Our businesses are becoming more unpredictable, due to rapid change in our environment. They are becoming more complex, as we integrate more technologies, business lines, functions, and cultures. We need to understand the impact of increased uncertainty and complexity.

 Watch for the effect of size and impact, complexity, and uncertainty when planning and managing your project.

Uncertainty and Complexity: What They Mean

Figure 1.1 shows a matrix of uncertainty against complexity. As with all two-by-two matrices, it illustrates just one simple view of the world, and a grossly simplified one at that. However, it does help to explain why so many of today's projects are failing and where to look to find better ways of managing them. First, let us understand uncertainty and complexity as intended here.

Uncertainty is a measure of the clarity and predictability of the outcome of a business venture or project. *Complexity* is a measure of the difficulty of effectively communicating between stakeholders on such a venture. The number of functional groups that need to be represented on the project team affects complexity. As technology becomes more sophisticated, so the need for more and different technical expertise is required. Technical people do not all speak the same language.

Figure 1.1 shows how traditional project management practices have evolved to handle more complex projects (such as nuclear power stations, offshore oil platforms, and satellite launches), as well as more uncertain projects (such as R&D, software development, new product development, and advertising). However, in today's world, everything is happening so fast that even the traditionally stable projects are becoming harder to predict, and the previously *simple* projects involve more complicated technologies and hence more companies and more complexity. This means that most projects are moving into the high complexity-high uncertainty quadrant.

The problem of managing these types of projects using modern project management techniques is that the techniques are an evolution of traditional project management, and the evolution has gone in just about diametrically opposite directions to address increased complexity and higher uncertainty. As the characteristics of the two paths taken in the development of project management practices are not complementary, they will not work when both sets of solutions are put together. The evidence lies

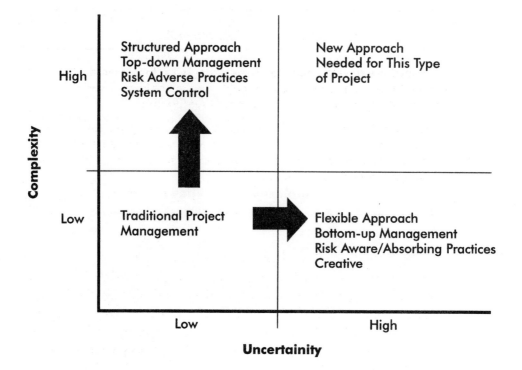

Figure 1.1 Uncertainty versus Complexity

in the frequently heard arguments over whether or not one approach to project management is better than another in a given situation.

 A simple and effective approach to project management is needed to address today's complex and uncertain projects.

1.6   Background to SMART Project Management

The start to development of SMART Project Management came in part from the analysis mentioned earlier; the other part of the process was the result of three different events. The first of these was the formation of a research advisory panel for my chair at the University of Calgary. The panel quickly identified a number of areas for research in project management that were important to industry. They all revolved around either solving specific problems or addressing the fact that project management was not evolving at the same rate as technology, industry itself, and the business environment generally.

The second event was a blinding discovery of the obvious—a simple definition of a successful project: *A project is successful if all the stakeholders are happy.* This gem of a definition is self-fulfilling. Interestingly, it has nothing directly to do with *controlling* quality, cost, time, scope, and safety (the traditional domain of project management). It does, however, have everything to do with knowing who your stakeholders are and with understanding what they expect from the project. This is because if we meet or exceed their expectations, we are going to be successful.

The last event was linked to seeking patterns in project failures. Here is one for the books—well, for this book, at least! In the numerous failed projects examined by us, the *ultimate* cause of failure was always the same. Cost overruns were due to poor estimates, missed elements of scope, and more; but in the end all was due to inadequate communications. Schedule overruns were due to work being more complex than anticipated, resources not being available, the scheduler being too optimistic, and more. Yet again, when we checked, there was a breakdown in communication at some point in all cases. The breakdown could be attributed to many factors, including lack of knowledge or experience, oversight, assumptions made, language, and, yes, even deliberate action or inaction!

Now, let's pause for a moment, and look at what we have—a matrix that says we need a new approach to project management, because our projects are too complex *and* too uncertain for conventional approaches (no matter how they have evolved) to work. Next, we have an identified need to develop a new and possibly different way to manage projects. Then, we see that success of projects is directly linked to having happy stakeholders, and failure is the result of a breakdown in communication. Is there a connection?

Try this. If we can manage stakeholders' expectations concerning uncertainty in projects, and we can overcome the barriers to communication created by complexity, we may have a new model for project management. If this is the problem, it is also a signpost to a solution. Our real challenge, then, is to discover the tricks of the most successful project managers, because they are probably solving these problems. This was the next step in the quest for a better approach to managing today's and tomorrow's complex and uncertain projects.

 Success of a project is directly linked to meeting stakeholder expectations, and failure is linked to communication breakdowns.

1.7   How Do We Find and Address the Real Challenge of Successful Project Management?

Who manages exceptionally well? How do we measure this? Best practices have a problem; we all believe that we use them. If we did not, why are we doing what we do? Benchmarking has a problem, too; in fact it has two basic problems, although they are not insurmountable. First, we all measure things in at least slightly different ways. For example, is insurance cost for a project part of the project's cost, or is it included in corporate overhead? Where do you charge time and costs expended on canceled or deferred projects—to the next project, to overhead, or does it *all depend?* If so, on what does it depend? When does project development—the piece of the project that gets it started—get charged to the project itself? Or does it? What about the cost of senior management time associated with your project? There are endless ways of accounting for these items, and each organization does things differently. Accounting practices, even within one organization, are not always consistent from one department to another or from one project to another.

In a recent benchmarking study, one of the measures for capital project efficiency in the oil and gas industry was the cost of engineering as a percentage of total installed cost for the project. How is this measured? What sense does it make to measure it? The original idea was to gain some evaluation of the effectiveness of strategic alliances set between owner organizations and their engineering contractors. Was there an optimum percentage? Was it a case of the lower, the better (we are getting the most value for money in engineering); the higher, the better (we are getting the most value for money in construction); or was it in the middle (we are getting the most mediocre results)? There is something patently wrong with the last option. The problem with the first one is easy to see when we suggest doing less engineering and ending with a much-too-expensive facility. The ratio is very low, but we have not achieved what we wanted. A similar argument will destroy the sense in the second benchmark; just charge double for your engineering, and you win on this score! For the investor, the measure is clear and simple: return on investment.

 The only truly effective benchmark for project success is the long-term return gained on the investment in the project.

1.8   Measuring Return on Investment for Projects

Now the new challenge is how do we measure this? It should be simple; unfortunately, it is not. We are back to accounting principles and to taking a holistic—businesswide—look at our projects. Let me explain with an example of a project being restarted as I write. The project cost over $200 million about ten years ago. If we include this investment (with virtually no return, except some knowledge of what *not* to do, assuming that we will not make the same mistake again) in the financial model, together with interest, then the new project will never be profitable. If we do not include it, to where do these project charges disappear? In the end, someone has to pay for this. The cost affects return on shareholders' investment; if we look just at return on shareholder investment as a benchmark, perhaps we will all have to become major banks in Canada. They keep breaking their own records for return on investment! Maybe this is what General Electric did when it started the hugely successful GE Capital Corporation. This is all still too complicated; we also need to consider the projects that contribute nothing to the bottom line yet need to be done to survive in business. We need to take another step back. In our quest for best practices, we asked a simpler question: Who is really smart about how they do business?

As this is an open-ended question, it is unlikely that we would have gotten very far. So we used our discovery of how success and failure are linked to uncertainty and complexity and asked questions around alignment of stakeholders, practices, processes, and anything else in the business of managing projects. To contain the questions, we developed a simple questionnaire, and set out to find some leads. In the process, we were able to identify industries, businesses, and individuals that were exceptional in one—and, very occasionally, more than one—aspect of project management. For example, we found a whole industry that delivers projects on time; it does so routinely, so much so that we would be surprised if it failed. We all know the industry; we are just not conscious of this skill that it possesses.

 If we want to learn from best practices, we need to find where consistent excellence is achieved, and then work out how it is done.

1.9   How SMART Was Developed

I hope you are wondering about the industry that delivers projects on time. Let me tell you a bit more about it before I tell you which industry it is. This industry does *not* use most of the following project management tools:

- Critical path method (CPM) scheduling: It may not even know how to spell CPM—and probably couldn't care less!
- Earned value techniques.
- Work breakdown structures (WBS) or the other structures—organizational breakdown structures (OBS), responsibility breakdown structures (RBS), and all the other BS's that are around in the world of classical project management.
- Many of the classical project management tools advocated in textbooks.

Now this is not true of all cases in this industry, but it is true in many of them. While we are about it, this industry is more successful (when measured in terms of business success, image, safety, and health of people working in it) than the construction industry or the military—both traditional users of classical project management.

Live entertainment is the industry to which I am referring. Imagine opening night at the opera. The lights dim as you settle into your seat with the taste of champagne still lingering on your lips. The overture is played, and the curtain rises. In dances the chorus—in cheap underwear, because the costumes were not ready. It is just about inconceivable, isn't it? Now try this. What time do you turn on the television for the six o'clock news? Stupid question, eh? What does this industry do to deliver all of its projects on time? Part of the answer can be attributed to the deadline imperative, but there is more. We know this because *imperative* deadlines are routinely missed on other projects in other industries.

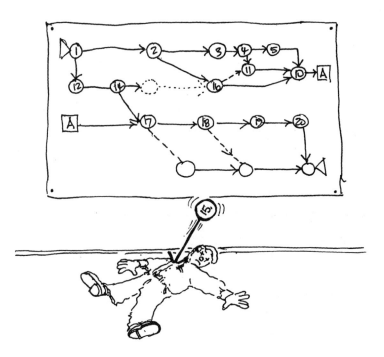

Inactivity-on-arrow scheduling.

So we looked further and found a pattern, which we (metaphorically) put in a small glass vial. We did the same with the tricks and wisdom of superstar project managers and companies that were particularly good at doing one aspect of project management. Then we took all these vials of wisdom and lined them up in some sort of order. What emerged was either a smart and effective way of managing projects, which was refreshing and challenged many normal practices, or we were sniffing glue. To discover which was the right approach, we experimented with the processes, tools, and tricks on real projects in industry. In some cases, the project teams knew that we were trying something different and new; in other cases, they did not. Although what we were doing was different, we said that we were training them in project management and gave no hint of the process being in any way special or different. Thus, we hoped to gain some measure of the impact of our intervention as both a new process and as an apparently established process that was not really experimental, just new to the team. In all cases, we worked with experienced professionals, so our benchmarking would be against at least the average performance of the organization or team.

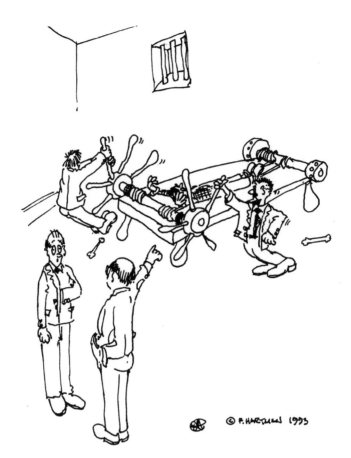

That's our client; we're trying to get a decision.

An important part of the new project management approach was that the teams could own and modify the model to suit their own cultures and business styles. As a result, what this book presents is not a silver-bullet or a prescriptive process that will lead to guaranteed success; I do not believe that those things really exist. What we have is a framework for success.

 There is no silver-bullet solution to effective project (or general) management, but using the best ideas from different industries and companies goes a long way toward improving performance by leaps and bounds.

1.10   SMART: A Framework, Not a Structure

SMART was never intended to kill creativity; on the contrary, it contains elements intended to improve our creative skills on projects. Any single and prescribed system for managing does just that; by definition, it tells us—step by step—how to do something. No room for creativity there! SMART is simply a set of general guidelines that will help you successfully manage your projects *your way*. It is important, however, that we recognize exactly what this means: freedom to do what you need in order to achieve your project objectives. But it also means that we need to be very sure that we are doing the right project in the first place! In a way, we are talking of controlled anarchy! (There will be more on this in the next chapter.)

You obviously know your business and types of projects, team, and culture far better than I do. So it follows that you will know more than I do about how to manage your project. What I offer, with SMART Project Management, is a framework that will make your life easier. It does so by taking you through a set of processes that will help in addressing the issues that are important to the success of your mission. Also included in this framework are tools and techniques that have been proven as useful in improving the success of projects. Finally, the SMART approach is cohesive; the *glue* that makes it so is its philosophy.

The philosophy behind SMART Management is described in more detail in Section B. Presently, it is important to stress just three things.

First, SMART Management is people focused without losing sight of why we are in business in the first place. If our enterprise is not successful, we are going to be out of a job anyway. Second, SMART Management is balanced. At all times, we need to be aware of the business, technical, and social issues related to the task at hand; this helps us keep the big picture in mind. In other words, we will try to keep the view from a few hundred feet above while we are negotiating the traffic of day-to-day issues at the operating level. Finally, we need to "go with the flow," which is not *wimping* out. If we use surfing as an analogy, we are saying that we cannot control the waves, but we can manage our surfboard to help us accomplish what we want done. This is not a new idea; the Zen serenity prayer nicely summarizes it: "Change the things that can be changed, accept those that cannot, and have the wisdom to know the difference."

Balance is the key to effective management of any venture. Focus management effort on the things you can influence or change.

1.11   The Structure of This Book

This book is written in four parts. The first part includes this chapter and provides the setting for SMART Management. The key to success is to know what it is and how to avoid failure. To do that, we need to understand what drives failure. With this under our belts, we move on to the next part.

Section B provides the principles and theory of SMART Management. It gives the underlying knowledge that helps us understand the way in which we need to manage projects and how to link the various tools, techniques, and processes that are detailed later. This knowledge is the foundation upon which the SMART framework is built.

The third part of the book, Section C, provides the SMART framework, laid out in the chronological order in which it is used on projects.

The final section, D, contains two chapters. The first one provides a maturity model. The model lays out the major phases of sustainable growth in capability when managing with the SMART approach, and helps determine what additional knowledge or skills may be needed to make SMART not only work for us, but also allow us to maintain a competitive edge into the future.

The very last chapter is filled with error messages. Really, this chapter is for those of us who like to buy books, but do not have time to read them. We are also the people who do not read instructions or user manuals when we buy new toys, technology, or software. We are also the people who have no time to plan a project—we have to get going—but seem to have lots of time to fix problems and redo work later. We are also good at panicking, which is why we need this chapter to help us find the information required to use SMART Management effectively.

 Even if you follow the best advice, and do things the smartest way possible, things will still go wrong. The key, therefore, is to recognize the problem and solve it.

Chapter 2

UNDERSTANDING
SUCCESS AND FAILURE

Traditionally, we determine the success of a project on the basis that it came in on time, was completed within budget, and did what it set out to do. The trouble is that what was included in the budget and what was to be done by a certain date are all too often unclear. Worse, we frequently do not realize at the outset how unclear they are.

John is a senior executive in a large engineering company. He and his team had been working on a specific project with a client and several other alliance partners for just over a year. The project was estimated to cost about $200 million. Contractual commitments determined the completion date. There was little doubt in anybody's mind what the project was to deliver.

John was concerned that the team was not functioning as well as it could be. He knew there were undercurrents of disagreement, but he could not put his finger on the precise problem. Could I help?

John brought the key team members into one room. I asked three questions about completion and success of the project. The answers were so varied that it seemed we were talking about different projects. The questions were simple enough. First, after we spent the budget and finished the project, we knew we were done because we had just delivered something. What was that something? Answers ranged from a mechanically complete process plant to one that had just completed twelve months of operation at expected productivity figures or better. The dates associated with these definitions are typically eighteen months apart. But everyone had the same "project completion" date in mind!

The second question had more to do with understanding success. When we delivered the final item, why was the project successful? Again, I received a large number of answers, this time ranging from the operators had accepted the facility to producing product from the new facility at $2 per unit less than the adjacent existing facility.

The third question was to discover who really voted on the answers to the first two questions. We found that we had not involved all of the right stakeholders; specifically, the VP Operations had not been involved.

We can complete projects on time and within budget, but if the stakeholders are not happy with the result, we will have a failed project on our hands. Equally, most of us have seen projects overrun budgets and schedules, and even not do what they set out to do, and yet they are lauded as being hugely successful. We really need to understand the differences between successful and failed projects in terms of the *real* factors that affect this perception, rather than just the traditional (classical project management) factors of safety, quality, cost, schedule, and scope. This chapter opens the doors to these other factors and sets the ground rules for successful (SMART) project management.

 Never assume you really know what a project is about. Ask the team members what they understand by success and completion, and know who else to check with to get the right answers.

2.1   Controlled Anarchy

In Chapter 1, I briefly, and perhaps dangerously, mentioned controlled anarchy. What is this all about? What we are trying to do is maximize our chances of success in business; this is what good management is all about. In order to do this, we need to use our brains, which in turn means that we need enough freedom from organizational and other restrictions to be able to do so.

My mother gave me some wonderful advice when I was still very young and I had asked her permission to do something. I cannot remember what I wanted permission to do, but I clearly remember the advice that I received: she told me not to ask. If I asked for permission to do something, she said, someone was likely to say no! I have used that advice often since then, and I offered it to my own children. The trick is to know when to ask and when not to ask.

I do not know of any cases of someone being chastised for being successful or for making people happy, except perhaps by the particularly unpleasant and vindictive folks we all come across from time to time. But is their opinion worth anything to you?

Therefore, controlled anarchy is all about being creative, successful, and making people happy with the results of what we do. It is about ignoring or working around foolish procedures and practices, with or without permission. It is also about understanding and supporting what our organization is all about. It is about constructive contribution. This is where the control comes in.

To what does this reduce in terms of managing our businesses and our projects? Simply put, it means:

- Understand what your organization is trying to do.
- Know your part in achieving this.
- Identify the degrees of freedom you really have to get your job done.
- Discard the artificial constraints to being effective.
- Remember that, as part of an organization, we need to work with it—not against it.
- Remember that failure is invariably due to breakdowns in communication, so be sure to communicate where and when needed.
- Respect people's ideas of what success is for your project, then manage expectations.

To do all of this well, we need to understand where we are going with our project, and we need to be clear about how our project contributes to the well-being and growth of our business or organization. If we keep helping the business to be successful, we will be successful as well. Our methods and processes will not be challenged, so we can be creative in how we deliver our projects!

 If we really know what our business is about and we work with the business to achieve its goals, we will have real freedom to be creative and highly effective. Policy and procedures will no longer be a restriction.

2.2   Defining Project Success and Failure

There are several aspects of success and failure to which we often do not give enough thought; acknowledging that there are degrees of success and failure is one of the most important. There are also perceptions of these results, and they are often not the same for all stakeholders. Not only that, but we change our own ideas as the project evolves. Thus, we spend much of our time as project managers trying to hit a moving target. The biggest challenge is not hitting the moving target but knowing where it is! So, the first trick in managing projects is to define what success means, and then get everyone to agree to the definition. That way, we know where the target is and how to hit it. When it moves—and it will move—then we have a way to follow it and keep stakeholders aligned.

The next obvious questions are:

- What if we do not know what the end result is (such as R&D projects)?
- What if we cannot get the various stakeholders to agree on what success is?
- What if we do not have time to get this agreement?
- What if people will not sign off on this definition of project success? (We will deal quickly with these issues now and address them in more detail later in Section C.) If we do not know the expected outcome, we cannot know when it will be delivered, what it will cost, its chances of success, and a whole lot of other things that our bosses or client will expect us to tell them. If we cannot get the stakeholders to agree on what success means at the outset, what hope do we have of getting them to agree at the end? And what chance do we have of keeping them all happy? In my experience (and that of many successful project managers), the start of a project—the honeymoon phase—is when we have the best chance of getting people to agree on anything. So even if you do not know the answer to these key questions, put down a best guess, and get everyone to agree to it. You will likely have to modify it as you go through the process, but you will at least have a basis on which to move forward with developing a project plan. When you get better information later, you can modify your plan and people's expectations around it.

If we do not have time to get agreement at the outset on what our project is all about, how much time are we going to lose in reworking things later, or even heading up the wrong path from the beginning? I suspect that the time we do not have for obtaining agreement is much less than the time we will waste later, and there is a lot of professional project management experience to back up this observation. Many of the senior managers with whom I work in improving project performance recognize the need for proper planning. It is often referred to as *front-end loading*, when you define the project you are going to undertake and ensure that you are working on the right one. This is imperative to the success of your project.

What do you expect if you build a $100 million project for just $43,462?

Success of a project should be defined in terms of outcomes. These outcomes (in SMART Project Management, they always comprise a set of deliverable items) should be agreed upon by the stakeholders, who will vote on whether or not the project is a success. The other elements to be defined are the limitations of time, cost, and other resources to be consumed in achieving the project objectives. If it is hard to pin down these items—and it usually is in the early stages of a project—then the assumptions and accuracy or inaccuracy of the guesses that are made should be stated. There are ways of doing this that are not offensive to the delicate ears and eyes of bosses and board members! (We will reveal more on how to present ranges of possible outcomes and address uncertainty in Chapter 9.)

If we do not identify success, we do not know if the intent of the project sponsors has been understood. Therefore, we cannot plan our project with any certainty. I have already mentioned that the primary, and possibly the only, cause of project failure is a breakdown in communication. Communication starts with setting and effectively relaying the measures of success at the start of a project.

 Success of projects depends on clearly defining what you are planning to do and then modifying the resulting plan, as better information becomes available.

2.3   The Shifting Sands of Stakeholder Expectations

By defining completion of a project, we are setting the expectations of stakeholders at the outset of the project. If stakeholders' expectations differ or are in conflict, this needs to be addressed. All too often we do not know about the differences in stakeholders' expectations until near or at the end of the project. Worse, stakeholders' expectations are not only rarely aligned with each other, but also they routinely change over time. Your own experience with this will serve to illustrate.

How many of us have had clients who urge us into action as quickly as possible, once we have been given a project to manage, then complain about poor planning later? How about the client who demands quality at the start of the project, shifts to schedule pressure as the project gets under way, then complains about costs as the project nears timely completion? In the end, we are uncertain as to what the client really wanted. Come back a few weeks after the project is complete, and, if everything works the way it should, the client will probably be happy. Any differences over the cost and schedule are quickly forgotten if the results of the project are otherwise very positive. The focus on money and schedule is rooted in the lack of comfort that most clients have with the natural uncertainty inherent in projects.

If none of this is new to us, why bother mentioning it at all? We need to be aware of possible shifts in priorities, and when and how these shifts in priorities and expectations will influence working relationships and the way we need to manage our project. (Once again, I'll give you a quick answer now and then get into detail later.) At this point, we need to be aware of priority shifts and how they may appear. To start this exercise, let me introduce the priority triangle (see Figure 2.1). Its original purpose was to help with research on alignment of project management tools, processes, and business drivers.

We undertook an extended study of over two hundred projects to better understand how different industries worked with project management. The results of the research showed that not only were priorities misaligned on projects between stakeholders, but they were also in a constant state of flux. If we look at a generic project (our study was based on seven different industries), we will see a general pattern emerge. This pattern is not typical of a particular type of project, and each project will vary. The point is simply to illustrate the fluctuating priorities of various stakeholders over the life cycle of a project, as illustrated in Figure 2.2.

So, what is going on? Our first observation is that two-thirds of this *team* did not get to vote in the first two phases of the project. The second observation is that the team members generally disagreed on

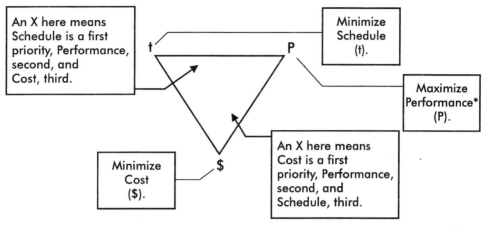

Figure 2.1 Priority Triangle

what is most important when they did get to vote. The third observation is that the three identified stakeholders changed their priorities at least once.

The shift in priorities is usually driven by what is important at the time to a particular stakeholder. What can we do about this? We can't reasonably hope to *control* the priority shifts that occur. Thus, we need to maintain focus on what we are trying to achieve and manage the different stakeholders' expectations as we work through the project.

 To keep our project stakeholders aligned, we need to understand their priorities and how they shift over time. Then we need to manage the project to accommodate those priority shifts.

 Never underestimate the importance of staying in touch with stakeholders' expectations.

2.4   Big and Small Targets—Getting Them the Right Way Round

When a project is completed, someone votes on its success. If we have set very precise and limiting objectives, our chances of success are diminished. By today's standards, Christopher Columbus' discovery of North America was a failure because that is not what he set

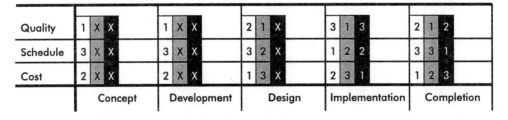

	Concept			Development			Design			Implementation			Completion		
Quality	1	X	X	1	X	X	2	1	X	3	1	3	2	1	2
Schedule	3	X	X	3	X	X	3	2	X	1	2	2	3	3	1
Cost	2	X	X	2	X	X	1	3	X	2	3	1	1	2	3

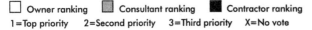

☐ Owner ranking   ▧ Consultant ranking   ■ Contractor ranking
1=Top priority   2=Second priority   3=Third priority   X=No vote

Figure 2.2   Priority Ranking by Project Phase

out to do. There are many examples of successful failures: for example, yellow stickies—the result of a glue that would not stick permanently—and crazy foam, albeit a fad—the result of a shaving cream gone wrong. The point is, success is not a measure of how precisely you deliver a project, but what the project does for the business or organization that sponsored it.

The old measures of having to be on time, within budget, and meet exactly what was requested in the project specifications has spawned some delightful cases of obtuse management. Sometimes, this manifests itself as downright foolish management. One example is the utility company that decided that all of its engineering projects must come in on budget; furthermore, no contingency would be allowed. It felt that since engineers manage projects precisely, these engineers should be fired if they get project estimates wrong. Considering that most of the projects done by these engineers are outdoors and susceptible to the weather, this is an astounding piece of logic.

The solution generated by the ingenious engineers was simple. All projects come in exactly on budget, except the last one in the year, which is usually over and sometimes under budget. They achieve this by charging overrun and underrun amounts to the next project. As for the contingencies that are not allowed, they are simply hidden in the base estimates. Of course, the result is chaos. Historical cost information is now fiction, yet estimates are based on these data and then *adjusted* to include contingencies. The result is compounded fiction, and the real control of these projects is totally lost. The benefits are that senior management is happy, because it sees precisely delivered projects. Cost inefficiencies, which must abound in this sort of situation, are actually an advantage, as this regulated utility is guaranteed a return on its capital investment. The more it costs, the greater the return. Even better, the engineers improve their ratios of overhead to operating revenue. Heaven help them, though, when they are deregulated.

This organization has made its project managers into big targets and the project objectives, small targets. Big targets are easy to hit; small ones are easily missed. What most smart project professionals want to achieve is making themselves small targets and the project objectives, bigger targets. That way, they are less likely to become scapegoats for the project, and the project is more likely to be seen as a success. This can be done; we simply need to know how, as well as to be aware of the practical limitations of such an approach.

The most obvious practical limitation is that project sponsors like to know with certainty to what they are committing. The fact that this is really not achievable is simply not a consideration! We need a way of maintaining management confidence in the project, while giving the decision-makers the information they need to be effective in their roles. Considering the real value of single-point estimates for time and cost is another way of looking at this. It is normal practice but not a real reflection of the situation or the information that decision-makers really need. Decision-makers will look at a project as an investment. For any investment, you need more than the cost and likely date on which you will see a return. Additional information includes the risk associated with the investment, which is essential to determine where the project fits in the business.

Let's look at an example to illustrate this point. You have a choice of investing in one of two projects of the same value and time frame. One will yield a return of 10 percent and the other one, 30 percent. Most of us, given this information, will pick the second project. But now add the following information. The first project has a 95 percent chance of being completed on time and within budget; the second project has a 15 percent chance of doing the same. Now which project would you pick? Add a bit more information. The second project, at a 95 percent probability, will cost ten times as much as the first one. The decision is easy now. Also, as a decision-maker, you have not picked a project on superficial values but on a risk/reward model.

Additional information about the probability of success adds a vital dimension to the business decision. Interestingly, it also adds a level of commitment from the decision-maker that will later help the project manager. The reason is simple. If a project manager is given a mandate to deliver a project for a specified cost and by a given date, it is clear who is responsible for failure. Success, all too often, is credited to the person least involved. However, with the added risk information, the project manager is effectively given a range of outcomes to meet. At least as important is the result that the decision-maker is now more involved, as he now has some ownership of the probability of success or failure to which he has committed.

 Working with ranges and probabilities, instead of single-point estimates, for time and money is not only more realistic, but also leads to better decisions and ownership by senior management.

2.5 Communication—The Only Cause of Failure

We should have seen from the last section that communicating a more complete picture of likely outcomes (based on schedule and cost information) improves our chances of being successful in managing a project. Communication at the right level and with the right people is at the heart of successful project management.

For several years, I have challenged project managers and others in the business to find a project with failures that can be attributed to any reason other than a breakdown in communication. Very few projects have been brought forward. In each case, when we worked backwards from the apparent problem, we ended with a vital gap in the communication chain. Let me illustrate with a few examples.

A large software development and implementation project was late and over budget, and the team was not working too well after almost two years of struggling with the project. The board of directors was upset with progress on this mission-critical project; thus, a new project manager had just been appointed. There were numerous identified technology problems; a review of the project revealed that several issues were at stake:

■ The project budget overrun was due to misunderstandings from the beginning about the scope of the project—essentially a communication breakdown.

■ The schedule overrun was due to innumerable incidents of rework on pieces of the software, as requirements were communicated after the work had been done.

■ Technical problems related to the capability of purchased software had been misunderstood, and hardware deliveries were not exactly as specified because of ambiguous specifications.

■ There were many other examples of problems that ultimately reduced to unclear, late, or incomplete communication.

On a large construction project, which apparently overran by over a billion dollars, there was a lot of fingerpointing going on. Several items emerged, pointing to communication breakdowns, not the least of which was a risk analysis completed at the start of the project, showing the actual final cost as being within the range of probabilities with a probability of occurrence around 85 percent. The project go-ahead was based on a target cost with a probability of about 50 percent. Not many of the complainants at the end of the project really understood that this target had a 50 percent chance of succeeding and, therefore, a similar chance of being overrun. The risk was not clearly communicated.

Sometimes we think we have communicated something, but in fact we have not!

 Communication is at the heart of effective project management. It needs to be timely, complete, accurate, and verified.

PRINCIPLES AND THEORY

30.3.93

It says: "This way up."

For the longest time, project management has been treated as either a tool kit or a process. Specifically, it has been seen as a set of tools and processes to deliver a predetermined set of requirements or products. This has led to a disconnection of project management from the business context in which it must happen in order to be truly effective. On the other hand, many people manage projects every day; yet they do not consider themselves to be project managers.

For some people, project management is still synonymous with use of the critical path method of scheduling. Many people today continue to look for tools and techniques, with an emphasis on tools, for ways to more effectively deliver projects. The result has been sustained mediocrity in both quality and delivery. As the saying goes, "To continue to do things the way you have always done them and expect different results is the first sign of madness." To step beyond this, in SMART Project Management, we ask that project managers not only try to manage their projects more effectively but also know why the tools, techniques, and processes that are used are in fact more effective. This additional knowledge allows the project manager to be more successful.

A common thread with the most successful project managers is the ability to make connections between different aspects of a project. Two other characteristics of such project managers are their capabilities to stay calm in a storm and to simplify the management process as much as possible.

 The best project managers will try new approaches, find the connections between the different aspects of the project and the team they manage, stay calm, and keep things simple.

It's the client—he's just canceled the flight.

Chapter 3

Strategically Managed Projects

W hen she was given the task of reorganizing the hospital's administration with a focus on patient service, Margaret thought she had a wonderful opportunity to make her mark, both in terms of quality care for patients and her career. After all, she started in nursing because of a personal need to contribute to society. As a senior administrator in the regional health-care system, she now had what seemed a heaven-sent opportunity to make some constructive changes. After two weeks, however, she found that the traditional ways were hard to overcome. There was resistance from some very influential surgeons and department heads, and the accounting department was putting what looked like major roadblocks in the way of any progress. A couple of weeks later, frustrated over and concerned about her project, she was being challenged by the chairman of the board over minor issues that were turning molehills into mountains.

Margaret was facing a predicament that many project managers see all too often. She had responsibility for a task, but no authority over the people on whom she needed to rely for success. Politics and turf issues were large stumbling blocks. The individual needs of departments and the personal needs of individuals were interfering with the greater purpose of the hospital. They were also at variance with the mission of her project. Dealing with these situations is difficult. We know from several studies (notably the one by Pinto and Slevin [1998]) that two of the leading critical success factors (CSFs) for projects are 1) a clearly defined mission and 2) support of senior management. Margaret seemed to have started with both, but she still had many of the same problems that many other project managers face. To understand why she had these problems, we need to first understand why these two CSFs are so important and how they can help a project manager get things done. We also need to understand the other CSFs that have been isolated by Pinto and Slevin and others.

In this chapter, we look at important cause-and-effect links between connected parts of project success that are either not well understood by many practitioners or not adequately addressed—often for apparently good practical reasons, such as there is not enough time to do so.

 To obtain effective authority to manage projects, we need to draw on the inherent authority granted by the institution or business that we are trying to serve. This authority lies in supporting and assisting the corporate strategy and being seen to do so. A key skill in harnessing such authority is found in the ability to understand and use the links between the many different aspects of a project, and thus understand how the project should be managed.

 The best project managers know how their projects support the corporate strategy. They use this knowledge to help them obtain needed support and resources to succeed.

3.1   Projects and Corporate Strategy

Many businesses today depend on project-based activities for their growth and long-term well-being. Many experts, including leading lights like Tom Peters, recognize this. Although ongoing operation is an important part of any business, it is the project elements that are usually at the cutting edge. These elements include process improvement, capital investment, adoption of new technologies, mergers and acquisitions, market studies, sales programs, and virtually any other special activity that will add shareholder value, profit, or corporate longevity.

There are many other projects that make up our day-to-day work life. They include small ones like moving offices, conducting internal evaluations of various sorts, and procuring a new computer. They also include larger projects such as selection and implementation of new accounting software, refurbishment of part of a building, or a factory shutdown.

Don't Park Your Brain Outside

Whatever the project, its size, or its complexity, it needs to be of value to someone in the organization if it is going to continue. The larger or more significant the project, the more important it is that the link to corporate strategy be clearly and firmly established. No one in her right mind will commit significant corporate resources and funds to a project that does little or nothing to further corporate objectives. The corollary is obvious: most people will support a project that clearly helps the corporation achieve its strategic objectives.

What does this tell us?

Projects do not happen in isolation; they are part of a bigger process: growth and survival of the organization. If we do not understand the larger process, we are less likely to be effective in managing the piece for which we are responsible: our project. Experience tells us that strange things happen on projects, such as senior management telling us that a project is extremely important and then canceling or delaying it. Impossible deadlines are set. And then the resources that are required to even stand a snowball-in-hell's chance in achieving them are taken away by the same people who set the impossible deadlines in the first place! We have all seen projects go through a *rush-and-stop* cycle. This cycle usually only happens once or twice on a project because, after a couple of these cycles, none of the players are willing to rush anymore. Nobody appreciates burning the midnight oil, giving up weekends with the family, and making other sacrifices to meet a deadline only to find that the deadline has been effectively ignored by the people who set it in the first place.

With all of these symptoms, and probably many more, we can see that uncontrollable factors will invariably affect the project as we try to implement it. So it helps to understand why we're implementing the project and why it is important to senior management. Let's put it another way. If it is not important to senior management, then we need to ask why we are doing the project in the first place and whether our involvement is even worthwhile.

Now you're going to ask, "Do I have a choice?" In the end, we always have a choice, although it may not be an easy one. In a most extreme situation, the choice is to work on the project or leave the company. If working on the project is going to be a career-limiting exercise, perhaps leaving the organization is not such a bad idea! At least you have control over how and when you take such drastic action.

If, however, we have one of those not-quite-so-desperate projects where the choice is not so immediate or obvious, then what do we do? Understanding the context and the relevance of the project to the corporate strategy now becomes important. If you cannot understand why the organization is doing something, then you should really find out, especially if you are responsible for managing that *something*. When you do find out, you may be surprised at how much more control and influence you have over the project itself.

 Projects are the building blocks of a business. This means we need to know not only how to deliver them, but where they fit in the business plan.

Let me give you an example. A large car manufacturer based in Germany wanted to build a parts warehouse in Britain. The company purchased land near one of the large London airports. It hired a project manager and told him that it wanted a modern and efficient warehouse for storing spare parts to service its customers in Britain. The project manager asked some seemingly stupid questions like, "Are you sure this is what you want?" Such questions were not well received; of course, this is what the company wanted! It needed to be able to guarantee a twenty-four-hour turnaround for any part required to service or repair one of its vehicles in Britain. Being sharp, the project manager realized that the corporate objective was not to own yet another warehouse, but to provide a better service to the customers. In relatively short order, the manager had identified a better solution.

After identifying that there was a steady stream of cargo planes traveling between Germany and Britain, he saw that the solution was a relatively simple ordering mechanism with a central distribution of parts coming straight off the aircraft onto delivery trucks. The company never built the warehouse; instead, it saved many millions of dollars by reselling the land, not building the warehouse, and not stocking large amounts of inventory in Britain. The car manufacturer negotiated guaranteed cargo space with an airline and installed a relatively simple ordering system, linking the British operation to its main warehouse in Germany.

Every day, and almost every hour during the day, trucks would be loaded with parts straight off an aircraft in response to orders placed just hours earlier. In fact, with the elimination of the central warehouse and the associated approximately twelve hours of turnaround inside the warehouse, the company achieved even faster delivery of parts than the originally anticipated twenty-four hours.

Although this is an extreme example, there are many very similar ones. On the other hand, there are many projects that probably should never have been undertaken in the first place.

It does not matter how well we deliver the project if it is the wrong one. It will still be wrong even when it has been perfectly executed and is on time and within budget.

The manufacturing sector has been more aware of this particular problem than some other sectors. In particular, it is aware that the selection of good ideas to be turned into products is often high risk. If you have three candidate projects and can only afford to develop one of them, how do you pick the best product? Even if we are not involved in the selection process itself, as project managers, we should understand the process if we want to be more effective in our roles.

 Proper definition and careful selection of the right projects in which to invest time, resources, and other effort is the foundation of good project and business management.

3.2   Project Selection

If we could afford to do every project that we wanted, we would probably have no problem selecting the ones in which to invest. Unfortunately, there are far more good ideas than there are money or time to develop them, which means that we have to weed out those projects that will add less value. Traditionally, we have used return on investment, net present value (NPV), discounted cash flow (DCF), or some other financial analysis tool to select a project. Part of this process has been riddled with problems, not the least of which is that we are often less than honest in presenting our particular cases. That was a harsh statement! Let's look at the reality of the situation.

3.2.1 Priorities

My project is the most important one in the world; if it wasn't, I'd be working on another one, and then that one would be the most important one in the world. Maybe I exaggerate a bit, but when I look at projects one rung up from where the project manager operates in the organization, what do I see? What's staring at me is a series of desperate, hungry, committed project managers, each with the world's most important project.

If I don't know how to use that word that begins with an "n," ends with an "o," and is two letters long, then I will end up accepting every one of those urgent projects, and they will all have the same priority. If I do know how to use that famous word, and say no to some or all of the projects, then project managers will quickly learn how to sell their projects more effectively to me, or they'll go off and sell them to someone else.

Perhaps, in your organization, you don't have a world in which every project is urgent, apart from those that are dumped in your lap because they are a crisis. Nor do you have those projects that are at least temporarily more important, and draw from the resources that you need to complete your project on time and on budget. If I guessed wrong, and you are like the rest of us, you have a problem. Frustrating as it is, the shifting sands of the business world force us to continuously adjust priorities on the projects that we have in hand. The resulting chaos is expensive, time consuming, and demoralizing. What can we do about it?

There are a few things that we can do to select projects, sorting the wheat from the chaff. Perhaps the smartest is to eliminate the 50 percent or so of projects that we shouldn't be doing in the first place (see earlier discussion). Once that's done, we need to understand what the business drivers are for the remaining ones.

 Be sure you are working on a worthwhile project. Yours must add value to the business that sponsors it. And you need to know exactly what that value is.

Just a note here: If you've done what most people do to select the projects that you *must* do, you'll still have all of the original projects to contemplate. Therefore, you need to consider: "If I can only do one project, which one do I pick?" The one you choose is your most important project. Now ask, "If I have to cancel one project, which one would it be?" This becomes your least important project. Keep bouncing from the top to the bottom of the list of those projects that remain until you have sorted them into two groups. The first group contains the priority projects; the second group is made up of those projects that can be dropped if you do not have the resources to complete all of the ones you feel should be done.

Then start again at the top, and ask the question: "What happens if I don't do this project?" If answering that question changes the order in which you have laid out your project priorities, test the priority change by asking whether the higher-priority project adds more value to the business than the lower-priority one. Now that you've done this prioritizing on your own, you may want to think about doing it as a group, involving the major stakeholders for the projects or perhaps the decision-makers in your organization.

But don't rush into this; before you go down this road, ask yourself another question: "Do I really understand what each of those projects is about?" If they are your own projects, you probably do. If they are somebody else's projects, you may want to go back and check that your understanding of the outcomes is in fact the same as that of the proponent. (In Chapter 4, we look at alignment and will ask three important questions that test our common understanding of the intent and expected outcomes of our project. We have been continuously surprised by the answers to these questions!)

 Picking the right project includes understanding the relative value to the sponsors of competing projects.

You may already have spotted it; we are drifting into the world of risks. The first risk on any project is that we don't really understand what we're doing or, if we understand, that we don't all understand the same thing! That's a hard risk to identify but a relatively easy one to fix.

3.2.2 Risks

Most of us are aware that projects have inherent risks and uncertainties. Generally, we can classify them into two broad categories, and then further group them in terms of how tangible they are. (The matrix in Figure 3.1 illustrates this.)

Figure 3.1 presents some examples to illustrate the range of risk types that we may encounter on a project. Tangible conventional risks are well understood by most practitioners, and we can develop our own list of these and use existing tools to manage them. Intangible conventional risk is a bit harder to manage, but we understand the need to do so even if we are unsure about how to reduce or manage it.

Latent risks are harder yet. First, there is a tendency to assume that there is nothing we can do about tangible latent risks such as contract dispute. We have to wait for the dispute to arise before we can possibly do anything about it. Second, we normally do not even want to waste time on intangible latent risk, because it is hard to visualize and even harder to predict. Arguably, it is virtually impossible to do anything about it. At least, that seems to be how most of these risks are managed.

Now let us look at these risks in a different way. Latent risks are ones that we can identify up-front and are often based on our experience from past projects. We can characterize them as those most likely to arise. At least, we will be able to recognize the symptoms.

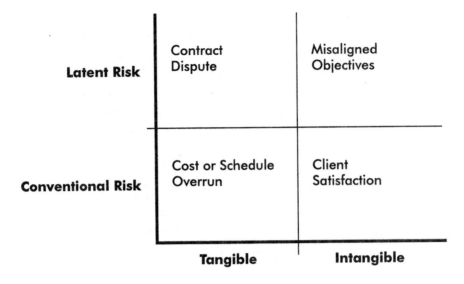

	Tangible	**Intangible**
Latent Risk	Contract Dispute	Misaligned Objectives
Conventional Risk	Cost or Schedule Overrun	Client Satisfaction

Figure 3.1 Examples of Risk Types

The whole issue of risk is covered in more detail in Chapter 9. For this discussion, however, it is important to realize that there are many types of risks and uncertainties in projects. We tend to stick with the definable, readily measurable, and quantifiable ones when we assess risk in projects. Today this is not enough. We also need to tackle the less tangible ones and understand their likely impact on project outcomes.

 We need to balance real risks and uncertainties with the potential return on investment in a project.

3.2.3 Rewards

How do we assess the likely outcomes and rewards of a project? The most common way of doing this is through some measure of return on investment. The most popular measures are as follows: internal rate of return (IRR), NPV, DCF, risk-assessed return, and return on investment.

Most businesses today typically will use at least two of these models to assess potential investment decisions. Each method of evaluating return on investment produces a slightly different result. This is why using two is good practice, as it provides an opportunity for a second view of the same issues.

Whatever the approach used to assess the potential value of the project, the process should include two other considerations as well. First, the link between the project and corporate strategy must be clear and visible. What does this project do to help the business or organization achieve its longer-term objectives? Second, the question of the value loss associated with not doing the project needs to be understood. Is this project needed for survival, to maintain market share, or some other such reason that does not specifically contribute to the bottom line? If so, then it will never get picked, based on IRR or one of the other techniques listed.

 Some of the most important projects for our organization are not likely to contribute directly to the profitability of the business. Measures of return on investment are not always obvious.

3.2.4 Lies and Distortions

What a harsh heading! Let me explain. When we propose a project, we are normally competing against others. We know that others' projects are presented in their best light. We also know that experienced senior managers and decision-makers will discount some of what we tell them as being overly optimistic. It pays us, therefore, to present our project case in the best possible light. Sometimes, as a result, this light is overly rose colored. We err on the optimistic side in all of our assumptions. Even the *facts* that we use are presented in the best possible light. (Of course, other people do this—you and I do not!) The result is one that can be measured quite easily in several different ways.

There are two ways to assess the effectiveness of our project selection process. First, if we are a publicly traded company, have a look at the rate of return on investment that appears in the annual or quarterly reports. Now have a look at the hurdle rate that is used for the approval of your project. You will note that there is often a significant difference between the two rates. If return on investment is at 10 percent in our annual report, then we may find that the equivalent hurdle rate for return on investment used by senior management is closer to 20 percent. Let us look at why this may be. Here are several possible explanations:

- Sunk costs, overheads, and other costs not allocated to a specific project need to be accounted for.
- The hurdle rate has been raised in order to compensate for the optimism traditionally seen in proposals.

- The real rate of return includes both successful and failed projects.
- The real rate of return is shackled to the dead weight of past investments.
- The real rate of return is also affected by the rate at which capitalized items are depreciated.
- Some or all of the above are combined to create a lower rate of return.

Let us look at a second possible explanation for the difference. Senior management has a real expected rate of return set at X percent. It knows that projects are presented to senior management with a very positive flavor. In other words, senior management needs to discount the rate of return or, as it has done, increase the hurdle rate, because the real expectation is $X - 5\%$. Now, the managers presenting the projects for approval and expenditure also know that they have a reputation for being optimistic. What does this mean? We have created a loop within which everybody plays games. The more we play and the smarter we are, the bigger the gap between reality and what people present when making a case for project approval and financing.

Now a question for us: How do we break out of this kind of loop and do things smarter? Before you answer, ask yourself if you are in fact in the loop. In reality, most of us are, to a greater or lesser extent. The drivers for this are as follows. First, if we fail with a project proposal, it is normally seen to be a personal failure. We must gain approval if we are to succeed. The corollary is that if we fail to obtain approval, we have just completed a career-limiting move. The second driver is that there is an enormous reluctance to throw away all of the hard work and commitment that we have made in taking a project from an idea to a decision or commitment point. Very often, we arrive at a *point of no return* too early in a project life cycle. To reinforce this, the third driver is that we do not like to leave on the table the costs sunk in developing a project to a specific point; it looks depressingly like wasted money. Thus, perhaps we need to take a fresh look at how we reach this point. Let's try that fresh look.

To take a different approach means that we need to ask some questions, which maybe we haven't asked quite as carefully as we might have in the past:

- What is the value of this project to the business?
- How is this value measured? Don't just look at the monetary value. We are likely to have projects where the value is longer term or not even measurable in hard money.

- How certain is the expected outcome of this project? Remember that very often we look at our projects through rose-colored glasses, discounting the things that could go wrong because they obviously don't happen to us!
- How clear is the outcome of this project? Some of the questions around this include:
  - How do you know that the project is complete?
  - How do you decide whether or not it has been a success?
- This next point is tricky, because the question has to do with whether your organization is a leader or a follower. Let me explain. Leaders are essentially the innovators in business, either through product or process. Followers are typically risk-averse organizations that follow with clones of other products and go for lower cost production. Leaders spend more money on research and development; they need to recover it by having the product in the marketplace early and charging a premium, normally through protected sales and production under patents and copy-rights. Followers focus primarily on reproduction of established products at lower costs and gaining market share. If you don't know where your business is on the continuum from innovator or leader to follower or refiner, you will have a problem under-standing the propensity that the organization has for taking risk. A finger on the risk pulse makes it a lot easier to understand how to align projects with corporate strategy.
- The final question has to do with projects that do not have a direct impact on the bottom line: "What happens if we do not do the project?"

Answering these questions should help us establish a line of sight between where the project is going and how it might contribute to the corporate strategy. Without establishing this link, we have no way of knowing how the project will be justified within our organization. With such a line of sight—clear links between where our organization is going and where our project may add a boost in the right direc-tion—we are well placed to start justifying the existence of the project. The bottom line is that if we cannot provide such a justification, and we fail to find a link between the project and where the business is going and how the project may help the business get there, then we should not do the project.

A clear and visible link between the contribution of your project to the business and the direction and objectives of the business itself is a powerful tool to help you gain the support of senior management. *This cannot be overemphasized.*

3.3   Risk/Return Models

The relationship between risk and return is well established and understood. In the context of most projects, however, this idea that the return on investment may be linked to the risk involved is mysteriously suppressed. We may wonder why. Here are a couple of conjectural ideas based on having been there and on observation of practices in industry:

- Projects are known to overrun budgets and schedules; we build this into our decision and then try to manage it by having the team work toward apparently immovable but aggressive targets. Then, when the project does not meet these artificial targets, we can still meet the larger real budget and schedule. This is usually achieved through application of threats and guilt, and we are very good at this!

- Investors and lenders like a sure thing. The *due-diligence* process is designed to provide some level of comfort in knowing that the required management and other expertise is built into the project and its team. If this is in place, there is no need to waste precious resources on contingencies and other luxuries. The appearance is that there is no (or little) risk.

- If we present a proposal for a project that has any uncertainty implied in it, it will be rejected in favor of an equally risky—or even riskier—project that is presented with assurance and the impression that there is no uncertainty in the outcome. We need to *appear* risk free if we want to survive.

- Despite the repeated reality of projects being late, requiring budget enhancements or massive scope changes, we choose to continue to put credence in the presentation of project proposals with little or no visible risk.

 The project sponsor needs to develop special skills to uncover hidden risks, and then assess them in some way. Only by doing this can she make any kind of rational decision in selecting and developing projects for investment.

3.3.1 General Issues

If we work in the *normal* world, where projects are brought forward for approval with little or no real disclosure of the risks, then the selection process that follows is, by definition, arbitrary. Most organizations today are seeking ways to become more informed, or less arbitrary, in the selection of projects in which they invest.

Good practice today does include some type of risk assessment as a required part of the project proposal process. The level of sophistication typically varies depending on the nature, complexity, novelty, duration, and size of the project. It also will be different between companies and, all too often, will vary by project manager or department within an organization. All of this makes it really difficult to compare competing projects for investment purposes.

Here are some questions to ask yourself about how you and your organization identify risk:

- Do you have a procedure for risk identification and assessment?
- Do you always follow the same process when you assess risk on a project?
- Do you have benchmarks for risk and risk tolerance in the organization?
- Do you include a probability of success in your estimates for cost, schedule, scope, and quality?
- Does your project exclude hidden contingencies that may have been added by you or others before being presented to senior management for approval?
- Do all parties to the project plan declare all contingencies?
- Are all optimistic forecasts properly identified as such?
- Is the corporate culture forgiving (within reason) of cost or schedule overruns, scope creep, or other classical measures of project failure?
- What is the ultimate measure of project success?

If the answer to the last question was anything but being on budget, within scope, and on schedule—or if the answers to any of the other questions was *yes*—there is hope that you are on the way to a consistent and comparable process for risk management in your organization.

 The model used in determining the risk and return on investment for a project needs to be sufficiently consistent across the organization to allow decision-makers the ability to compare projects.

3.3.2 Consistency in Presenting Projects for Approval versus Creativity and Other Issues

The main disadvantages to a consistent approach to measurement and reporting of potential risk on projects lie in the need to have corporate standards and in the lack of flexibility that this creates. Any movement toward corporate standards will require awareness of these standards across the board and the education and communication costs associated with it. It also tends to reduce the scope for creativity and innovation if overdone and bureaucratized. Lack of flexibility is of particular concern to many who promote projects within and to companies or sources of funding.

We need flexibility for two reasons. First, to allow us to be truly creative in the development of our project proposals. Second, to allow us to present our proposal in the best possible light. This second element is often taken to excess. The "best possible light" often excludes the things that can go wrong. It may include hidden contingencies. It may also include untested assumptions and opinions presented as statements. All contribute to the increased potential for approval of the project. They also increase the potential for subsequent cost and schedule overruns.

 If we really want a project to go ahead, we will find a way to help convince the decision-makers to accept and approve it. Often this means that later we will be asking for more money, time, and staff in order to complete the project.

3.3.3 Avoiding the *Sunk Cost Trap*

Starting a project based on wrong or misleading information sets up the project, its team, and the corporate sponsor(s) for failure. This is such a common problem that it even has a name: sunk cost trap. Let's examine how it works.

The root of the problem is at the project approval stage. Here the proponents paint—deliberately or otherwise—an optimistic picture of the project and its outcomes. The project is approved on that basis, and work starts. Once a sufficient amount of time and resources have been expended on the project, such that it is politically difficult to withdraw, the request for additional funding is made. This approach is well known on large government-funded projects; it is probably just as common in the private sector, just less visible. Arguably it is easier to disguise the problem in the private sector!

Substantial sunk costs on a project are a good deterrent to project cancellation, even if people know the project we are doing is the wrong one or is doomed to failure.

The solution to this problem lies in avoiding it in the first place, or in providing appropriate checkpoints in the development of the project at which the sponsors can reapprove the project if specific criteria are met. This process is also well understood in some sectors and is often referred to as a *stage-gate process*. As we deal with this a bit differently in SMART Management, we will refer to these places as *checkpoints*. (Stage gates are well documented in the literature. How to implement an effective checkpoint process on projects is described in Chapters 8 and 9.) Checkpoints allow the project sponsors and the project manager to set points at which the intent and likely outcomes of the project can be reassessed in the context of the overall business. This in turn helps to ensure that the project is still aligned with the sponsoring organization's needs. Through this predetermined review, the project team and other stakeholders can be realigned with the project objectives, and these objectives can be adjusted, where needed, to meet the current situation.

 Checkpoints, set correctly and with appropriate criteria, can be used to validate, modify, or cancel projects with minimal expenditure on wasted effort.

3.3.4 Killing Projects When We Should

A significant number of projects do not yield the expected return on investment that was anticipated when they were first approved. A number of formal and informal studies show that the difference between expected and actual return on project investments can be in the range of 4 to 6 percent. Whenever I mention this to senior executives, the statistic receives knowing nods. (We have seen the reason for this phenomenon in Section 3.2.4.)

Any process that helps identify projects that should not proceed and eliminates them at minimal cost and wasted effort is probably useful.

 A stage-gate or checkpoint type of process will help reduce the chance of good money being spent after bad on inappropriate projects.

That leaves just two problems. First is the project that should proceed and will not because of this type of screening process, and the second is the project that should not proceed but is made to look good in the light of the adopted screening process. In other words, no screening process is foolproof; to make one more useful, a number of additional ingredients need to be added. A measure of the risk involved or the potential for success is the first of these. Another consideration is the impact on the business of not doing anything. Examples of this type of project include replacing obsolete equipment and systems, addressing the impact of a new competitive product, or adjusting to a significant shift in the marketplace.

 It is not enough to look just at the expected return on investment of a project. We also need to consider the probability of success and the consequences of not doing the project.

3.3.5 Getting the Right Balance between Risk and Return on Projects

If we need more than just the return on investment in the selection of projects, what else do we need to consider? A few factors that may drive projects ahead, despite any other considerations, include the following:

- An exceptionally low risk: If the project shows a reasonable and solid return, and the risk is particularly low for both execution and operation, then a low return may become attractive compared to other projects in the portfolio.

- The business imperative: Some projects are needed simply because *not* doing them will damage the business significantly. These types of projects need to be assessed in light of the eliminated consequences of not proceeding if we are to evaluate the real return on such an investment.

- Intuitively *right* projects: Probably one of the hardest project types to evaluate objectively, these projects should not be dismissed simply because they are hard to assess. There are many projects in the history of mankind that only passed this test and none of the others, and the proponents of these projects did very well. Examples include the dry photocopy process, yellow stickies, and the fax machine, as well as many more innovations.

- Market opportunity: Many market opportunities occur at times and in situations that preclude proper analysis or are of such significance that they demand a response. Recently, one of my clients went ahead on a project that would fail any rational test: The return on investment could not be justified, based on the risk involved, and the return was likely to be small or negative. If the project failed, it could mean the demise of the entire business; the penalties for delays were huge. The technology did not exist and needed to be developed to meet the project requirements. Yet, if it succeeded, the company would be in an important market that is needed for future growth.

- Technological advantage: Either because you have a technological advantage or because you want to create one, this driver can bring otherwise insignificant projects to the forefront. Technological advantages may be simple, but could lead to innovations or cost breakthroughs that make you more competitive or return a larger profit—or both.

- A *loss leader* project: These projects are undertaken because of perceived future opportunities for business, or because they are expected to lead to other and more profitable projects with some sort of competitive edge as a result of the first one. The value of the first project lies in the competitive advantage created or in the increased market share or revenue generated.

None of these opportunities, however, can be fully taken advantage of—or even recognized—if awareness of these types of criteria for selection of projects is unknown to the people who come up with the ideas or are in the field looking for business opportunities.

 The right balance between risk and return on a project is not always obvious. Soft issues and strategic needs for a particular project can help hide real priorities from senior management. Project proponents have a responsibility to clarify this to senior management. Senior management has a responsibility to keep staff informed of strategic needs for the business and how these and business tactics may be changing over time.

3.4   Senior Management Support and Other Critical Success Factors

There are several studies on CSFs that need to be examined to ensure success of projects; notable among them is the study by Pinto and Slevin (1998), mentioned earlier. All the different studies undertaken have had some common results. For example, among the top few

CSFs, two routinely reappear: 1) the need for support of top management and 2) a clear mission statement for the project.

When we look at these two and try to understand not just the symptom, but also what underlies these important elements for project success, an interesting pattern emerges. The question that leads us to the pattern is: "How do we obtain support of senior management?" The answer, in a generic sense, is that we appeal to senior management's need to do its own job. This means that if we find a clear way to help the business, senior management will likely support what we are doing. More specifically, if we can provide a clear link between corporate strategy and the objectives of our project, then we can demonstrate how we will help achieve corporate goals by doing the project. It's simple really. And you have probably spotted the rest of the pattern. We cannot provide the link that we just identified unless we have clear goals for the project we are undertaking.

Now we can close this loop. If we have a clear goal for our project that is directly linked to the strategic needs of the organization, it must be couched in terms of three components: 1) business needs and implications, 2) technological needs and implications, and 3) social and societal needs and implications.

 Successful projects need support from the boss. Understanding how the project helps achieve the organization's objectives will go a long way toward getting that support.

As with all factors that need to be present for project success, the underlying issues need to be identified and addressed. Only by doing this can we find the best way to put the right elements in place for project success. Now let us look at the other factors identified by Pinto and Slevin (1998).

■ Project mission: The objective is to have clear and well-defined goals and general directions from the outset. This is often difficult to do on many projects. The way to resolve this is to do the best job possible of defining the goals and objectives, even if they are subsequently going to be proven wrong. The advantage of this approach is that we are defining the intent at the outset. If it changes, we can readily see the change later, as it will show as a difference between the intent and the modified plan. Thus, we develop a better way to identify and manage subsequent change to a project. More importantly, we have the makings of a tool to help us manage the expectations of our project stakeholders. The importance of this becomes obvious as we work through the remaining critical success factors.

- Top management support: This is the willingness of top management to provide the necessary resources and authority or power for effective project implementation. The link to clear goals has already been identified. Now look at senior management expectations. As long as the project is meeting these expectations—whatever they are—we will continue to get support. It is when these expectations are no longer being met that support dries up. So we need to manage expectations, and we need to keep them managed in line with corporate strategy and objectives.

- Schedule plans: This is the detailed specification of what the action plan is for implementation of the project. It is a tool to help manage expectations of our stakeholders. Often it is presented at a level of detail that does not pass the Idaho test (see Chapter 9). We do not plan at the same level of detail for the whole life of the project at home. The accuracy of the plan, including resource requirements, needs to be assessed and declared if we are to let the sponsor know the degree of precision in our plan. The default assumption (typically the wrong one) is that we can do the project within the limitations of time, money, and other resources identified in the plan. If we cannot, it becomes our fault, as project managers.

- Client consultation: This factor is about effective communication with all of the stakeholders affected by the project. We need to listen to them and consult effectively with them. Part of this process is closely linked to managing their expectations. Listening to a customer without feedback and appropriate management of expectations will simply reinforce the current expectations, even if they are unrealistic.

- Personnel: This CSF is about putting together the right team with the technical and other skills required for completion of the project. Implicit in this is also the ability to obtain the team's commitment to success. In the real world, we often do not get the resources we would like; all too often, others assign them to us. They may not be the best people for the job in hand; they may not be interested in the project. Yet, we still need to work with them, and help them make the project and themselves successful. There is a degree of risk in this situation, which needs to be understood. The sponsors' expectations also must be managed in order to be in line with reality.

- Technical tasks: This factor deals with the availability of the right technical expertise to serve the needs of the project. The extent to which the available resources meet the need—which are in-house and which are out-house—must be understood and assessed. The risk of resources not meeting the technical demands, not being available for the project, or other risk factors are commonly not assessed at the outset. The expectation implied in the plan is that the resources will perform at whatever the industry average is, or at the level assumed in the estimate for cost and elapsed time.

- Client acceptance: Pinto and Kharabanda (1995) define this as the final stage in the project implementation process. In the SMART approach, I define it as the start of the implementation process and link it closely to the CSF, client consultation, listed earlier. Leaving client acceptance to chance at the end of a project is an unacceptable risk. Defining the criteria that constitute client acceptance at the outset is critical to lowering the risk of failure. (Defining success in terms of deliverables is discussed later in Chapter 8.)

- Monitoring and feedback: This is an important part of the project management process; it is also one of the most misunderstood elements in practice. The evidence is in the large number of projects that suffer from one or more of the following symptoms. There are *surprise* delays or cost overruns, as the project comes close to completion. We have dissatisfied end users or customers, or there are quality problems. The scope creeps (usually upward). There is a disconnection between team activity or performance and the project plan. Maybe the project monitoring and feedback process is too slow or cumbersome to be effective. In SMART Project Management, the way in which the project is monitored is linked to the way that it is planned and to the project priorities.

- Communication: Breakdowns in communication are a primary cause of project failure. The communication issues for a project must be identified and addressed as an integral part of the project planning and management process. Who needs to communicate to whom about what and when needs to be included as an integral part of the plan for implementation.

- Troubleshooting: Classical project management emphasizes the need to not just find problems, but also to address them once they are found and then adjust the project plan. More current thinking includes early warning systems in the project implementation system. In SMART, we try to go beyond this and build in the flexibility needed to accommodate the inevitable troubles that will plague any project. The preferred sequence for doing this is as follows:

1. Identify potential problems and plan to avoid them.
2. Failing being able to avoid them, identify contingency options to address them if they occur.
3. Keep stakeholders involved, as the project is adapted to suit the most recent changes.

 The studies to determine project CSFs have gone a long way toward helping us understand what needs to be done for successful projects. Understanding what lies behind these factors helps us make success a reality.

If there are connections between CSFs for project success, then they need to be understood in the context of our projects. Some of the most obvious and general ones are as follows:

- The project must serve a valuable purpose in achieving corporate objectives.
- Alignment among stakeholders—in understanding what the project will achieve and what it needs for success—is necessary.
- The stakeholders deciding whether or not the project is a success should be involved in the definition and approval of the project.
- As projects occur in an ever-changing business environment, the expectations of the stakeholders must continuously be realigned with what is actually happening on projects.

The logical starting point for identifying the real project objectives is answering the following questions: Who are the stakeholders voting on the success of the project when it is done? What, in their opinions, will make the project a success? How do they (and the project team) know when the project is finished?

These questions need to be couched in a specific way to get the answers we need to start the planning process. (This is discussed in more detail in Chapter 8.)

 The steps for success in any project will depend on many factors. To discover what they are, we need to know what questions to answer. It is the answers to the three key questions mentioned earlier that will shed light on the issues to be addressed in planning for and achieving successful projects.

As it turns out, this is much more consistent than a person,
and the results are better, too!

Understanding the Project Objectives in a Business and Social Sense

Further study of the CSFs identified by researchers shows not only a linkage between them that points to the underlying issues, but also the underlying issues themselves tend to suggest that there are drivers beyond just business and technical considerations. For example, if communication is a big element in the success of a project, then what do we need to do to make it work well? Now consider the telephone calls you have not returned and the ones you have not had returned. Eliminate the ones that were not returned for sound business reasons (for example, because they were a waste of time) or for technical reasons (such as you could not get to a phone, or because the wrong number was recorded). Probably you still have most of those unreturned calls on your list! What do they have in common? There is no personal or social value in returning them; so, you don't. If we still need to have the

Don't Park Your Brain Outside

communication implicit in the original call, we need an incentive for that communication to take place, and it needs to happen in a timely fashion.

The third dimension we need to consider in management of projects, beyond the technical and business issues, is that of social issues.

 The business issues on projects are not always clear. The social issues are rarely even considered. Social issues are the ones most likely to get in the way of success. Therefore, we need to know what they are and how to deal with them.

A large part of the solution to social problems in the management of projects lies in real and effective alignment among the many different stakeholders on the project, which is addressed in the next chapter.

Chapter 4

ALIGNMENT

Keith was an old hand at software implementation. He was working on a project that had been under way for about a year—this was just another soured project. The whole team, he could see, was no longer enthusiastic—if ever it had been—about the system, the technology, or even the organization for which it was working. However, the project was a large new accounting system, and specific parts were required to meet a new reporting regulation. The board of directors was keenly interested in seeing it finished; specifically, the board needed it in place before the reporting grace period expired. Penalties for failing to meet the new government regulations would be severe and would take some explaining to shareholders and others. There were six groups working on this project, and each dealt with one major component of the system. Michael had just been appointed to the project as *overall project manager*. His mandate was to get the project done as quickly as possible. Because he knew Keith, he sought his opinion regarding the project's status. Keith told him; none of it was good news. It fit the description of a runaway software project on every count. The required deadline was demoralizing. The budget was inadequate. The team was tired. Key people had left. Keith knew that others were planning to leave, too. Vendors and subcontractors were not responsive and seemed to have lost interest.

Michael did not have much time to assess the situation or to get the project moving again. But, he did not feel that he had a team that was working well. Management was upset. The accounting department did not think that the project would ever get done and was looking for other solutions. Michael's problems, as with many technology projects, were not technology problems. What he was seeing were largely the symptoms of a lack of alignment between stakeholders. This mystical alignment was needed in three areas. First, the objectives of the project needed to be aligned with corporate objectives. Second, team members needed to align their own interests with those of the project, or vice versa. Finally, the management tools and techniques needed to be in line with the project priorities.

Alignment is a complex and tangled issue that we unravel in this chapter as we look at some of the key elements involved. Specifically, we need to look at alignment from three points of view:

1. The project needs to be aligned with the corporate direction of the stakeholder businesses.
2. The project team members need to be aligned with the project and what it is to achieve.
3. The tools, techniques, and processes we use to manage the project need to be aligned with what we are trying to achieve and the priorities involved in doing so effectively.

These three views start with a strategic objective and end with specific detail that reflects the importance of selecting the right tools for the job. Alignment issues are, by definition, connected; without alignment, we will have unnecessary energy waste as we churn through our projects.

 Alignment of the project, its stakeholders, and the team results in improved efficiency in the delivery of the project.

4.1　Why Alignment Is Important

On projects, it is particularly clear that we need to get things right the first time, whenever possible. To understand what is right, we need to be sure that we all agree on the definitions of what we are trying to do and how we will measure success. It is also important to realize that success is not an absolute; it usually lies within a range of possible outcomes. All too often, we try to define success in terms of absolutes. The only thing of which we can be absolutely certain, in that case, is that we will not be successful!

So what does this mean? First, if we want to be successful, it means that we must all agree on a definition of project success. Next, it means that we can agree on a range of outcomes—including the must-have, want, and would-be-nice parts—and know which outcomes fall into each of these three categories. Because we now have degrees of success, we can achieve alignment more easily.

Part of the process of alignment is to soften the project objectives so that there is some flexibility in adapting, to best address conflicts and other issues that may get in the way of success.

4.2 Corporate Strategies

I am constantly surprised by how often the average working person in an organization has little or no clear picture of its corporate strategy. This is often not his fault. He has no real access to this information, and, if he did, it is probably obfuscated to the point where it means nothing to anyone except the person who authored it. Even that person may no longer be sure what it means! And we do not like to ask about it, because we know from experience that this is typically seen as a *stupid question*—even by those who do not know the answer. This makes it really difficult to be aligned with the corporate strategy.

4.2.1 Sponsor Organization

Step one on the road to alignment is to make sure that we know both what the corporate strategy is, and that we understand the implications of that strategy for our project. At its simplest, we need to understand how our project will add to the corporate strategy. What is it we are doing that helps the sponsor organization achieve its objectives?

In order to make this link, we need to be sure that the project contributes something useful and relevant to the success of the business. We need to understand whether it is a long-term component or one where the impact is more immediate. We need to know this, as the time horizon for the management team expectations for a return on the investment in our project will be dictated by the answer.

To test the reality of the contribution that our project will make to corporate strategy, we need to identify the project objective in simple and clear terms that relate to the corporate strategy. This is then presented to the project executive(s) who will sponsor it. If the executive can see the value and make the link to the corporate objective, the chance of success for our project is enhanced. Now let us go one step further. If we can link the success of the project to one or more of the measures by which the sponsor's performance is assessed, the chance of getting sustained support from that sponsor is considerably enhanced.

The project must clearly contribute to the objectives of the sponsor organization as a building block for its corporate strategy. This helps the project manager define and focus the project mission while obtaining the support of senior management.

If we look at the top two critical success factors as being the *result* of rather than the *driver* for good project management, they take on a different complexion, one that supports alignment between the corporate strategy and the objectives of the project that we are trying to manage. Alignment with the sponsor is the first step.

4.2.2 Partner Organizations

Partner organizations are cosponsors of the project. They can be separate organizations, or they can be departments or divisions of the same parent organization. Either way, the opportunity for the manager of a multi-sponsor project to get caught in the middle of corporate politics is very real and potentially damaging to her career. As a result, there is a real need, from a personal survival perspective, to make sure that these sponsors are truly aligned.

We will have different types of partners for our project, which means that we will have different agendas and needs from these partners. It is unlikely that all objectives will be naturally aligned; the converse is probably more true. There is a good chance that the objectives of the project partners are in real or potential conflict.

A common example is capital investment. Often, organizations manage operations and capital expenditure through two different departments, each with its own budget. Typically, operating costs can be reduced by spending more on the capital investment (automation, maintenance interval, reliability, and so on); hence, we have two stakeholders with misaligned agendas.

What makes a partner interested in a project? If we apply the Wall Street motivation theory, there can be two reasons: fear or greed—or possibly both. Partners in a project are involved because they want to take care of their own interests. We need to identify these, and we need to be aware that they will likely change over the life of any significant project. The changes may be real or simply a differing perception of the same drivers. Whatever the motivation to become involved in the project, the partner will need to see the potential for gain in some form.

Don't Park Your Brain Outside

Partners will be motivated by gain-driven incentives that might include one or more of the following:

- profit
- reputation
- market opportunity
- public relations
- achievement of objectives (particularly important to nonprofit organizations).

On the other end of the spectrum, drivers for involvement may include:

- loss mitigation
- beating the competition
- loss leader for future opportunity
- change (improve) image through performance or other achievement
- audit: meeting mandate of organization.

You probably noticed that the first and the second list are basically the same, seen from different perspectives: positive and negative. Either way, the partner's motivation should be based on achieving the objective. If the project is a success, he will be better off than before the project. To gain the partner's attention and, later, trust, we need to be sure that we understand why he is involved and what he really needs to get out of that involvement.

 The business of a partner organization needs to be better off as a result of the project's success. This helps us find the links between the project and the partners' strategy.

4.2.3 Support and Service Organizations

These project players are further down the food chain. Their motive for involvement in the project is usually pretty clear: long term or short term, they want to do business and make a profit. This is a reasonable perspective from which to operate, and it should be respected. The behavior of the supplier will be influenced by whether there is a need to maintain a long-term relationship. If the business is one that is of a long-term nature, then service is likely to be driven in part by the need to maintain good business relationships. If involvement in the project is likely to be a one-time deal, the service quality may be driven primarily for short-term profit. Longer-term objectives relating to reputation, references to future clients, and business development will likely be less significant.

It is not intuitively obvious to most project managers working for either the buyer or the vendor in this type of situation that the profit motive is not necessarily in conflict with success of the project. If we think about it, a profitable supplier will be more able to focus on meeting the client's needs. One that is losing money will look to recover that money from the customer through shortcuts, claims for additional payment, and other behaviors that are potentially damaging to the client. Only if we are really lucky will we have a supplier who is truly creative and can solve her profit problem without damage to the project.

 Involvement in a project needs to be good for the suppliers of goods and services. Normally, this means that the support organization will make a reasonable profit and has a valuable business opportunity. This allows the supplier to focus on providing quality and timely service in support of the project. Consider also the converse. It is not obvious to everyone!

4.2.4 *External* Organizations

Organizations external to the project include regulators, the general public, financiers, insurers, and many others. We normally think of them as *outsiders*. But are they? I do not think so. We are often better off with these outsiders as part of our project team. Let me give you an example.

This story is quite commonplace. I have seen many like it in my career as a practitioner and in studies of projects. You can replace the insurer with regulators who save steps in the process, as well as eliminate costly mistakes before they are implemented. Or you can replace the regulator with financiers. Good investors bring some in-house expertise in the industry with them. They do this directly because the expert is on staff, or they do it through the due diligence process. In this process, the potential investor will have external experts independently assess the investment. The sidebar, The Friendly Banker, illustrates just one example of what happened to a new consulting business as a result of seeking financing for the next step in its growth.

 Some *external* groups are not as external as we think!

Another interesting phenomenon is the relationship between involvement of external (or any) stakeholders and the extent to which they will *own* success of the project. I think it was Machiavelli's advice to keep

He monitors productivity. Since he started with us,
everyone has been much more focused.

your friends close and your enemies, closer. One of my brightest students returned as a guest speaker for a course. He told how he gets stakeholders involved if he thinks that they might get in the way of project success. His simplest solution was to ask for their advice. Most people love to give advice. Few people deliberately will give you bad advice (and if they do, it is often obvious, and you simply ignore it). This method has had interesting results. A particularly smart adversary commented one time, after having been asked for advice on a number of projects: "I hate it when you seek my advice; I get sucked in, and you have a successful project when I want it to fail!"

Some external parties can be difficult to manage. For example, many construction project owners are reluctant to involve unions in early project planning, because they are afraid that they will lose bargaining power later. Special interest groups, particularly local and amateur ones, are hard to work with because they need so much time to be educated about the objectives of the project, the technology involved, the potential risks and opportunities, and so on. Well, if you think this way, you *may* be right, but think again. Most of these groups are not interested in the entire project; they are only concerned about the bit that will

The Friendly Banker

This small engineering consulting practice had been in business for about three years. It had grown steadily and had a number of opportunities coming its way, which made the principals seriously consider rapid expansion. They went to the bank to request a line of credit for financing extended operating costs through the more difficult stages of the expansion. They presented what they believed to be a realistic business plan, based on their experience with the business to date.

The bankers were willing to consider the application, but they knew enough about the expected new clients to identify a significant flaw in the business plan. The principals of the engineering company dealt with clients who paid in thirty days; the bankers knew that the proposed new clients generally paid in ninety days. Therefore, the partners would need three times the requested line of credit to finance the expansion with the prospective new clients. Operating such a line of credit would be expensive and may not return the planned profit.

As a result, the partners negotiated payment terms up-front with the new clients, something they had not previously considered. The expansion was a success; it could easily have been a disaster.

---

affect them. Keeping them informed helps manage their expectations and will typically reduce the potential for subsequent antagonism. It may even result in a significant cost saving.

The sidebar, The Sweet Sour Gas Plant, illustrates a success story; not all interventions with or by external stakeholders result in such success. Open communication, overall, has shown itself to be more effective than trying to hide issues from the public. This is good for several reasons, not least of which is that it is ethical!

 The more involved external parties are, the more they own success of the project. There are, however, diminishing returns in benefits versus the effort and cost of involvement. Balance these factors.

Don't Park Your Brain Outside

4.2.5 Individual Stakeholders

In the end, nothing happens on any project or in any business without the active intervention or action of people. The difference between the best organizations and others lies in the people they employ and how they are allowed to perform. In many organizations, there are real barriers to the effectiveness of their primary resources. An important part of the process of removing barriers is to allow people the room to perform effectively. This is sometimes referred to as *empowerment*. But, as that word has rightfully fallen into disrespect because of abuse, let's use another word.

How about *enabled?* Now let me define the term. I mean that each employee is allowed to do his job as independently as possible and reasonable for efficiency. To do this, each person on the team needs to have a clear and consistent picture of the end product of the project and what his role is in achieving it. This is what alignment at the team-member level is all about.

 It is people that make things happen on projects. They are, therefore, the single most important part of successful project management.

Once team members understand the objective of the project and how that objective relates to corporate strategy, it is an easy step to see how the effort of each individual contributes to the success of the project and the business. This link is surprisingly energizing. The energy stems from a simple need we all have: we want what we do to matter. If we can see how this works for the project, we can gain a lot of internal fortitude to handle the mundane and enthusiasm to overcome the difficult.

 If we address the interests and concerns of individual stakeholders, we increase our chance of successful delivery of the project.

One last step in alignment of individuals with the success of the project remains: bringing out any personal hidden-agenda items, such as expectations of a bonus, promotion, recognition, new experience, or career progression. Usually they are quite reasonable expectations;

The Sweet Sour Gas Plant

Sour gas is called that because it contains a lot of sulfur—nasty stuff to burn and corrosive to transport. Therefore, soon after sour gas is removed from underground, it is processed to remove impurities—especially the sulfur. One such plant located in the Western sedimentary basin had to ship the resulting sulfur across extensive farmland, which the farmers did not like. Active consultations with stakeholders eventually resulted in a planned spur rail line—used to ship the sulfur—being replaced by an underground heated pipeline.

The alternative solution resulted in substantial savings—estimated in the region of $50 million—over the life cycle of the project. This solution likely would never have been considered had a specialist interest group not raised a serious complaint.

invariably, they are not voiced, and so they are not considered in the project plan. Many of them can be easily accommodated, some take a bit of effort, and some cannot be included in the plans. If we allow these hidden-agenda items to be voiced, we at least know that they exist and that they have been acknowledged. This in itself is a big deal for most people. It's nice to know that our own aspirations are important. A word of caution here, though: Just paying lip service to the process of discovering people's personal agenda items is probably worse than not asking about them. If we cannot hope to address their personal aspirations, we need to hear them, at least, and explain why they cannot be addressed. Reasonable people will accept explanations, most of the time.

 A big part of the needs of individual stakeholders is addressed simply by just listening to—and sympathizing with—those needs and concerns.

In addressing the personal requirements or preferences of team members, we need to be sure that the team understands that the project can only accommodate *some* of these needs *before* we solicit them. Then, if a need cannot be met, it's a normal event—not a case of someone having their expectations falsely raised and then dashed to the ground.

We achieve alignment of individual stakeholders with corporate strategies and the direction of the project through a combination of including stakeholder needs in the project plan and managing expectations, explaining why some of their needs won't be met—or some compromise between the two.

The principle of letting people know that there is no guarantee of success, or that circumstances—and therefore, the project—will inevitably change can be generalized to all aspects of the project. As soon as we know that there is a problem that cannot be fixed or reversed, we should let the affected stakeholders know and give them time to adjust their expectations. (We'll discuss this further later!)

 It is better to eat crow when it is young and tender, rather than when it is old and tough!

4.3 The Project Team

Who is on the project team? For most of us, this is a relatively small group. It normally does not include people in supplier organizations providing goods and services to the project. Often, it excludes regulators, and, all too often, it even excludes clients! In SMART Project Management, we include all of these groups because we need to include everyone who contributes to the project's success. As this makes for an unusually large and cumbersome team, we use the target organization model for defining the project team (described in more detail in Chapter 10). For now, it is important to appreciate the need for different levels of communication between different parts of the project team. The more involved a person is, the more complete the communication needs to be. As we work with people who are less involved, so the communication is more focused and specialized. It also needs to be more carefully conducted, as miscommunication is more likely to occur. The same holds true for alignment: The closer people are to the project, the more important alignment becomes. With a properly aligned team, we are more likely to succeed because we reduce *churn*, rework, misunderstandings, opposition, antagonism, and all those other counterproductive emotions that occur when teams are unaligned.

The SMART project team is bigger than the traditional project team. This makes it harder to manage, as a team, but easier to deliver the overall project.

Team alignment and how to achieve it is described in Section C. We are trying to achieve a common understanding of what is important to project success and, probably just as tricky, what is not important to that success. If everyone on the team has a real understanding of what matters and what does not, then priorities and management of the inevitable compromises are easy.

One of the biggest causes of frustration in any job is wasted effort. In this category, we can include rushing to get something done, then seeing the result of all that effort languish forever while something else takes priority. Worse than this is when such extraordinary effort is rewarded by the results being declared "surplus to requirements"! If we know this is likely to occur on a project, we should do something about it. One way is to allow members of the team to decide what is important and what is not. This is rarely done in practice because people often display poor judgment; yet the real cause of *poor judgment* is that involved people were not adequately informed of the project priorities and so were forced to make an assessment in a vacuum. If the entire team shares a common view of success and what it takes to get there, we enable the team to perform much more effectively.

 The project team needs to understand what is important for the success of the project.

It is not enough to merely convey a project requirement to the members of a team and expect them to pick up this set of ideas and accept them unilaterally. Most of us are human enough to want some say in or influence over the project. This amount of say and influence may be severely limited by practical considerations. This said, we can—and should—provide some opportunity for buy-in by participants. One way to do this is to help each person involved in the project make a personal link between project success (from her point of view) and personal success. The type of link needed may take many forms. Some examples include the following:

■ personal achievement
■ recognition
■ career opportunity

- personal or professional challenge
- promotion, bonus, or other tangible reward for accomplishment of specific project objectives.

Whatever the reward—and it need not cost anything except a bit of extra effort to recognize success—the time taken to establish this link for everyone is important, as it will motivate, help build the team, and save endless hours in subsequent management and supervision.

 What is important to the success of the project must be aligned with what is important to the success of the team and the individuals on the team.

It is not always possible to achieve alignment of personal expectations with requirements of the project. In such situations, project objectives must take precedence. The primary reason is that we need to keep individual expectations sufficiently consistent and aligned in order to avoid internal conflicts. If we cannot meet individual objectives, we need to manage the situation immediately. Do not pretend to meet expectations, an act that leads to serious disappointment, anger, loss of credibility, and more. Recognize the limitations of any situation and acknowledge defeat if you must! In my experience, you earn more respect from honesty than from lying and making false promises.

 If individual team members' needs are not aligned with the team's overall objectives, the misalignment needs to be addressed through management of stakeholder expectations.

4.4   Management Tools and Metrics

The final area in which we need to consider alignment is between what is important to the project and what we plan and measure. Consider any of the projects on which you have worked, and you will likely see what is shown in the following sections.

What We Talk About

The messages on the wall: mission, key results, CSFs, and so on will be quality focused. We will talk to our client (especially at the outset) about the quality of results, controls in our process to deliver client needs, and more of this nature. There is a heavy focus on quality in the words we produce.

What We Measure

The things we put together as a baseline for measurement and for day-to-day project control will typically be based on a schedule. Milestones, deadlines, weekly checklists, progress meetings, and more are a big part of the routine for project controls. Yes, we will also have budget concerns, but much of that will relate to work hours being expended, as this (quite rightly) is seen as the most volatile element in project controls. What we measure has a predominance of schedule-related action and focus.

What the Business Drivers Are

The reason for most projects is to improve the business of the sponsor organization. Whether this is through introducing a new product; discovering new mineral deposits; building a factory, warehouse, or office; reorganizing the organization; running a marketing campaign; adding or modifying information systems; or a myriad of other projects, the bottom line is better business performance. Return on investment is the driver in the private sector; efficient use of taxpayer money is the guideline in the government sector. Either way, projects usually happen with a motive largely focused on cost.

Now which of these three is really important? We send mixed messages to the project team by talking about quality and measuring schedule and then complaining about costs! Awareness of mixed messages and a bit of care in managing the project controls leads to significant reduction in misunderstandings.

 What we measure to assess how well we are doing on a project is often not connected to what is important or how we planned the project.

No doubt, you've experienced the boss complaining to you about budget overruns and demanding appropriate action to fix the problem. You take that appropriate action, and then you get complaints about the inappropriateness of your actions because they affected the quality, scope, or schedule of the work. What is wrong with this picture? Apart from it being such a common occurrence that we can relate to it regardless of where we work or what business we are in? The problem is that our bosses and clients send us mixed messages all the time—and they are powerful messages aimed at the currently perceived project crisis. What's happening is normal. Our client or boss is simply keeping an eye on the ball, as it bounces from one priority to another. In Section C, we

Of course, we do not expect any increase in price
because of this design clarification.

will look at the use of the priority triangle to understand the dynamics of project priorities better. Meanwhile, we need to be aware of two things.

First, we need to recognize that priorities shift over time and are usually different at any one time for different participants in the project. Second, we need to realize that an overall set of priorities for the project needs to be developed for stability in management. Finally, if we are objective about looking at our own behavior, we will note some similarities with the picture that started this piece. It is quite likely that we routinely send mixed and confusing messages to our project teams, too!

 We send important signals to the team by what information we request and appear to value. If it is the wrong information, it is probably the wrong message too!

Chapter 5

REGENERATIVE WORK ENVIRONMENT

Reality is what you perceive. This seemed to be getting in the way of progress for the team on Gary's project. He was not the project manager; there was not really any special person in charge of the whole project. In the early stages, marketing seemed to be in charge. Then the research and development group took over for a while. Now the project and all of its problems were with Gary, who was in manufacturing. He had to make the whole thing work. He was being hounded by marketing because the project was already late. The technical team that had worked on product development had mostly been reassigned, and it was hard to find the people who were needed to solve the remaining technical problems. There were many problems, including trying to procure the right parts, making modifications to the design to accommodate production cost improvements, and developing the right product testing program. The other people involved in the project included the client for this new telephone and the executive who was the corporate sponsor for the project. Stress was high, and there always seemed to be other projects on which people needed to work, whether or not they were more important to the organization. Gary's primary problem lay in the attitudes of key people toward the project.

No matter who was responsible for the project, the real issue to be addressed was the work environment, which was not cohesive in any way. The project lacked any clear leadership. Communication was clearly a problem, since people did not take the time or make the effort to work on the project. These and other issues related to helping team members work together are discussed in this chapter. The time urgency for this project should not be lost. Fast-forming and effective project teams have certain things in common. In this chapter, we look at those factors and how they affect the success of the team—and therefore the project—on which the team is working.

 The right work environment for a project is important, and this can be strongly influenced by the project manager.

5.1   Having Fun at Work Is Serious Business

In this chapter, we will look at ways to make our project a great place to work. Let's face it; life is short, projects are demanding, and it is all too easy to burn out the team when delivering a continuous stream of successful projects, or even just one large project. Having a bit of fun on the way is powerful for purely business reasons; there are some neat social and other side effects, too!

Perhaps the most important aspect of a regenerative workplace is the ability to work safely. By this, I do not only mean a physically safe place to work, although physical safety is extremely important. So, let's start there. It makes good sense to avoid situations in which people are placed at risk for loss of health, limb, or life. Quite apart from the ethical and legal considerations, it makes good sense from a business point of view. If nothing else, a good safety record will lower insurance and other costs. When it is relevant, many customers will look at safety record as a prequalifier for suppliers of goods and services. Another good reason is simply related to productivity. This is easily observed by visiting a clean, organized, and safe construction site or manufacturing facility, then visiting one with poor practices in safety, hygiene, lighting, and ventilation. The difference in productivity can be quite profound.

Safety, however, goes beyond the physical aspects and includes other factors that make us feel that the work we do and the environment in which we work is safe in terms of our future, reputation, job security (as far as that can be real nowadays), career, and so on. These softer issues also form part of a safe workplace and need to be understood and managed.

 People are more productive in a safe work environment than in a dangerous one.

Just being safe in our workplace is not enough to get startling performance; we know from our own experience that other things are needed. In fact, being safe can slow us down because we get comfortable, and this can lead to complacency, being overrelaxed, and other diversions. What is it that keeps us charged and energetic? Cahoon and Rowney did a study in 1996 investigating stress in the workplace. They found low stress and high productivity in what they dubbed a "Regenerative" workplace. These workplaces had a number of features in common:

- open communication
- ownership of work
- propensity to take risk
- trust.

These features exactly match four of the five that I identified in my own review of best practices in project management. My fifth one was *fun* (with a special definition). Because of this coincidence in findings, I was able to make an important link. When we field-tested SMART Project Management, we found that our teams seemed to miss the second step in team development, based on these four steps: 1) forming, 2) storming, 3) norming, and 4) performing.

I was anxious to understand why, partly because I was no expert on teamwork, and I was worried about missing the storming phase symptoms. So I spoke to Al Cahoon, who pointed out that in truly regenerative organizations, the storming phase would disappear. Ah, here is the link: Storming is not part of the normal team-forming process; it is a symptom of not doing the teamwork stuff as well as we could.

 A positive and happy workplace is even better than one that is merely safe.

Now that we know that leaving the work environment to chance is going to slow down the team-building process, we realize that we need to create a positive work environment. As project teams are truly temporary—they last only as long as the project—we need to build them as quickly and efficiently as possible. We need to be proactive in creating a good working environment for the team, also considering the typical conditions in which project teams find themselves, including some, or all, of the following partial list of challenges:

- multidisciplinary and cross-functional teams
- interorganizational or intraorganizational teams

- people who do not get along
- divergent objectives for groups within the team
- differences in culture
- differences in language (even if we all speak English)
- varying sense of urgency
- people who are committed versus others merely involved (In a bacon and egg breakfast, the chicken is involved, and the pig is committed!)
- one group, or even one individual, from a dominant culture (often the project sponsor organization) trying to impose its, or her, culture, rules, and policies on the rest of the team. The team is then disenfranchised and disadvantaged, because it does not know how this particular culture works.

 We need to *plan* a good working environment; in most situations it does not *just happen*.

5.2   Effort Well Spent

You have probably been there and done that; I am talking about the touchy-feely team-building stuff. For many project managers, as well as for many technical people, the standard team-building exercises are, at best, frivolous breaks from routine. At worst, they are time-wasting exercises dictated by management. This attitude is understandable in many cases. Even if the team-building exercise was a success in reality, it's panned because of its segregation from the normal business of getting the project done. As many of the people we find on typical projects have self-selected themselves for this type of work, they are probably task oriented, which means that they do not like to waste time doing things that don't appear to directly contribute to the end result.

 Many project managers tend to be results (or task) oriented. As a consequence, there is a tendency to diminish or ignore activities that do not seem to directly contribute to the delivery of the project.

There is no point in trying to change this mindset. First, there is some basis for it, and, second, why fight it? Instead, here is a different approach: spend time on doing the right things. This effort will save you even more time later when the team is working and delivering more results than were originally planned. And the chances are good that it will do it more creatively, faster, and better than average.

 Time spent in nurturing a good work environment usually results in saving many times over the time, effort, and cost involved.

Since the original work that identified the earlier-mentioned five ingredients for effective teams, I have isolated two more ingredients, the result of field-testing and observation: creativity and tribalism. We now have seven elements with which to work. Following is a description of the seven elements. (How to get them to work for you is described in Chapters 10 and 12.)

5.3   Seven Ingredients of a Regenerative Work Environment

Why seven elements for successful teams? Frankly, I do not know whether or not this is a complete list, or even if they can accurately be called seven separate elements, for they are closely linked. The seven elements are presented in the order in which I have introduced them to teams when field-testing SMART Project Management; the order evolved from these tests. As the elements are so closely linked, there is a bit of a chicken-and-egg challenge in getting them to work for you. The following sequence seems to work best, but bear in mind that it is not the only one for creating high-performance teams.

 There are seven elements that, when present, will help teams form and work well together.

5.4   Open Communication (No Hidden Agendas)

Hidden-agenda items usually are the result of someone wanting something that doesn't align with his perception of the team's objectives. These hidden-agenda items will likely need to be addressed at some point. When they are, it is often too late to deal properly with them. Furthermore, they will have caused odd behavior, time wastage, and other grief along the way. The obvious thing to do is get them on the table in the beginning. This is easier said than done, but, once started, we quickly find that three things happen. First, the hidden-agenda items often turn out to be resolvable. Second, we find that there is better alignment of the team (see earlier). Third, we open up further communication, as people realize that it is acceptable to bring up issues that appear to be tangential to the main thrust of the project.

An obvious trap needs to be mentioned and avoided: do not set a precedent by allowing anyone to wander off the meeting agenda at any time. It is clearly not effective. To avoid it, have an agenda item for early meetings and then for later meetings when new people are brought into the team. This agenda item should create an opportunity for people to air their own hidden-agenda items. I like a cheeky approach to this: I label the item *Hidden-Agenda Items*! This tends to get some constructive discussion going on the subject of open communication. It also serves the purpose of being candid, setting an example for the team.

Open communication implies that we share information with others—not all information for everyone or on a *need-to-know* basis. There is a balance between too much information and not enough information, and this balance needs to evolve as the project progresses. I tend to start with too much information, for the purpose of getting used to sharing knowledge. Teams are usually pretty good at giving feedback; if you give a team too much information, its members will quickly let you know. If you provide too little, you often will not know until something has gone wrong—and that is too late!

 **Open communication is closely linked to the only absolute rule in SMART Management: Never hide a problem.**

This rule prevents a worse problem. If we have a problem and hide it, we instantly have three problems: 1) the original one, 2) the fact that someone is expending (often considerable) effort in hiding it, and 3) the fact that we are missing the best opportunities to fix the original problem.

 If the only—or at least the primary—cause of failure in projects is a breakdown in communication, then open communication must surely be the antidote to this poison!

We should start with introducing open communication in the early planning stages of a project. For example, use the planning process to identify all of the things that define success for a project and as an incentive to elicit people's expectations.

 It is easier to get dialogue going in a group where people know and trust each other. If we can take advantage of this type of situation, it's easier to get started with open communication by example. If, however, the team is new and people do not know each other, then we need time to build sufficient trust and allow people to feel comfortable about opening up. This is part of the *safety* issue discussed earlier. Patience is required.

 Open communication needs to be developed, and we rely on trust to help achieve it. This makes the process a bit chicken-and-eggish!

There is little room for patience in the high-pressure world in which we live today. So, if we need to kick-start the open-communication piece, one way is to use incentives and lead by example at the same time. Try telling the team what is in the project for you and how you intend to get what you want. For example, you may be after a promotion. If you introduce this information properly and professionally, you are showing the team that it is quite acceptable to have an agenda item and declare it. More so, you may recruit help in achieving your objective!

Any experienced project manager will spot the obvious problem with what I have just said. Declaring such an agenda item carries a risk, too: people will know how to get at you later. Fair enough—if you are not willing to take the risk, why ask anyone else on the team to do so? Even if this happens, we have not given up on open communication yet. You still need it, just try it at a different level. Consider explaining the corporate objective and how the project fits into and helps achieve it. The chances are pretty good that this will be a first and unusual experience for many of the team's membership!

The Project That Nearly Died

One particularly quiet person, sitting in a project planning meeting, spoke for the first time when challenged with exclusion of his project agenda items if they were not declared at that particular meeting. He said that he was at the meeting only because his boss had sent him. His boss did not want the project to succeed. (A turf battle was taking place.) The team member's job, as he understood it, was to figure a way to scuttle the project!

You could have heard an ant's burp after that announcement.

The issue was discussed with the boss in question afterward, and the project went ahead without hitches—because the turf issues were resolved up-front. In fact, it is likely that we had a better result than originally planned, but that is a matter of perspective!

If all else fails, let people know that the measures for success of the project will only include those declared—and agreed to—by team members at the planning stage. Any changes afterward and the requestor needs to find the budget and schedule extension required to handle the change when it is made. It is amazing what comes out of the woodwork with that challenge!

 For open communication to take hold and work, leadership is required in developing it. Failing that, some real incentive to get effective open communication going can work for you.

5.5 Ownership of Your Job

No doubt you have had the experience of being micromanaged, and you know that it is no fun for the managee. Often it is no fun for the manager either.

We limit the opportunity for creativity when we tell people how to do their jobs. The more we can increase an individual's autonomy, the higher the potential for performance. The need for alignment is obvious. Good alignment is based on effective and open communication. You can see the links for yourself; I do not need to spell them out. If I did, I'd be guilty of a form of micromanagement. I mention this, because it is easy for us to fall into bad habits without being aware that we are doing so, although the recipient of micromanagement notices pretty quickly. With open communication, we should feel free to comment and point out these flaws as we go.

 Virtually nobody likes to be micromanaged. When we micromanage others, we are often unaware of what we are doing!

One of the most common flaws in management is to try to make our problems someone else's. We recognize this when it is done to us but are less likely to recognize the same behavior when we do it to others. No doubt you have been through a similar experience as the one described here.

You are busy getting something done, and it is near the end of the day. Your boss walks into your office (or wherever you are) and hands you a file or some other token symbolizing the passing of responsibility to you. If you are smart, you refuse to take it, and she ends up putting it on the desk. The first part of this ritual is complete. The next step is to tell you that something must be done. It is vital. You are the only one who can handle it. So do it. Here is what is going through your mind as the rest of this ritual unfurls: "This is your problem. There must be others who can do this. If it was really vital, why so little notice? Who is going to be in more trouble if it is not done—you or me? It cannot be done in the time you are asking. ... " I will stop there, as the thoughts might get worse! In essence, you do not own the problem. More importantly, you do not want to own the problem. Thus, you will resist it. If the work does not get done, the problem will still not be yours.

When was the last time you did this to someone on your team? Bad question, I know. Now, let us try the same thing, but do it right this time.

The boss walks in and explains that something has changed—this opens up the door for you to negotiate changes in your priorities. She then says that the change has resulted in a bit of a crisis, and she would like your help in resolving it. (You note the invitation to participate.) Maybe she pauses, waiting for you to ask what is going on (using your natural inquisitiveness to suck you in). Perhaps, knowing you are familiar with this tactic, she just carries right on and explains the situation, inviting your comment. ... I need not complete the picture. You can see where it's heading. This is still the same exercise: "Stop whatever was urgent today; this is more urgent!" The end result, however, is different. You've had the opportunity to accept the change, negotiate new priorities in your work, and then discuss options to resolve the problem. You own whatever work you take; there will be genuine commitment to get things done.

 We are more likely to perform to deadlines and other targets that we are involved in setting than those dictated to us by others.

Once you have committed to doing the impossible, you will find a way to achieve the result you need. You will go the extra mile even, if needed. This is human nature: we all take pride in a job well done. If we are not constantly being asked to put out fires, we will happily pitch in when needed. And we will work hard to meet a deadline to which we've committed. If this is true of you and me, it is probably true of most of the team members who work on our project.

 Most people who commit to delivery of something will work hard to meet that commitment.

Given that we need a bit of flexibility in managing our own work, it follows that others need this as well. Consider today's role as analogous to that of the conductor of an orchestra. Individual members need to play the right tune at the right time to achieve the desired result. The conductor will discuss and agree on the artistic interpretation of the piece with each of the individual players or with groups of players, but how the instruments are handled and played is left to the professionals. Turning up for rehearsals on time is a matter of professionalism. (It is unusual for musicians to be late for rehearsals. It is not unusual for people to be late for meetings. Maybe we can learn something here!) The boundaries of where the musician has total control, where coordination and agreement is required, and where each player must comply with the requirements of the conductor are agreed and respected. In an orchestral setting, such understandings are known through culture, training, and tradition. In the case of projects, the boundaries are not so clear. They need to be clarified, and expectations should be set at the outset. Projects and project teams work better when all has been agreed at the outset and then managed afterward, especially when new people join the team.

If we own and control our own work, we are usually happier than when others try to dictate all the details to us.

5.6   Propensity to Take Risk

I do not know of anyone who has been fired for following organizational policy. Doing what has always been done is safe. Most businesses exist "to make money, not take risks." Not true—there are few businesses that make money with no risk attached. We need to be aware of our business' risk-taking profile if we want to understand what is and what is not acceptable to the organization.

 Few organizations fire anyone for following policy.

There is a safe path, preferred by many in middle management. Unfortunately, following policy and procedure without challenging either will not improve performance.

 The first sign of madness is to keep doing the same thing while expecting a different result!

Trying new ideas is a real challenge for many organizations. Often, the larger the organization, the harder it is for it to move away from established practices. Many executives in such organizations have limited power over change, as the more effective changes span more than one area of control. Both large and small organizations that consider themselves to be business leaders will tend to respond to a request to try a new process (in my case, a way of delivering projects) with the question: "Who has tried this before?" In other words, we are only leaders as long as someone else has done it before. The reason is quite rational: if someone else has tried it and been successful, then the risk of failure is lower than with an untried process. Understanding this reluctance to take risk and the reasons for it is important.

 Many business leaders prefer to do things that previously have been done by someone else, so maybe they are not leaders after all.

There is a shift in the corporate view of risk taking place. Increasingly, companies are recognizing the uncertainty element in conducting business. This is partly driven by the increase in uncertainty that is generated by accelerating change in technologies, markets, international and national politics, regulatory requirements, and more.

Risk analysis tools are more accessible. Risk taking is a significant part of the decision process. We need to move away from merely being responsive to our market and toward influencing the marketplace or creating new markets. This is in turn creating a new mentality regarding corporate operating style. There are many responses to the changes we are undergoing, but one emerging trend seems to be that companies are reworking their internal structures and procedures on an ongoing basis. This is still largely being done by step changes from one static form to another. How many of us see corporate reorganizations in some form on a regular or frequent basis? The logical next step is to have continuous and rapid evolution.

Such corporate evolution will require that we consider more flexible corporate policy and procedures. A framework more akin to a set of general guidelines with few rules will likely emerge. In the meantime, we must content ourselves with some controlled anarchy!

 Part of any organizational policy must be that it is acceptable to breach policy. But you may want to have some organizational policy about this!

Even before organizations adopt more flexible policies, it may be that we need to adopt them on our projects to help them succeed. If we work on large, complex, and volatile projects, we need more structure in managing them than we do in managing smaller and more routine ones. Either way, there needs to be recognition of the real risks involved. The obvious risk of having an incorrect budget or schedule is a starting point. We are all intuitively aware of the many things that can—and do—go wrong on projects, such as:

■ delays in decisions and approvals
■ unavailability of staff and resources
■ false starts, due to misunderstandings or changes
■ technology problems (lots of these to choose from)
■ too-high productivity expectations
■ ill, vacationing, or reassigned key personnel
■ restricted access to or delay of information
■ we could go on forever.

That's not what I meant when I said,
"Make sure the team is tied into the plan for the project."

Now let's look at the problem using an analogy that highlights the key issues for us (see sidebar, Commuting to Work).

We need to be able to accept, live, and work with the very real uncertainties in the planning and execution of projects. This is often at variance with the expectations of the sponsor organization, which is why we started this discussion with the need to build in some procedural flexibility at the project level, even if the host organization has not reached this point in its evolution at the corporate level.

 A propensity to take risk is all about accepting the realities of risk-taking and its consequences—both good and bad.

The point is that we cannot escape risk and uncertainty. This is true in almost anything we do, and it is particularly true of projects because of their very nature. Projects involve different disciplines, are difficult to plan with any precision, can be influenced by many variables, and involve an end customer and a work environment that will inevitably change in some way after the project has been planned. We must not stick our head in the sand and pretend that there is greater certainty than there really is.

Commuting to Work

Ask any group of people how long it takes them to commute to work, and the typical reply will include a range of times, such as ten to twenty minutes, or forty minutes to an hour and a half. Often, though, the odd person will say, "Exactly seventeen minutes." She is probably wrong in her precision, and if not, there will be unusual circumstances around the precision.

Let's stay with the normal response. Why the range, when it is something we do every day, probably have more control over than most of the work we do, and the trip is relatively short and fairly predictable?

Compare this to the precision we employ when forecasting project completion. We have never done a project like it, it involves lots of other people and companies, and we have to guess at what might happen. Yet, we work with amazing precision—often accurate to the day for completion of projects that are months and years long! This is accuracy to within a fraction of 1 percent, compared to the relatively sloppy 50 percent or so for commuting to work.

If we look carefully, this makes little sense—even after considering the consistency of average commute times (smaller range) and the opportunity on a project for give and take in the longer time span that is available.

 Risk-taking is an essential part of project management.

So if there is real risk in a project and we need to acknowledge that it is there, it follows that we then need to create a work environment in which it is relatively safe to work with this risk. Gone are the days when the label *project manager* was synonymous with *scapegoat*. If those days are not gone, they should be! The entire team working on a project should be indemnified from consequences that are genuinely beyond its control. But we need to be careful, as many things fall into a gray area, such as *normal* weather conditions for outside work or *normal* time for obtaining a license or permit. These elements are largely beyond the control of the project team. However, identifying the risk and having a contingency plan for the abnormal is within the control of the team. As these are things that often are not *normal*, we should recognize them and address the problem.

Don't Park Your Brain Outside

A propensity to take risk is an essential ingredient in developing effective project teams.

5.7   Creativity

Most people enjoy being creative. If you think about the *good* days at work, you will probably find that many of those days included one or more of the following creative happenings:

- You solved a challenging problem.
- You had a neat idea for improving the business (a new product, a better way of doing something, a marketing concept, and so on).
- You inspired a coworker to do something special.
- You were particularly productive, as a result of a better approach to your work.
- You obtained some new insights into the business, or part of it, as a result of putting together data from various sources.
- You were part of a group that had a wild (and possibly hilarious time) tinkering with some ideas, trying to get out of the conventional box of thinking about how you tackle daily issues.

Whatever our business, being creative within our own sphere typically does at least one of two things: it gives us a charge, and it helps our business to be a bit more competitive.

 One of the things that keeps our jobs interesting is the opportunity to be creative. Arenas in which to do this include problem solving, developing ideas and products, analyzing information, and improving processes.

Most organizations discourage creativity through careful placement of roadblocks in culture, procedure, approval systems, and more. Our society also puts many barriers in the way of creativity—for example, the ways we educate our children and orient people in our organizations. At school, we teach people to spell, color between the lines, that the sky is blue, and that the grass is green. Then we punish or penalize people who do not conform. I always understood that William Shakespeare (did I spell that correctly?) could not spell. Consequently, he invented hundreds of phrases and new words for the English language. I wonder, how creative would he have been if he had been taught to spell?

In our organizations, we strongly encourage people to *fit in*. How often do we hear (or say) things like, "That's not how it's done around here," "We can't do that; we do things differently," or "That will not be approved because we have never done it before." I am sure that you can find many more such indicators of creativity-stifling behavior. We all stifle it, because we are conditioned to do so. Let me try something.

In this paragraf; I hav spelt many of the wurds inkorrecklie. I'm pretty shure that yew will still understand what I yam trying two say. As eye move on, the word swill change. The in tent is two ewes asthma-knee knew an din appropriate words that still pass spell checkers.

You get the point. Did you feel that I was losing it for a while? Were you uncomfortable that the quality of the book had deteriorated? How about the story mentioned earlier in this chapter of the project that nearly died? Did you feel uncomfortable or shocked when I mentioned the ant's burp? Frankly, I hesitated writing that because I was worried about how you might react! We are conditioned to standards of behavior that are sometimes appropriate; other times, they simply get in the way of creative thinking. We do not like to take risks.

 Most organizations have built-in barriers to creativity, not the least of which is a perceived low willingness to take risk.

I have already mentioned that we unlearn creative thinking at school. We continue to get training in or receive reinforcement for noncreative habits throughout our lives. We need to be trained back into creative thinking. A wonderful book—and an easy read—is *A Whack on the Side of the Head* by Roger von Oech. This is a good start on the road to recovery of creative skills. Buy it, read it, and share it with your project team members.

 We unlearn our ability to be creative at a very early age. We need to be trained back into the skill.

The way we think about a particular problem or situation is colored by many things, such as culture, political outlook, genes, sense of humor, education and training, family circumstances, religion, and much more that will influence our view of what is happening and our response to stimuli. The creative process is very personal. Some of us are happy in a group-think environment, while others in our group are far more creative if left alone to work on problems and opportunities. Project managers need to harvest the skills of each individual on the team and get them hitched to our project wagon. (Boy, did I mix up my metaphors there!)

 Creativity comes in many forms and needs to be nurtured if it is to help the team, project, and business. Creativity is a personal and individual thing that may work in isolation or in a group setting.

Finally—I said it before, but here it is again, because it is so important.

 People who are being creative are usually having fun, too!

5.8 Fun in the Workplace

Let me define *fun* in this context; there are two parts to the definition. First, conventional fun is great, and I would always encourage it as long as it does not get in the way of doing what should be done. Second—and more specifically in this context—I am talking about those actions that make us feel satisfied and happy with our work. There are few things that contribute to feeling that we had a really good day at work. The list is short:

- We achieved something that was a challenge or that was particularly important to us—or both.
- We got peer recognition for something that they perceived as special or well done.
- We got corporate recognition for an achievement and how it helped the business. In other words, a boss pointed out to us that we had more than earned our keep by doing something special.
- We had a chance to be truly creative and either constructive or productive.

Think back to the last time that you went home feeling energized and looking forward to going back to work. (Can you think back that far?) I would be really surprised if one or more of the four things on the list had not happened to give you that positive feeling. If this could happen virtually every day, then we would really have a great place to work.

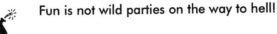 **Fun is not wild parties on the way to hell!**

Go for Fun—All the Way!

Shortly after delivering a presentation on fun at a seminar, Andrew Smith phoned to tell me that he was lucky to still have a job! Inspired by my presentation, he had tried to implement fun in his company. Here is what happened.

At a senior management meeting, he introduced the subject of fun and started writing the word on a flipchart. About two-thirds of the way through, the chairman of the board, who knew me, interrupted and said, "You've been talking to that Hartman fellow. You're going to write 'fun.' We're not in the business of having fun. We are an engineering company, and we are here to do engineering and make money."

At this point, my new convert turned around to look at what he had written and then said to the chairman, "All I've written so far is 'FU.'"

Only after he realized what he'd said did it occur to him what others had heard!

Apparently, the rest of the day was a lot more fun than most people in the room had had in a long time!

The moral (if there is one) is to go all the way if you plan to have fun.

We have seen the very short list of things that make for a positive work environment. We will look at how to make these things happen for us in Section C.

 Fun is about creativity, recognition, reward, and achievement.

We do not live in a perfect world, nor should we try to do the futile and create a workplace that is perfect. What we need is a balanced, safe, and fun place in which to work. With the right direction, we can put up with a lot of daily trivia, boring activities, grind, and general stupidity if these few important elements for a regenerative work environment are in place.

 Having fun makes up for a lot of other shortcomings in the workplace.

We earlier discussed trust. Working with people we trust is easier than the converse. Fun goes a long way toward addressing this issue and helping to develop and nurture trust in our team.

To come to grips with this is easy. When was the last time you had a lot of fun with people you mistrusted? Stupid question! When we think about it, so is the converse. How often do we mistrust the people with whom we are having fun? We can use fun to help nurture a happy, productive, and safe workplace. We can also use it as a gauge of the level of trust (and, therefore, of effective and open communication) in our team.

 It is difficult to have fun with people you do not trust. Equally, it is harder to mistrust people with whom you can have fun!

Teams and individuals having fun also display a few other common traits, listed below. They are interesting to observe and note if for no other reason than they are worth noting, because we have some people in every organization who frown on fun as being unbusiness-like.

- We are more productive when we have fun.
- It's easier to be creative.
- It's easier to build and maintain trust.
- We reduce absenteeism.
- Health is generally better.
- Working overtime when needed is less difficult for everyone.
- We are more willing to go the extra mile.

 There are sound business reasons for having fun.

Once we understand the ingredients for fun in the workplace, they become relatively easy to incorporate. We will discuss this in more detail in Chapters 10 and 12. For now, let me introduce another concept: tribalism. Yes, you read it correctly, and we will look at it in more detail in a moment. Tribalism is something in our human makeup that can be harnessed for our businesses and projects; others have done so previously—with success. Adding the fun ingredient to our tribal culture is not only relatively easy, but it also helps us with the tribal identity.

5.9   A Tribal Culture

So what is this tribalism thing? We are all members of one or more tribes. First, we are part of the family tribe at home. Often, we are members of two or more family tribes through marriage. We are also members of the workplace tribe and maybe a sports or hobby tribe, too. Within each tribe, we speak the tribal language, wear tribally acceptable costumes, fit into the hierarchy, and respect the tribal symbols. In exchange, these tribes will protect us from the enemy outside the tribe, by sticking together in adversity. We are accustomed to doing this, and it is true, to a lesser extent perhaps, of most corporations and departments or subgroups within them.

 We belong to more than one tribe at a time, and we are accustomed to this. Tribes have certain ingredients: language, symbols, culture, defense of members, hierarchy, traditions, and induction to membership.

Some of us are old enough to recall IBM's one-time tribal costume: blue suit and white shirt. Most of us, at least in North America, recognize that the Harley Davidson tribe does not wear a full-face crash helmet. We know that the machines they ride are *hogs*.

In helping teams develop new skills that are anathema to corporate culture, I have used this tribal instinct to help the team build its own enabling culture without having to mess with the entrenched corporate culture. We can do things within the security of the team that would be too dangerous in the mainstream of the organization.

 Tribalism is part of our human makeup. We should take advantage of it to make our teams more effective.

One additional benefit of tribal cultures is that the approach helps level the playing field in interorganizational and intraorganizational project teams. Many of us have worked in teams that are dominated by one group, imposing *its way* of doing things on the rest; it is often the sponsor organization. The problem is not apparent when we are part of the dominant group; we see efficiencies in everyone doing things in an orderly fashion and in a way that is consistent with the client group. All the rest (who will typically not say anything about the situation) view this as a set of rules that they do not fully understand or that may be in conflict with their own organizations. They may not buy-in to the way that the client does things and so on. In the end, the team is working on two levels: one group knows the rules and how to work around them; the other group (usually larger) does not. The result is seen in inefficiencies, friction, misunderstandings, and more.

 The tribal culture of the team needs to be strong enough to allow members to work on a level playing field. (No dominant external culture sets the rules and processes for project delivery.)

When a team forms, the SMART approach is to allow it to develop its own rules. We know from theory that this is true, but we end up force-feeding one dominant culture with the result that the storming phase exists, and the end result is often one that needs more maintenance than really necessary. The project manager will play a significant role in setting team culture. Increasingly, my observation is that the dominant types (my way or the highway) will produce less effective teams than those that are more flexible and sensitive to the needs of the team as a whole. It pays to listen to what individuals suggest with regard to how the team should function. Everyone brings scars and successes from past experience, and it's all different and usually interesting stuff! Do not confuse *dominant types* with strong charismatic leaders. The latter persuade by personality, example, and other leadership skills. The former coerce.

 The culture of the team is strongly influenced by the members and the team's leaders.

A relatively small investment in effective team building at the beginning of a project pays for itself many times over in increased productivity and better communication. These facets, and others derived from having fun and being creative, help nurture trust.

 A good tribe will nurture trust among members.

5.10   Trust

In the end, trust is a vital ingredient in regenerative organizations. It is also the hardest component to define, create, and support; it cannot be bought. Where do we start? One way is to look at the types of trust with which we might work. Although not yet a scientific construct, we can consider three types of trust to which most people relate: 1) ethical based, 2) competence based, and 3) emotional based.

In a team context, we often think of integrity-based trust. We ask questions like:

- Is it safe to disclose information?
- Will people listen to my concerns?
- Will I get honest or political answers to my questions?
- Will people tell the truth? Hold back vital information?
- Are people likely to sacrifice me for their own advancement?
- What happens if I ask a dumb question? Make a mistake? Suggest something outrageous?

There are many more questions like this, and they all challenge the personal and group integrity of the team. We gain confidence as we test and see results, and as we gain experience in working with others on the team.

On an individual basis, we relate to work, tasks, and individual contribution. We all know that we have to earn our reputations, and we have to re-earn them in each new situation. Our professional or trade reputation is based on competence. Some examples of competence-based trust questions include the following:

- Will the job get done?
- Is that person a self-starter?
- How much supervision is required?
- Can I rely on that person to do what he says he will do?
- How productive is that person?
- What is the quality of his work? His track record? His reputation with previous bosses or clients?

Emotional trust derives from being able to work for someone because we want to, rather than because we have to!

 There are different *flavors* of trust. The most important ones are integrity (personal and professional trust), competence (trust in technical capability), and leadership (trust that following you will result in a positive outcome).

A regenerative organization is a *Catch-22* situation; trust is the cornerstone of such an organization. Yet, we need all of the other ingredients if we want to develop trust in our team. Thus, we need to set about earning trust. As leaders, we need to be fair and consistent in our dealings. We need to have reasonable, yet challenging, targets and objectives. We need to demonstrate trust wherever and whenever we reasonably can, to show that we mean business. One easy way to do this is to start relying on people to do their jobs. This should be the easiest of them all. After all, we expect others to rely on us and not feel the need to micromanage what we are supposed to be doing.

 Trust is earned. It is easier to earn and nurture in a regenerative work environment.

We all know that trust may take forever to build, but it takes only moments to destroy. Trust is temporary; it needs nurturing. Mistrust tends to be more permanent. We need to keep an eye on the trust ball throughout all of our work. And remember: trust is a two-way street!

 Trust needs to be maintained.

If we work at maintaining the other six elements of a regenerative work environment, it will help us maintain trust. The link is probably obvious, but here is another way of looking at it. Monitor the openness of communication, how much fun people are having, how willing team members are to be openly creative, and so on. If you spot a drop in performance in any of these areas, it is likely a symptom of fallen trust levels—time to take action!

 Trust will develop if the other regenerative work environment elements are present.

Chapter 6

TRANSITION: MANAGING CHANGE AND UNCERTAINTY

"I shouldn't be here!" That was the opening line from Karen to Arne. The occasion was the launch of a drill ship for a Norwegian company. Every contractor who had contributed to the project with goods or services over a certain value had been invited. Karen had just discovered the cut-off for contributions. Her product was a water treatment plant that converted seawater into drinking water by reverse osmosis. Arne was the project manager, and, his curiosity aroused, he asked Karen why she felt she should not be at the celebration. Karen coolly said, "Because you paid too much for our product!" Not surprisingly, Arne was upset and wanted to know why Karen would make such a statement, implying that her company had cheated him, at such an event. Karen replied, "Actually, you cheated yourselves. I thought you might want to know how." She explained.

When Arne's company put out the bid package, they sent bidders a detailed document, some four inches thick, with precise and complete specifications: materials to be used, dimensions, finishes, and more. At about the same time, Karen's company received a similar request for installation in a cruise ship being built in northern Italy. These specifications were, in Karen's opinion, much more precise and demanding. Arne's company's specifications told Karen's company how to build the plant in such detail that her company could not use its own expertise, the latest technology, or standard parts or materials. The cruise ship-builders, on the other hand, simply specified the required performance. As a result, the Italians got a standard off-the-shelf product with better technology at a fraction of the cost of the one delivered to Norway.

Arne wanted to know how three pages could produce more precise and rigorous specifications than the four-inch-thick bid supplied by his company. Karen explained that the Italian specification simply stated the amount of water to produce and reminded the bidders that the passengers of the ship would likely be rich Americans with lawyers!

With technology changing so quickly, we need to revisit who does what on a project. Fast change is a relatively new phenomenon. It has crept up on us, and we are only now starting to feel the impact of rapid change on our society, as well as on the way we think and how we manage. How we manage projects, the tools we use, the contracts we write, and much more have roots in what we did over thirty years ago. Very few of the assumptions made then—and on which we base today's management tools and processes—hold true any longer. It follows that we need new and more responsive tools now. We also need to better understand issues such as risk, uncertainty, and the propensity of things to change. This higher uncertainty, its causes, likely future implications on projects, and how to manage these implications are explored in this chapter.

Arne's lesson was that it is better to leave how something is done in the hands of the experts. Often, performance specifications are better than detailed technical ones.

6.1   Rate of Change and What Is Changing

You may have noticed how many organizations are constantly redefining what is meant by *core business*; this is a result of change. Another symptom of rapid change is the amount of outsourcing we are doing as compared to even a few years ago. Yet another sign is the shift in skills at every level. For example, not so long ago, we hired *programmers* to help us build software; now these same people are much more focused. We have specialists within the boundaries of hardware and operating systems, languages, and applications. Today's requirement would be for a client server specialist in C++ programming of user interfaces for the Dunn and Bradstreet accounting package. Skills in object-oriented programming may also be required.

You may say that we are seeing this change only in high-technology companies; this is not true. Even the tradition-bound construction industry has moved from requesting "ten welders" from the union hall. Now it is asking for two mild steel-pipe welders; one stainless steel, down-hand welding specialist; and so on. We may even see requests for Mary or Fred specifically!

Technology is the driver. As we double available technology every few years, we see three things emerge. First, we need more specialists. Second, we cannot afford to keep all of the specialists in-house, so we outsource those skills. Third, because of the need to outsource, what was a routine in-house process a few scant years ago is now a complex contractual arrangement with several specialist out-house suppliers and all of the coordination and other headaches that this produces.

 Technology is doubling every three years or so. We are only just starting to see the impact of this on how we do business.

It is not just technology that is increasing; so also is our knowledge and understanding in many other areas including human behavior, ethics, history, politics, economics, anthropology, social science, medicine, and much more. All of this knowledge is creating new challenges. People who know and understand more will inevitably be more competitive that others, all things being equal. Access to knowledge and the ability to harness it effectively requires a new skill set.

 Knowledge overall is doubling every five years or so. New management skills are already being demanded to manage enterprises in this emerging world.

One of the fascinating challenges we face is the need to communicate effectively and precisely. My own observation is that this is getting more difficult. Remember the problem with the word *function* (Chapter 1)? Not only the word has been recycled in the past decade or two, but also, as language is a living thing, we have changed the meaning of the words we use, and we are making those changes faster than ever. Evolution seems to be different from one part of the world to the next and from one organization to the next, but all of this increases the challenge in communicating exactly what we intend.

 It is getting harder to describe what we intend; therefore, it is harder to achieve our objectives.

One of the other significant shifts we have seen in society is greater involvement by the public in what affects us. There is also greater

What Changes Have We Seen in the Past Fifteen Years?

Some significant changes happened between 1982 and 1998, a span of just over fifteen years. Think of the new technology that became available during that time: fax machines, then modems, public access to the Internet, yellow sticky notes (and we get them in different colors now), cell phones, notebook computer (with color monitors and graphics yet), handheld computers, cloning of sheep and mice, huge leaps in development of artificial limbs and other body parts—and the list goes on.

On the political front, we have seen new countries form, old barriers come down, new trading partnerships emerge, and much more.

On the social front, emancipation of races and genders continues to move forward slowly or, in some opinions, too slowly or too quickly.

And there are many more fronts.

awareness of what influences our lives, which in turn has led to increases in regulations to control what is being done in the name of progress. Regulations in the environmental arena, as well as in other areas, have grown at international, national, regional, and local levels.

There are very few projects that are not affected by regulatory requirements or potential future requirements. They range from labor rules to safety, and from compliance with national technical standards and codes to voluntary industry standards.

 The number of regulations with which we have to work continues to increase exponentially.

We have meandered over just two areas of development and change. The experts in projecting or predicting the future tend to look at what has happened in the past ten to fifteen years to predict what might occur in the next five.

When we look at how much conventional thinking about project management has changed in the past fifteen years, we find it has changed very little. Many experienced practitioners are aware of this and are looking for better ways to manage projects. Some improved versions of classical project management are emerging; one example is Prince 2, out of the United Kingdom.

It is reasonable to expect the same quantum of change in the next five years as we have seen in the last fifteen. Are we keeping up with these changes in how we manage projects?

Basically, there are two issues related to all this change and how we manage projects. The first one is that we have a different type of project to manage. The second challenge is that we are working in an environment where change continues apace, and this means our projects will likely change as well. The dynamics of today's world already have made it more difficult to bring in projects on time and within budget. This trend will doubtless continue, so we need to rethink what we are doing about change and uncertainty in projects.

 There is so much change that it is getting harder to predictably deliver projects on time and within budget.

6.2   Predictability of the Future

It is not an original thought, but the only thing that we should never predict is the future. Yet, think about it; put together any plan for delivery of a project, and predicting the future is exactly what we are doing! Hence, perhaps we need to redefine what we mean by planning and the planning process.

 Just about the only thing you should never try to predict is the future!

In practice, the solution is really simple. We plan at different levels of detail, appropriate to the time horizon with which we are working. For example, we may plan to meet major milestones spread over the entire project. Then we plan in more detail, identifying the deliverables needed, for, say, four weeks ahead. On a weekly basis, we reduce this to a daily list of what needs to be done to maintain the schedule. Generally, the habit is to plan at one level of detail for most or all of the project. Yet, this may not be detailed enough for the beginning and will undoubtedly be too detailed for the end. One of the results is that we spend too much time updating schedules, or we reach a point where we give up trying to work with the formal project schedule, because it is much too hard work for the benefit received.

Another problem is that we give up before we start. Why bother with plans and schedules if you know they are going to be wrong, or because the future is too uncertain?

In managing research projects—software, new product development, oil and gas exploration, and others—I keep hearing the same rationale for not planning. The future is too uncertain, so there is no point in trying to plan; we are exempt. Despite these protestations, I have yet to see any project that did not benefit from appropriate planning.

 Everything we do now will end some time in the future. So we must do *some* predicting.

The trick to predicting the future is to base as much as you can on expert opinion and track record, and then be vague. Let me explain, because this sounds unprofessional. There are different ways of being vague. One is to generally be unclear about what you mean; the other is to provide a range of likely outcomes. It is the latter that I am advocating, and I offer two reasons for doing so: credibility and reality.

Forecasting the likely outcome of future events is, in itself, not logically credible. Yet how often do we see the incredible being demanded in terms of what a project will cost, when it will be finished, and exactly what the end result will be. The truth is, we can reasonably guess within a range. We can go further and put probabilities on the range of outcomes. We can even go further than that and do the same for each element of the project. This idea is not new either; it originated in the 1950s and was labeled PERT. With today's computing power, we can move beyond the severe limitations of PERT by using Monte Carlo analysis in conjunction with PLO estimating (deliberately a bit more colorful than PERT, for reasons discussed in Section 6.3 and Chapter 9). A range of outcomes is a more credible forecast than a precise cost or completion date, final scope, or quality definition.

Dealing with ranges for the sake of reality is easier to see with an illustration. The story in the sidebar, Picking a Project, is about an investment committee that has to choose between two new products. The company can only afford the investment in one of them, so it has to choose which one. To make the problem impossibly simple, I have eliminated many of the variables and imponderables that normally go with this type of investment decision, so we can see more clearly the huge impact of using better data for the delivery of a project.

In practice, when companies have overcome the natural aversion to range estimating, better project investment decisions are being made. Over the next few years, I predict these companies will do better than others.

> **The better we get at predicting the future (or the more informed the prediction is), the more successful we will be.**

There are several interesting books written by well-known futurists. The *Megatrends* series by J. Naisbitt and P. Aburdene (1990) and *The 500-year Delta—What Happens After What Comes Next* by J. Taylor and W. Wacker (1997) are only two of them. Futurist books make good reading and give a sense of what might be coming down the pike in the next few years. They provide insight into how project managers draw their conclusions and make their predictions, which could help us predict and plan our own projects. It is also helpful to try to gauge where the rest of the world might be when our project is completed, and what this could mean to the project itself.

Futurist books offer some help for longer-term predictions.

One of the most important aspects of any plan for the future is managing people's expectations around what is a reasonable range of outcomes. Most customers like precise dates, budgets, and specifications. It also sets their expectations in such a way that the chances of delivering and meeting them are pretty small. Being practical about forecasts includes using ranges, or, if we stick with single-point estimates, then attaching a probability of success to them. This sends a message to the buyer about the realities and precision of our forecast.

 Be practical about the limitations of any predictions you make. Manage expectations.

6.3 PLO Estimating

In the 1950s, an inspired team working on the Polaris Missile invented the program, evaluation, and review technique (PERT) for scheduling. The team felt that the uncertainty involved in the planning of projects needs to be reflected in the plans. It decided to include *optimistic*, *likely*, and *pessimistic* estimates in its forecasts, which complicated the scheduling process. Thus, the solution—smart for the time—was to reduce the range back to a single number, accomplished by adding together the pessimistic estimate, four times the likely estimate and the optimistic estimate, then dividing by six. The result is a number skewed toward the likely, somewhat adjusted to reflect the range of outcomes that may occur.

With access to better analysis tools, and with some imagination, we can build on this basic idea to create something better. PLO estimating is one solution. I have replaced optimistic and pessimistic with *perfect* and *outrageous* to add a bit of color and get us thinking. Perfect is the time, effort, or money required to achieve our objective under optimal conditions. Outrageous is what it takes if we badly mess up and everything else goes wrong, too.

 PLO estimates are so called because we capture perfect, likely, and outrageous guesses of what might happen.

So, why the color? Simply because we can get so much more out of the process if we think of it a bit differently. On the few occasions when I have seen PERT actually used in industry, the approach has been mechanical in nature; it lacked the flair that brings out the good part of the process. Here is an example of what can happen when you turn people loose (in a regenerative team) with PLO estimating.

First, we collect useful data about how uncertain an activity is; the bigger the range, the more uncertain it is. Next, we can ask why the range is what it is. For large ranges, we will get reasons why a particular activity or deliverable might take so long or cost so much. These reasons are based on the informant's experience, and they are invariably insightful. If the person likely to be doing the work is going to give you this information, you will quickly garner the experience and expertise of that person and put it to work to help your project. This person also feels that he is contributing as he explains exactly what can go wrong. More importantly, he probably also knows how to fix the problem, which is worth even more! (This is so important that we will revisit it in Chapter 9.)

 Range estimating helps us mine team members' expertise.

Next, once we have collected the PLO estimates and reworked our plans to accommodate the changes resulting from knowing how to fix the unearthed problems, we can identify the parts of the plan that will need the most attention. This is easily done. If there were just two deliverables that were required at a particular time in a project and both required ten days to complete, we would not know on which one to focus. If, however, the PLO range for these was nine to eleven days for one and four to twenty-five for the other, we would quickly see that the second deliverable is more sensitive to uncertainty than the other. We can now focus our attention on the more volatile items in our plan.

 The range of an estimate can tell us a lot about what is happening, and it leads to some interesting questions.

If we now perform a Monte Carlo analysis on the information we have collected, we can get a sense of the project's risk profile. (This is discussed in more detail in Chapter 9.) One of the fascinating things about this analysis is that it helps us understand why so many projects go over budget and schedule.

The typical project schedule and budget are based on a set of individual estimates for components, the likely cost, and budget. Intuitively, this would seem to be the estimate with a 50 percent or better chance of success. Look at the typical PLO estimates that are generated; they will have the same number as we would normally estimate for the likely. However, the outrageous is more likely further away from the likely than the perfect estimate. For example, if something is likely to take five days, the perfect time may be three days, but the outrageous may be ten days. A Monte Carlo risk analysis will typically show a result similar to the one presented in Figure 6.3.

You will see in Figure 6.3 that the chart plots cumulative probability against the variable that was modeled in the simulation. For projects, that variable will typically be project duration, budget, or effort (work hours) required. In Figure 6.3, project duration is used for illustration purposes. Also in the figure, the overall PLO estimates for project duration are 100 days (perfect), 145 days (likely), and 200 days (outrageous). You will see that the likely duration has a probability (P_L) that is significantly less than 50 percent!

 If we analyze the results, we find that the likely estimate is actually quite unlikely.

It makes sense to give our customer, client, or boss a range of outcomes for the project; it is sane and wise to do so. We know from our

Don't Park Your Brain Outside

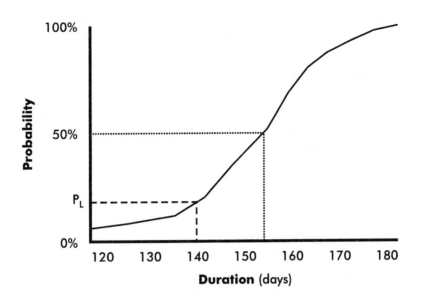

Figure 6.3 Sample Monte Carlo Simulation Result

own experience that most clients do not like to receive this type of estimate. Who would commit to a home project when the renovation contractor tells us that the new kitchen will cost between $15,000 and $45, 000 and will be done in three to nine months' time? I would not! This means we need to deal with such dichotomy.

Having said that I did not like the idea of an estimate and schedule for my kitchen renovation as described, I would be happy with one that came in another way. To show you what I mean, consider the situation where I have two quotes that are identical, except for one piece of information.

The first quote says that the project will cost $20,000 and will be done in eight weeks. The second quote says the same, but it provides some additional information. First, it states that the quote is based on available information, but the contractor may find structural or other problems when the existing kitchen is removed. The quote includes a reasonable amount—$2,000—for fix-up. If we use slightly different materials, they may be cheaper and faster to obtain, which could influence the cost and accelerate the completion date. Some suggestions are included.

With just this information, I would tend to pick the second contractor, because I feel more comfortable with the additional information. Here is the secret to packaging range estimates: do so in a way that makes the client more comfortable than with the single-point estimate, and it will be accepted.

 The only problem with range estimates is that people like giving them, but they do not like receiving them. So we need to package the results.

Range estimates are good for helping us understand the uncertainties in our plan, but they fall apart when we try to manage according to them. Therefore, we need to convert the ranges into targets. We will work to achieve the target cost, completion (and intermediate) dates, and other estimates; they serve several purposes. Targets require some decisions on the level of risk that we are willing to take. They create an opportunity for the team to buy-in to what we are trying to achieve, and we can use them to build-in the time and other resources needed to accommodate learning curves for the team. The entire process of arriving at a target helps us understand the main issues in delivery of the project. We are well ahead of the regular project scheduling process.

 When we are done, we still have a single-point estimate, but we have a qualified and informed target rather than an optimistic guess.

6.4 More on Big and Small Targets

I see companies repeatedly embarrassed by the results of their projects. Many of these projects are not even recognized as projects; they are just a part of the business. The stories in the sidebars, Broken Promises and A Big Accounting System, show what I mean.

Using ranges, probabilities, and additional information that comes out of risk management in planning of projects helps all participants do a better job.

 Companies and bosses do not like to be big targets.

For the longest time—and it still continues today—the term *project manager* has been synonymous with *scapegoat*. This is because most managers responsible for projects do not like failure. They do not like to be associated with poor performance. If your project contributes to such poor performance, it must be your fault, as you were the project manager.

 Your project becomes a big target if someone made a mistake when approving it in the first place.

The bigger the target, the easier it is to hit; so we want our project objectives to be as big as we can reasonably obtain while balancing business needs with practicality. As most of us do not like being big targets, we should seriously consider the tools that make us smaller targets. Typically, the bigger the project target, the smaller the project manager and project team are as a target!

 Use of range estimating and other uncertainty management tools makes you, your project, your boss or client, and the sponsor organization a small target. That is good.

6.5   Accessible Risk Analysis

If you had tried to perform almost any type of risk analysis in the early 1980s, you would likely have used a mainframe computer and needed special programming. On one project, where a Monte Carlo analysis was required to meet specific contract requirements, one run cost almost $2,000 and took four days to turn around! Today, the same analysis can be completed in minutes on a personal computer with a software package that costs less than $500.

The advent of powerful and easy-to-use software for risk analysis has opened many opportunities for quick and easy additional evaluation of projects. In theory, at least, we should be able to choose better projects with better plans and deliver them more reliably as a result.

 There is a growing number of tools available for risk analysis.

Obviously, all of the analyses in the world will make no difference to your project unless something useful is done with the results. That said, I still see many projects that go entirely without the benefit of any risk analysis for the project delivery itself. Many of those that do undergo risk evaluations result in little or no change in the plan to deal with the discovered risk. The real benefit of any risk analysis lies in the action we take to mitigate the risks. I do *not* mean fobbing them off to someone else; often, that solution is expensive and of little ultimate value to the project.

Using risk-analysis tools will not get rid of the risks. Discovering the risks, determining which ones require action, then doing something about them will help minimize risk impact.

6.6   More on Managing Expectations

I recall upsetting a group of owner representatives on a very large (multibillion-dollar project) by suggesting to its members that the biggest risk they had was not knowing what they were doing. I should have known they would be upset; in fact, I *did* know, and the shock effect served my purpose. I wanted them to look at the defined result of their project. Specifically, I wanted them to agree with respect to when the project was finished and what success looked like.

The date was agreed for completion, but the spread of ideas as to what *finished* meant spanned about eighteen months—or however long it took to get from a mechanically complete facility (one definition) to a commissioned and operating one (another definition), to one that had been operating without fault and with a fully trained team of operators for a year (yet another definition!).

If that wasn't bad enough, these different things all happened on exactly the same day—as if anyone in the room could reasonably predict something to that accuracy four years later! The team members were already upset at the range of expectations; they were right to be. Yet, it was better that this happened at the outset (when there was plenty of time to fix the problems) than at the end (when the client would be upset and the project late and probably over budget, too).

Give a customer or a boss a firm estimate, and they will expect performance to that estimate.

A really interesting observation, made when we tested SMART Project Management, was the shift in attitude of management as observed by the team. This shift had to do with the positive involvement of management in the project; I eventually linked it to the *process* of planning the project. The link was the result of a wise colleague's comment made many years earlier.

Ivan was an astute manager and had a wealth of experience gained from rising from having been a carpenter to vice president of a large integrated design and construction company. His comment, which obviously stuck with me, related to client satisfaction; he said that it is important to have client buy-in. His actual words were, "You have to make them [clients] a party to the crime. That way it is in their best interests to help you be successful."

Give a client or boss a firm date and budget for completion of a project, and you are entirely to blame if something goes wrong. After all, you set the targets. Even if you did not set the targets and only tried to find a way to meet the one dreamed up by the client, you own them once you produce a plan that shows how you intend to achieve them!

On the other hand, if you negotiate a set of targets that has an associated level of risk, then the client has to pick a level of risk associated with the target that is then set. The client is now part of the decision, and, whether she likes it or not, she is now party to the crime. Invariably, we have found that there is greater support from people who have a stake in the outcome of a project as a result of their involvement in the target setting.

A Big Accounting System

Eighteen months into the project, the problem was pretty clear to the board of directors: the original $24 million budget was spent. The completion deadline lay in tatters—about six months back. The ultimatum: Give us one more realistic budget and one more date for completion for the new accounting system; meet them, or look for another job—and not in this company or even in this industry!

The importance of the project was linked to new regulations requiring reporting of certain types of income. The threats were real and coming from the taxman.

The new date and budget presented were based on soft completion criteria, and there was a probability attached to them. If the board wanted to take a bigger risk, it could quote an earlier date. If it wanted to play it safe, the board could use a later date. Board members had the needed information to respond intelligently to those looking to them for leadership. The project met its new targets and, in the end, was considered a success.

 If the client or boss is party to the crime, he will be more inclined to work with you rather than against you.

Any cynic will stop at this point and mention the obvious. We routinely go for firm quotes for work; be it construction, software development, technology acquisition, insurance, or a myriad of other things, this holds true. Then we usually pick the one that gives us the *best value*. Unless we have an excellent excuse, this is the cheapest bidder—or maybe the one who made the biggest mistake. Or, just maybe, you have the contractor or supplier who saw the biggest opportunity to make money later!

Most of us who have been through this type of procurement know that it is very unusual for the initial bid and the final cost to be the same. Yet, we persist in going for the lowest initial price rather than the lowest total cost or even the best value over the life of the project.

 Don't kid yourself with *firm quotes*.

6.7   Using Uncertainty to Your Advantage

There are many examples of realism being a part of the decision process. Let us look at one such story, based on a personal experience, when I was just starting a new company to provide project management services. (See sidebar, A Complex Project and a SMART Client.)

Competitively tendered fixed-price projects and other mechanisms to place risk firmly in the hands of someone else generally lead to trouble somewhere and with someone. Unlimited trust, on the other hand, results in much of the same. A happy balance between the two requires honesty and realism, which seems like a healthy way to start a sustainable business relationship on a project.

Most people prefer honesty and realism to impossible targets and false hope, and the difference in what we try to achieve between these approaches can be minimal.

6.7.1   Team Motivation

Teams with impossible-to-achieve targets will ignore the targets. If the team buys-in to a challenge, and a range of *acceptable* outcomes are offered as a safety net if the targets are missed, then the team is much more likely to take the challenge and meet it.

We know from our own personal experience that we do not take kindly to stupidity from our boss or client. We tend to ignore plans and budgets that we do not believe can possibly be met.

It is easier to motivate a team when its members believe they stand a chance of success.

6.7.2   Success

I mentioned a safety net; consider this. The last time you had someone do some work for you, you probably had a range of outcomes that you would accept. Be it having the car serviced, rugs cleaned, or a meal at your favorite restaurant, you had an expectation. On good days, you are delighted with quality of product or service. On other days, it is ho hum. Yet, on other days, you are disappointed. There is a range. Should there not be for your projects as well? Do we know what it is? Have we discussed this with our client? Why not?

A Complex Project and a SMART Client

This client was a sophisticated pharmaceutical company; people in Canada were going to take on a large expansion to their plant. They not only were going to introduce new technology in several areas, but also needed to keep the existing facility in operation throughout the new construction, renovation, and reconstruction of the existing facility. I persuaded the client to let us bid on the work, although we had no previous experience in the pharmaceutical industry. I suggested that this was an advantage, as we were therefore eager learners and would try all the harder. We did, and we thoroughly researched our project before bidding. The project was tendered on a fixed-price, design-build basis including all of the new required process technology.

I was briefly elated when the clients called after tenders closed; they wanted to meet with me to discuss our price. It turned out that their curiosity was aroused by the fact that we were almost 30 percent more expensive than the next highest bidder. They wanted to know why; I showed them our bid and risk analysis; then I explained where we thought the project could go wrong. If they wanted a trouble-free fixed price, the estimate showed what we felt it would take. If they wanted to increase the risk of claims, changes, and other problems, we could talk about a lower price and perhaps a cost-plus contract.

We got the work. It was completed without problems and on time. I assume that the clients were happy because we negotiated (no bid) their next project.

 Too often we define success as an absolute. It is not. There are shades of success, from marginal to outstanding. We should know the limits.

6.7.3 *Control*

Face it, once the planning is done and expectations are set, all we can do is the best job possible to meet those targets set for our project. Control, as such, is largely gone; we had it while we were making planning decisions.

However, we do retain control (or at least some influence) after planning on one really key item: the expectations of the key stakeholders. We need to keep managing them.

Of course, the report is blank. We only report the good news.

What happens on projects after planning is largely management and reporting; there is little left to really control. We need to stay very conscious of this!

 Control of a project happens before most people are involved; after that, it is monitoring of performance.

6.7.4 Expectations

I gave my favorite trick away a moment ago: Manage stakeholder expectations. The project and its world will change over its lifetime, unless it is a very simple and short-duration one. As things change, we often forget to keep our stakeholders informed of the impact of those changes; this is a significant failing on many projects. Awareness of the real impact of a change is important. (Techniques to help with this are described in Section C.)

 In the end, if we meet or exceed the expectations of the key stakeholders, we will be successful.

Chapter 7

SMART: PUTTING THE PIECES TOGETHER

Carol and Greg didn't have time to do everything. The project was large, and, as co-managers, they had split up the responsibilities for getting the show on the road. Carol would look after the hard issues—such as schedule, budget, risk analysis, procurement, and the production of technology—and Greg was to work on the soft items. In particular, he was to build the team, address public concerns, deal with marketing, develop the project team's culture, work with external parties on cooperation, and generally be concerned with the welfare of the project's many participants. It was not long before Carol and Greg were tripping over each other, arguing about how things should be done and what the priorities were for a successful project, and even getting into turf battles.

The hard and soft issues on a project are inseparable, and most books on project management present both aspects. Yet, too often, one of them dominates the other, reflecting that particular author's background and expertise. Normally, hard and soft issues are dealt with separately by a project manager; however, consider the following questions: Without trust and open communication, will you get good information for your schedule and estimate? Without an appropriate contracting framework, will you be able to build a cooperative working relationship with your suppliers and contractors? Which comes first, the soft stuff or the tools and techniques? In this chapter, we explore interrelationships among the different elements of good project management, and we discover that balancing and integrating all aspects is important at all times. The mix of tools and practices that are needed for a project will be dependent on the style of the individual manager, the team, the project, and more. While we explore these elements, we also need to view the project in its true perspective: a part of business of the various stakeholders. The relative importance of the project and the individual stakeholders' businesses will vary over time, and will probably not coincide with all of your plans and needs as the manager of the project!

Just as a dentist needs tools, knowledge of how to use them, and the competence to identify the problem, so project managers need to know their tools, how to use them, and when to use them to solve the right problems. A holistic and balanced approach is needed.

 Good managers balance understanding of the problem with knowing which management tools to use and how to work with people to achieve the best possible results.

7.1   A Holistic Approach

Virtually anything that we do to maintain or improve shareholder value in any organization is a project. Projects start with an idea, are selected because they are seen to be of value, are implemented, and then are handed over for someone to operate or use the result.

Interestingly, many of the projects that we do are not recognized as such; therefore, they are not implemented as effectively as they could be. Typical projects that are often not recognized include the following: corporate reorganizations, training programs implementation, key staff recruitment, marketing campaigns, litigation, and lobbying.

Another group of projects typically managed by people who may have a lot of skill and talent, but have little or no formal training in project management, include: maintenance of facilities, safety training, retooling of production lines, research and development, mineral exploration, sales campaigns, political campaigns, and acquisitions and takeovers.

The list of projects that we undertake and manage with inappropriate tools or inadequate training is huge. Fortunately, most of our competition is in the same boat; otherwise, we could not compete. The competition could do the work faster, cheaper, and better with the right management tools and training to support these efforts.

 The majority of project managers do not know that they are project managers!

Don't Park Your Brain Outside

Project management is described by many as *technical*. They believe that it has to do with construction, defense, or aerospace projects; is encapsulated in critical path scheduling; and is a bunch of tools based on a systematic approach. Project managers prepare estimates, schedules, and work breakdown structures. We then complicate all of this with acronyms like EAC, BCWS, and others. *Not so!*

First and foremost, project management is about people. After all, it is people who do everything on projects. If they use tools like computers, hammers, or telephones, they are just proving that humans are smarter than animals. If they use techniques such as scheduling, earned value, and sensitivity analysis, they are merely using tools. The bottom line is that we need to harness the skills, talent, and enthusiasm of the people involved in a project if we want to be truly successful. All the rest is a framework with tools to help us on our way.

 Good project management is about harnessing the skills and energy of people to achieve a planned outcome. This is a blend of people skills and a systems approach.

Projects do not happen in a vacuum; they are usually the result of someone wanting to achieve something. In business, they are normally driven by corporate objectives. In the public sector, projects are ideally driven by a will to improve services to the community and give the best value for the taxpayers' money. In the world of volunteerism, we undertake projects to improve the lot of people, animals, the environment, or some other cause. Any of these projects will have some sort of *customer*, the recipient of the benefits. If the customer is happy, and if other major stakeholders (such as the project team, regulators, neighbors, and so on) are also happy with the result and the process of getting there, we will have a successful project.

The project is more than just delivering something. It includes defining what we deliver, ensuring that it is worth delivering, and making sure that the customer is happy with the result.

In the end, any project worth undertaking results in value added to or on behalf of the sponsor. The sponsor—and what that person or group of people really wants—is, therefore, of utmost importance to the success of the project. We need to understand the need that the project is going to fill. We also need to understand how well the client understands what is expected. It is not unusual for the needs of a client to be unclear, or for those needs to be expressed in uncertain or ambiguous form, or even as a solution—and the wrong solution at that!

One of my favorite characters is an old client of mine, who would tell me exactly and unequivocally what he wanted, brooking no discussion or disagreement. We would deliver what he asked; he would say it was not what he wanted. We would point out that he had insisted and would not entertain any discussion. He would counter with, "I relied on you as a professional to provide professional advice. You failed because I do not like what you have done." Another way he handled the situation was to ask for advice and then follow it, get what we recommended, and then say it was not what he wanted: "You are supposed to be the experts. You should have gotten it right!" In the end, he'd be happy if we met his overall expectations. Invariably, it was because he saw the value of the end result—or at least his boss did!

 The bottom line is that project management is about delivering added value.

7.2   Maintaining a Balanced Scorecard

The debate over whether project management is a people business or a systems approach to management has been raging for a long time. The answer is that it is not just both; it is more. A balanced scorecard is favored in the SMART approach. Now, let us look at what we need to score. Consider the following project management scorecard (in random order):

❑ corporate objectives	❑ workplace expectations
❑ accommodation of idiosyncrasies	❑ individual needs
	❑ systematic approach
❑ challenging performance targets	❑ achievable results
	❑ detailed planning
❑ flexibility	❑ fun
❑ project performance	❑ legal issues and contracts
❑ trust	❑ corporate priorities
❑ project priorities	❑ analysis
❑ gut feeling or intuition	❑ team recognition
❑ individual recognition	❑ family and personal lives

The list is not exhaustive but serves to illustrate the span and nature of the sorts of things that we, as managers, need to balance. Experience and wisdom will help develop a framework for managing them. The framework will vary over our working careers, as our own personal knowledge and experience builds and affects our perspective of what is going on. As a consequence, we need to stay aware of the many factors that influence project outcomes, whether or not we think they are important. Others will have different weightings on the same factors; they may even have different factors on their scorecards.

 We need to balance not just our own scorecard, but also the scorecards of other stakeholders.

7.3 Quality (and Scope), Cost, and Time—You Get Two Out of Three!

While driving through the Rocky Mountains in 1997, I needed a small cotter pin to hold my trailer in place. (We had mysteriously lost the old one.) There was a sign in the hardware store, where I finally located one, which read:

> You can have it FAST,
> You can have it CHEAP,
> You can have the BEST.
> Pick any two.

This seemed to me at the time to be the epitome of the project management dilemma! How often do we ask for—or get asked for—an impossible mix of quality, cost, and time performance? The right balance and the management of expectations around that balance need to be obtained if the project is to be managed effectively. (How this might be done is described in Chapter 8.)

 Many projects demand an irrational mix of quality, cost, and time for a given scope, which inevitably leads to compromise; too often, it leads to disappointment.

As the project evolves and adjustments are made to the definition of success, or the circumstances and environment change, the stakeholders need to be kept informed and adjustments made to expectations.

 Any compromise needs to accommodate the expectations of the stakeholders. Or the stakeholders' expectations need to accommodate the results of the compromise.

If we know that the project will change, and we know the best options for accommodating and managing the change, we can respond quickly and efficiently. The priority triangle (described in Chapter 8) is a tool to help us understand the relative priorities of quality, cost, and time. With it, we can develop ground rules for future compromise, and, in this way, the stakeholders are prepared for the types of responses that we will make to changes and the inevitable reworking of schedule, budget, scope, and quality. As people are predisposed to certain types of management response and have some say in setting the ground rules, they will respond more positively to change and its implications.

 It is easier and faster to make the inevitable compromise decisions if the ground rules for doing so are already established.

7.4   Processes Need to Consider People and Results— in That Order

We have already discussed the importance of stakeholder buy-in to the project plan. This type of buy-in is just as important for the process that we will use to manage the project. It is, however, easier to obtain, as most people are willing to adapt to how a project is managed. The first step in developing an effective project management process is to select the tools that we think will be needed to do the job. There must be a greater return than investment in the use of any tool. In some instances, team members will see no value in using a particular tool. They either will not use it, or they will pay lip service to it; the result is the same either way: it will not work for you. If we cannot sell a tool and its value to the team, we should probably not be using it! When people are asked to contribute information to the management process, some form of a return needs to be made to them. It could come in a number of ways; it could be that it helps them coordinate their own work, stay on schedule, or get the help they need, or it provides them with recognition. There are many ways that a particular management approach will help the team. We just need to know how and then make team members aware of the benefits.

 The processes that we adopt for management of a project need to be accepted by the team. If they are not, the processes will either work poorly or fail.

Look, if it really was a good idea,
someone would already have thought of it.

Too often, we ask team members for information but do not offer any feedback or value in return. A one-way street for information has a negative impact on most of us.

On too many projects, planning tools add little value to the participants. As a result, they are ignored, which leads to the tools' ineffectiveness. It is a spiral argument. For example, consider on how many of the projects you have worked that the schedule was checked daily by everyone on the team so that everyone knew what needed to be done and where the bottlenecks were. Not too many, if any, I would guess. For a schedule to be effective, it needs to be of value to everyone as a daily working tool. (There are many ways of achieving this, and we will look at some of them in Section C.)

Another example of effectiveness of tools is the value that is associated with completion of any task on a project. Some we celebrate, and some we do not. Unfortunately, we tend to celebrate those deliverables that were a challenge and fun to produce. The really boring ones rarely get appreciated, making it demotivating to work on the mundane and unrecognized parts of the project, and those are too often the action items that go awry. Again, balance is important.

 In addressing the systems needs of a project, consider how they will work for the people who need to use them or who contribute to their effectiveness.

7.5   The Key Resource Is ...

The key resource on any project is people. This has already been said many times, so I will repeat it again only once (for now).

 Nothing happens without the intervention and involvement of people.

I repeat this, at the risk of beating it to pulp, to prepare us for what I think is the most important single issue in managing projects: working with people. Many of the approaches we see to project management—especially those that carry labels like *systematic, systems approach, structured, phased,* or ... any one of a number of words that put a focus on tools—tend to trivialize the delight (and frustration) of working with people. I suspect that, based on my own experience and observation, the majority of project managers today still come from technical backgrounds—engineers, accountants, lawyers, scientists, pharmacists, systems analysts, or another professional trained to be logical and structured. It is not a bad training, but it tends to get us focused on the wrong stuff at times.

 People are volatile, arbitrary, creative, emotional, and a bunch of other things that make us highly unpredictable and individual. These traits also make us exciting, challenging, and—if we do it right—fun to work with.

7.6   Most Volatile, Unpredictable, and Hard to Manage Is ...

We know that the most volatile resource on any project is going to be the people who work on it. People have their own lives to lead. We get sick, happy, emotional, tired, energized, and frenetic—any one of which and more will affect our performance. Productivity is highly volatile on a day-to-day basis. Moreover, we vary from one person to another. Different things motivate and depress us; we are all good at some things and not so good at others—and those things are not the same!

Machines and materials, on the other hand, are more consistent. Their performance in many respects can be measured, defined, and predicted much more easily.

Now look at how we allocate resources on projects. We need seventeen programmers, or three geologists, or maybe six carpenters. We assume that they all will behave uniformly, have the same skill sets, and work to the same timetables. At least this is implied in the normal planning and resource allocation processes. If this were not bad enough, we then use technology to do some resource smoothing, and we actually try to use the results to help us manage the project. Several things happen as a consequence.

First, have you noticed how often noncritical activities (those not on the alleged critical path) cause us grief? The reason is simple: we tend to allocate the best resources to the critical activities. They will (by definition) take the same or less time than allocated. The activity stays on schedule. The less-than-best resources then work on the less-critical activities and take longer than expected, thus making these activities critical instead—the result: delays. Worse yet, we tend to blame the people who caused the delay. In fact, we, as managers, are responsible because we did not ascertain the skill levels and expertise of the individuals relative to each other—or, if we did, we did not take the differences into account when planning.

 Materials and equipment behave much more consistently than people do! Therefore, focus management effort on the people who can help the project.

7.7 Keep the Big Picture; Pay Attention to the Detail

One of the advantages of the job I do is that I get to see some exceptional managers at work. Being able to do two things very well is one common trait of really successful managers generally and project managers in particular. First, they stay in touch with and aware of the *big picture*, and they pay attention to detail at the same time. Second, they are continuously aware of the links between the different aspects of their work or project. The second facet is a product of understanding the big picture. Let me illustrate.

Consider a large project with much of the specialized and highly technical work being outsourced to a number of specialist companies.

Here are some links. The selected contracting strategy will affect risk apportionment, trust development, how the team will interact, open communication, the budget and schedule, quality of the end product, and more. Now pick any one of these affected items, and see what they affect. Complicated, isn't it? Primary and secondary impacts may be large or small. To be really effective, we need to understand how any one decision on a project will affect not just every other element of the project, but also the businesses that are linked to the project, the people involved, and the entire environment. Any one of these may bounce back to hurt the project. Many of the consequences of single decisions and actions are not recognized, and we receive the predictable body blow to our project. With our twenty-twenty hindsight, we can see the links; twenty-twenty foresight is a whole lot tougher.

 Project management is like juggling: you need to keep your eye on more than one ball at a time.

By the time we have become good at spotting all of these connections, we will probably have mangled a few projects. It will generally be impossible to watch all of the issues with equal and rigorous attention at all times.

 The trick is to know which ball to watch at any given time.

Defining and controlling the balls we will juggle in our projects is the subject of the next section of the book.

How SMART Works

In this section of the book, you will find the basics of the SMART Management tools and an outline of how to use them. Just as giving someone a set of dentist's tools does not make him a dentist, so just reading about the SMART tools is normally not enough. The SMART Management tools are designed to be simple to implement. However, without a detailed appreciation of *why* they are used (see Section A) and *how* they work (see Section B), they will not achieve what you desire.

In the following chapters, we build on the first two sections of this book by adding the mechanics of SMART Management. These mechanics and their associated tools are presented in the sequence that most projects will require them. As with dentistry—where we hope the dentist will not use every tool for surgery—we do not need every SMART tool on every project!

This section starts by describing, in general, the project charter, then goes on to develop the specific tools and processes to be considered at each phase, from project definition, through approval, to completion.

Only the basic tools for SMART Management are included; there is not enough room in one book for all of them. What is here, though, should get us going on the road to better, faster, and cheaper (in the best sense of the word) projects.

Planning Processes— The Project Charter

Planning a successful project has to begin with the process of picking the right project. Try the following quiz, and answer the questions, based on the project you are working on now—or the last one you worked on if you are not on a project at present. For the purposes of this exercise, "I don't know" is an acceptable answer!

1. My organization's mission is to:

_____

_____

2. My project helps achieve this mission by:

_____

_____

3. The corporate sponsor for my project is:

_____

_____

4. My project will increase the value of the business by (action or result):

_____

_____

5. The project was approved by (person, level in organization):

_____

_____

6. I was involved in setting the budget and schedule.

_____ yes _____ no

7. I have control over the resources required to complete the project.

_____ yes _____ no

8. This project ranks _____ in the priorities of the business.

9. The importance of this project will be affected by (people, politics, other factors):

_____

_____

10. The ultimate (final) customer for the results of my project is:

_____

_____

There are no right answers, and there is a good chance that you do not know the answer to every question. If you do know the answer, you will probably find that others have different opinions! The point of the exercise is to gain a sense of some of the hard-to-measure elements that affect the potential success of our projects; we often have no time to seriously consider them. How and why our project was created and selected are vital pieces of information for successful project managers. This knowledge gives us insight into the politics, business rationale, and opportunities for leverage for our project over resource shortages, funding, and other issues, as they arise.

 There is power in knowledge. Some of the greatest power that a project manager can wield lies in understanding the business and other drivers for a project.

There is a good chance that your project was not picked on a scientific basis; it may have been a political decision. Possibly, it was based on the *gut feeling* of some manager or executive, or it may have had careful feasibility studies completed and complex analyses undertaken before a decision was made at a senior level—or even by the board of directors. Often, even these rigorous exercises are based on assumptions and fuzzy data. Whatever the process for selection of the project, it is important that we know what it is and how it works. We need to know this because the process gives us clues as to what may influence success or failure. We also need to understand the real rationale and purpose behind the project if we are to successfully manage it. All too often, we are given a project to manage without the appropriate background about its development. In such a case, although we do know what is to be done and how to do it, we may not know what we are doing!

The real start to any project is when the original idea for the project is conceived. This is followed by the development of the idea, a feasibility assessment, and funding for the project itself. The function of a project charter is to help define and communicate the objectives of and constraints for the project. It's the business plan for the project. Putting the charter together may be done quickly, or it may be negotiated over a period of years. The original idea for the project may well be modified in the process of developing the charter. In the end, the final charter will define what the project is to achieve and the measures of success, together with who will decide whether these measures have been achieved. Such a charter, whether it is a formal document or an informal result, needs to be based on correct early decisions in the development of the project. This is more likely to happen if an effective process is used.

In this chapter, we look at simple but powerful processes for development of an effective project charter and, in doing so, develop the information we need for success.

 A project manager needs a license to spend the project budget and use other resources. That license needs to be properly documented, together with the rules by which the project is to be piloted. The license also needs to be renewed at critical points in the development of the project.

The license that the project manager needs is embodied in the project charter.

Not all of the ingredients of the project charter—listed in the sidebar, Project Charter—Contents—are needed on every project; clearly, the list is overkill for small or really simple projects. The charter need not be complete when the project is approved. But if we include a table of contents with our charter, reflecting what the final document will contain, we can readily see that the project is not completely defined when it is approved. This is useful in managing stakeholder expectations.

The first significant happening on a project is to have it approved and funded. This milestone is preceded by a series of steps leading to sanction of the project. Sanction needs to be based on sufficient information to make such an important decision, and this requires some sort of business plan for what is being proposed.

> ## Project Charter—Contents
>
> 1. Project Mission, Key Result Areas, and Critical Success Factors
> 2. List of Key Stakeholders
> 3. Clear Definition of Completion and Success
> 4. Schedule
> 5. Estimate and Budget (not the same thing!)
> 6. Risk Assessment and Mitigation Plan
> 7. Checkpoints
> 8. Communications Plan
> 9. Procurement (includes all outsourcing) Strategy and Plan
> 10. Performance Specifications
> 11. Project Policies and Procedures
> 12. Anything Else That the Project Team May Need

8.1 Picking the Right Project

Remember that projects are all about improving or maintaining shareholder value; any project we do needs to be justified in this light. But, let us consider what it really means. There are projects that we can readily define in these terms such as adding a new product, building a new factory, or improving business processes. This assumes that the business plan for these projects is supportable and shows the value to the business of doing the work prescribed. What, then, about the projects that do not add any such obvious, tangible, and measurable value?

Projects such as corporate reorganizations, marketing plans, system maintenance, and new accounting software package purchases and installation are harder to quantify and measure. In these cases, it may be necessary to consider the expected marginal improvement to the business as a result of implementing the project and the expected outcome if the project is not implemented. These issues are harder to assess. This means that we need to start by understanding the drivers behind project selection (as described in Chapter 3). The next step is to put in place a consistent approach to project selection.

Project selection is the starting point for this chapter. How the project needs to evolve and how to track and manage project changes follow. We need to monitor the project in terms of shareholder value.

Don't Park Your Brain Outside

The project will inevitably change in many ways over time. As success is related to meeting stakeholder expectations, we need to keep them aligned as the project evolves. The charter is the project manager's license to spend money; the license clearly needs to be linked to the perceived value of the investment.

 No project should proceed until the project manager is able to understand and explain how the project helps the business achieve its objectives. This is the link that helps the project manager explain to the project team how shareholder value is enhanced. It is also the basis on which we get support from senior management.

8.1.1 Portfolio of Projects

Every project happens in the context of other projects. Of particular importance to us, as project managers, are the other projects being implemented by our own organization, as they will most likely take away resources needed for our success. These other projects are also organizational investments; they are a part of a portfolio of projects. As with all portfolios, some investments are more important that others; some will provide a greater return, and some are more risky.

The less important our project is in this portfolio, the more likely it will be adversely affected by others. Clearly, we need to understand where our project is in the pecking order. We also need to be aware of shifting priorities that projects undergo as the business environment evolves. Through this awareness, we are able to better predict the future impact of staff transfers, slow down, or withdrawal (temporary or permanent) of funding for our project.

 Knowing what is going on around us helps us to deal with changes in support for and priority of our project.

8.1.2 Project Selection

For most of us, the project selection process is beyond our control. For many of us, as project managers, it is not even a part of our scope of work. Yet, what happens at this stage in the development of a project is critical to its success. We need to know the drivers behind the project: business motivation, supporters and detractors, urgency and priority, sustainability, and more. It is much easier for us to manage a project if we understand why we are doing it.

If we know why we are executing a particular project, it can lead to very different solutions. You may recall the story of the car manufacturer who wanted to build a warehouse (see Chapter 3). The sidebar, So *That's* What We're Doing, features another story to reinforce this point. We can see clearly that understanding the real drivers for a project is more important than delivering exactly what was requested on time, within budget, and to quality expectations!

 The final product of a project may be completely different from the one originally envisioned, and the project is still a success.

 The first step in selecting a project is to define it correctly!

Once we have defined the success of a project in terms of its fundamental objectives, we can then define it in terms of a solution. Once a possible solution has been developed, the scope, cost, and time frame for delivery may be estimated. All of the assumptions, together with enough detail about the discarded alternatives during the feasibility study stage, should be recorded so that the basis of these decisions remains available later in the life of the project. This saves a lot of subsequent rework and erroneous assumptions with their consequences.

 A log of the decisions made in selecting and defining a project will help the project manager and the project team make better decisions later in the development of the project.

The selection of the project for funding and implementation will occur at a level in the organization where budget control is held; this can be anywhere from within a department to a board-level decision. The decision-makers need enough information to make the most reasonable choice, particularly if there are competing opportunities for use of the funds. Probability of success of the project is all too often missing in the decision-making process. It needs to be assessed in terms of the technology, commercial benefits, social impact, scope, quality, and probability of delivering within budget or schedule. The probability of delivering a project within budget and schedule is rarely addressed on any but the largest projects. The probability of success generally improves over time, as better information becomes available and as potential risk events are overtaken by history and become fact. The conversion of forecast to history usually reveals optimism in the forecast. In other words, actual results tend to be worse (more adverse to project success) than was originally planned, which means that the return on investment also reduces over time.

The budget is fixed; it's the project we still need to decide on.

The predictability of success generally improves as the project progresses. The return on investment often declines as predictability increases.

8.2 Project Approvals

Approval of a project usually does not happen once and for all. We are accustomed to seeing projects started but not finished, or we see projects given a high priority only to have the key resources taken away at a critical point. Whether done formally or informally, our projects are reassessed and reapproved on an ongoing basis. Recently, while discussing myths in the workplace, someone suggested that the biggest myth in her workplace was that a project got approved!

Constant review of a project is prudent. As we saw earlier, the project's value likely will decrease as budgets and schedules are exceeded for legitimate or other reasons. It pays to predetermine the points at which the project is to be reviewed; there are several reasons for this:

- We can chose the points in time where it makes sense to reevaluate the project.
- We manage stakeholder expectations at each point, as the project (and the charter) evolves.
- We create opportunities to realign stakeholders with the project's plans, direction, and objectives.
- It's easier to obtain initial approval of the project if those responsible for the decision know when and under what circumstances the project will be presented again for verification or validation and, if necessary, reapproval.

Implicit in this process is that we have identified key points in the development of the project, when we will likely need to obtain approval for the next tranche of spending. This is a useful exercise in itself. There are several ways to do it, modeled after the stage-gate process often used in manufacturing. Common stages where projects may undergo reapproval are the:

- prefeasibility stage (to fund feasibility study)
- feasibility stage (to confirm feasibility and fund development work)
- design stage (to confirm conditions are still favorable and to fund detailed design and development)
- implementation stage (to confirm that objectives are still being met and that return on investment is reasonable, before the largest commitment is made)
- preprocurement stage (just before awarding the largest contracts and committing to this expenditure).

These stages may be interspersed with others, or some may be omitted, depending on how risky, complex, expensive, and long (duration) the project is. At each of these stages, the risks associated with successful delivery should be reduced, compared to the previous stage. Selection of how many review points you want and when they should occur may be within your control or influence. If it is, consider the needs of all stakeholders, and suggest a balance between the need for senior management control and the independence of the team doing the work.

For each of the reapproval points, we need to predefine the information and deliverables required at that time. If those requirements are met, then approval of the next stage should be automatic, subject only to changes in organizational priorities. If they are not met, then we can anticipate several options for action, based on how they are not met—which may identify how we respond to different situations that are likely to occur.

Projects need to be approved, based on both value and risks involved in their execution. Probability of success is rarely included in the evaluation process—often with devastating results.

8.3   Checkpoint Process (SMART Off-Ramps for Projects)

Checkpoints are not a new idea; they were originally developed to help manage new product development. The concept is simply to stop projects that are not panning out and to do so as soon as possible. We need *off-ramps* that allow us to cancel or change a *wrong* project without it becoming career limiting. It also prevents spending good money after bad. There are many projects that reflect more money being spent than was necessary before they were canceled. The more we spend on a project, the harder it is to stop it.

 Checkpoints and off-ramps should be set at key points in the evolution of a project to reassess the value of the planned work and to proceed, modify, or cancel the project to suit the changed circumstances at the time.

Look at the sidebar, Setting Review Points for a Project, to see how these points may be determined and set.

Don't forget that we first need to consider the business drivers for the project. Once a sound business case has been made and can be supported, look at the social impact of the project and ensure that the benefits justify the impact, if any, on people. Afterward, the technical and process-related issues can be addressed; they are probably the easiest.

 As the project and its environment are dynamic, the business, technical, and social needs for a project will likely change over time. At key points in the development of a project, its viability and relevance need to be reassessed and the stakeholders realigned with any change in direction.

8.4   Mission Key Result Areas and Deliverables

The next step in the development of an effective project charter is to provide some focus on the intent and validate it with the project team and key stakeholders, a process that can be handled in a number of

Setting Review Points for a Project

1. Identify stakeholders who need to be involved in the review process.

2. Discover the concerns of each stakeholder, and ask when he feels that he would like to review the project.

3. Identify from this list which points in the life of the project are of common concern.

4. Based on this information, establish a set of preliminary points at which the project will be reassessed.

5. For each of these points, identify the range of outcomes that may be reasonable for cost, completion date, and other factors at that time.

6. Identify the deliverables that may be required for each point in time.

7. Prepare a proposal for review and agreement among voting stake-holders as to when the project should be reviewed and to determine criteria for a *go*, *modify and go*, *modify and resubmit*, or *stop* decision at each decision point.

8. Remind all key stakeholders that these are preliminary checkpoints that will be confirmed as the charter evolves.

different ways. If you follow the steps outlined in this sidebar, you will have predefined the success of the project, at least at a high level. It is important to realize that it does not matter if the first draft of the deliverables breakdown structure (DBS) is not complete or totally correct. If and when things change, we now have a basis for identifying and managing the change.

 We should never leave determination of project success until the end, when the project has been completed. We need clearly and definitively set criteria for success at the outset, and a well-constructed DBS will help achieve this.

Now that we have seen the basic mechanical steps, we still need to cover two points. The first is to look at what else we may achieve while building the first draft of the DBS. The second is to work through how the DBS may be developed to achieve these additional objectives.

Establishing the Mission, Key Results, and Main Deliverables for a Project

These steps should be followed:

1. Identify the main stakeholders for the project and ensure that they are present or represented when you develop the mission, key results, and deliverables defining success of the project.

2. With this group of people, develop the keywords that should go into a mission statement for the project. Do not try to finalize or wordsmith at this point.

3. Repeat the exercise for the key results required for project success. The principle here is that the mission is met, by definition, if the key results are all met.

4. For each key result, identify the deliverable items that, if delivered, will—again, by definition—meet the requirements for success with that key result.

5. Work through Steps 2, 3, and 4 until nothing new emerges, and the keywords or items are in the right place.

6. Finalize the wording for each element; this gives you the first draft of the DBS for the project.

7. Ensure that all participants agree on the meaning of each keyword in the DBS. Record keyword meanings in a project lexicon so that no later confusion results.

8. We have just defined success of the project in terms of a number of deliverables. If we deliver these, we have met all of the key results, and, if we have done that, we have achieved the mission—by definition!

9. For an example of a process and what it might look like, see Sections 8.4.1 and 8.4.2.

 Developing the DBS is one of the first steps in planning a successful project. We can combine this activity with a number of other objectives and save time and effort while improving the outcome of the exercise.

8.4.1 What Else May Be Achieved

While preparing the first draft of the first part of a DBS, there are things that can be done in parallel. First, start building our team. In Chapter 4, we discussed the SMART definition of a project team; it is far more inclusive than the conventional definition. As we also include the client, suppliers, and stakeholders who can influence the outcome or whom we affect by executing the project, we approach SMART team building differently.

Part of effective teamwork is open communication—the antithesis of hidden agendas—so in developing our DBS, we begin with it. If participants understand that the definition of a successful project is implied in the DBS, then they realize that they need to get their hidden-agenda items covered in the included deliverables. If these items are not part of our DBS, they also are not part of the project's success. As we record who participated in the development of the DBS and other elements in the project charter, it is difficult to keep hidden-agenda items hidden!

To keep the exercise positive, we focus on common objectives in which all stakeholders are interested. If there are none, we work on the most common ones. We never ignore the conflicting issues; we simply defer the discussion on these elements until we have some common ground from which to work.

One way to get all participants involved in the process is to use yellow Post-It® or similar notes. All participants write down the words for the mission, key results, and deliverables on separate sheets. These are then collected on a wall chart or flipchart that has been divided into four zones, as shown in Figure 8.1.

In Figure 8.1, we have separated our working surface into four areas, as recommended. Three of them have already been discussed; the fourth is the parking lot. As we do not discard any ideas, those that the team generally feels are not part of the project will be *parked* in the parking lot until they are discussed. Once consensus has been obtained regarding how these items will be considered (each on its own merits), they can be included in the project or omitted. If left out, we note them as being beyond the scope of the project.

If we handle the process well, we will see discussion and consensus occurring. Inclusion in the idea makes all the participants in the exercise *party to the crime*. They will all own the result. More to the point, they will have been forced to either declare hidden-agenda items or accept that they are not part of the project.

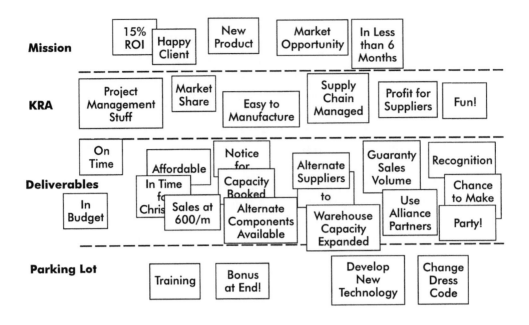

Figure 8.1 Building the Deliverables Breakdown Structure

 Done correctly, developing the DBS will start the team-building process in a directly relevant way. The process will open communication and start to develop ownership of the plan.

8.4.2 How Do We Develop a Deliverables Breakdown Structure?

Whether we use the yellow-stickie method (described in Section 8.4.1) or another approach for facilitating the process, we need to be aware of some of the *tricks* for making a DBS work for us. Start by looking at panel A in Figure 8.2. There are five dots; we recognize that without counting. Now look at panel B, which is a bit different; there are nine dots. You will have to group, sort, or count these dots to discover the number. For the vast majority of the world's population, the point at which instant recognition stops and the need to count starts is between seven and eight.

Try not to exceed seven key result areas (KRAs) or seven primary deliverables for each KRA.

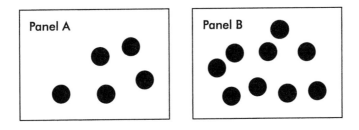

Figure 8.2 Perception Limits Test

 So, here is the first trick: Never have more than seven children to each parent in a breakdown structure like the DBS.

To make sure that we do not *waste* our seven KRAs on obvious items, here are a couple of simple guidelines. First, put all the traditional project management items that are standard for most DBSs in the first KRA, which will likely have the following deliverables:

- safely executed
- on time
- within budget
- defined and managed scope
- meets quality expectations and standards.

When you start using SMART Management, it sometimes helps to also reserve one KRA for *fun*. (The concept and the importance of having fun at work were covered in Chapter 4. It is expanded in Chapters 10 and 12. I mention it again because planning to have fun helps break the ice and establish the importance of team health and the well-being of individuals at the outset.)

 Two of the KRAs should be reserved for project management *stuff* and fun, respectively.

The intervening KRAs should address the concerns of the key stakeholders or stakeholder groups. In the example shown in Figure 8.1, we can identify corporate interests (marketing, finance, and the boss) in the second KRA. Manufacturing and perhaps the design group are in the next one. Purchasing and perhaps the project manager may be in the one after that. The remaining one covers the suppliers.

The KRAs should be developed in such a way as to ensure that the divergent interests of the different stakeholders are represented and considered in the process.

In Figure 8.1, ideas that did not fit in the project, as seen by the participants as a whole, ended up in the parking lot. These must not be ignored. Each one needs to be discussed by the team, and the contributor needs to be brought on board with the consensus decision on how that item will be handled.

 Any *parked* ideas must be addressed by the team; consensus must be obtained regarding how such ideas are to be considered.

Each KRA needs to be defined in terms that make it as clear and unambiguous as possible; for the reasons discussed in Chapters 3 and 7, we use deliverables to do this. In other words, each KRA is reduced to a set of deliverables that define what the KRA may mean in terms of what needs to be produced by the project team to keep that stakeholder happy and meet the intent of the relevant key result.

The deliverables shown in Figure 8.1 illustrate how this may be achieved. If a particular deliverable is still too general, it can be broken down into smaller components. Each of those can then be broken down into smaller components and so on until clarity is achieved. If a deliverable cannot be fully defined at this stage, we can readily see it and reflect the uncertainty in our plans and in the charter.

The key result identified in the sidebar, Example of Defining a Key Result Area, was broken down into three prime deliverables. They were then further broken down to specific smaller components, and dates were added in some cases, where they were perceived as critical to success. Watch these as we move through the planning process, because we will check them later when we develop our 3-D schedule.

 Break down deliverables until either they are sufficiently clear and unambiguous, or we cannot define them more clearly at this stage. Identify the deliverables that are unclear; they represent a scope risk.

Example of Defining a Key Result Area

Key Result Area: Obtain Market Share

Deliverable 1: Affordable
    Cost of Manufacture < $15 per Unit
    Cost of Shipping and Distribution < $1.72 per Unit
    Marketing Costs Excluded

Deliverable 2: In Time for Christmas
    Stock in Warehouse: 4,000 Units by October 15
    Cost of Packaging < $0.84 per Unit
    Production Capable of 600 Units per Month by End of November

Deliverable 3: Sales at 600 Units per Month
    Channels Established by End of August to Meet Sales Objectives

8.5   Key Result Areas

KRAs in the SMART context are those factors that we need to address in terms of process and procedure in order to keep our stakeholders happy. If they add costs or time to the delivery process, we need to advise the affected stakeholders. In this way, we can verify that the tradeoff of time and cost is worthwhile in the stakeholders' opinions. For example, if the number of gates or reapproval points for a project seems unrealistically high for the team, the resulting additional cost and delay should be assessed, and the people requesting them should be informed of the results.

Specific procedures and processes required for any reason should be noted and included in the plan for delivery of the project, including such items as safety training, obtaining regulatory approvals, orientation of new staff, and much more. These items are all too often forgotten in our delivery-focused approach to project planning; thus, they get missed when estimating time, money, and resources required to do the work properly.

Remember that the specific KRAs that will lead to project success will vary from one project to another. We need to really understand these key results. The underlying issues for these KRAs need to be developed, so the project manager can develop appropriate strategies for project implementation.

8.6   Three Key Questions

Planning once is not enough, as we have no idea until later—sometimes too late—whether the one plan is correct. Therefore, in SMART Management, we plan twice; the second planning process starts with three simple but vital questions. Yet, on all of the over sixty projects where we have used these questions to test alignment of the stakeholders, we have never seen a situation in which two stakeholders came up with the same answer to any one of them. These projects spanned several industries and ranged in value from a few hundred thousand dollars to several billion dollars.

The three questions in the sidebar, Yet Another Project Heading for Trouble!, are asked in the order listed for testing alignment of a team with itself and with the objectives of the project. When planning, however, we should ask them in the reversed order.

The question, "Who gets a vote?," is intended to identify the key stakeholders for the project. This is a check on the assumptions made in developing the DBS.

The question, "What have you delivered that makes this a successful project?," is intended to bring out any remaining hidden agendas. It is also to make the stakeholders think about the project in terms of what is driving it, rather than what the product of or solution for the project might be. For example, the product of the project might be a report, but the driver is to understand what went wrong with a design that led to a building collapse. Or the project may be to build a factory; the driver is to increase production, perhaps to lower operating costs, or maybe to improve the access to raw materials or to the marketplace.

The question, "What have you delivered that tells you the project is complete?," brings expectations around completion into focus.

As I have never seen a project where the answers to these questions are the same, I believe that they do not have to be. But we do need to discuss the different answers and achieve alignment on how we are

> ## Yet Another Project Heading for Trouble!
>
> A project to implement a new accounting system had been going for over a year. The project had good news and bad news. The good news was that it was apparently 70 percent complete. The bad news was that the budget was already 140 percent complete, and the schedule was over 110 percent complete!
>
> Before asking questions, I confirmed that everyone had the same new completion date and budget in mind. Responses to the question, "What have you just delivered that tells you that the project is complete?," were varied. They ranged from, "The beta test is complete"—with no hint of fixing any bugs—to, "We have completed a full fiscal year since being in full use of the whole system." These definitions are about eighteen months apart.
>
> In response to the question, "What have you delivered that tells you that the project was a resounding success?," replies varied from, "The users are using it"—a nonreply really, as the plan was to turn off the old system when the new one was running—to, "We have reduced accounting staff by at least thirty people." Some of the thirty people were in the room when this was announced. It was the first time that they had officially heard of it, and it was the primary business driver for the project!
>
> That many of the stakeholders had never been consulted quickly became clear from responses to the question, "Who gets to vote on the first two questions?" These stakeholders included senior executives and, of course, the thirty people who were being laid off!

going to address the differences. For example, in SMART projects, we often see a series of *completion* dates for different stakeholders. The discussion about success brings out a range of issues from profitability for contractors (at variance with the perception of *value for money* by the client organization staff), to breakthrough technology (at variance with the organization's propensity to take risk), or market expectations (at variance with what can realistically be achieved in the time available). Resolution of these variances helps the different stakeholders appreciate the challenges that others face, which leads to better communication, a more realistic plan, and a balance among the demands of the different stakeholders. The result is alignment of project objectives.

This balance is most easily achieved at the outset of the project, before expectations have drifted off course and become hardened.

Alignment of stakeholders is vital for project success. Definition of and consensus on what constitutes project success is most easily achieved early in the project development process.

8.7   3-D Schedule

Starting with the answers to the three questions discussed in the sidebar, Yet Another Project Heading for Trouble, we can pinpoint the end of the project and the deliverables required at that point. This is the start of the 3-D scheduling process.

The three D's in 3-D scheduling stand for *drop-dead dates*. The process objective is to identify the last date by which a deliverable needs to be produced before the project as a whole is delayed. The process is equivalent to the backward pass in the calculation of float or slack time in a critical path schedule. The mechanical steps for developing such a schedule are listed in the sidebar, Building a 3-D Schedule.

The result of the exercise is a timeline on which all of the deliverables critical to the project are laid out in the order in which they are required. Figure 8.3 illustrates how a 3-D schedule may appear.

Producing the 3-D schedule is difficult, because we have to think backwards from a complete and successful project, undoing it until we have worked to the present time. In doing so, do not be surprised if the number of deliverables is different from the one determined in the DBS.

Planning backwards helps us in two ways: 1) it produces a more *honest* assessment of the real duration required to complete a project, and 2) it helps unearth the deliverables that we missed during the first round of planning.

Once we have made the adjustments to the schedule that are necessary to make it realistic, we can then add the earlier-derived checkpoints or off-ramps. When it comes to managing the project, we will use the 3-D schedule to help coordinate different activities and assess progress. If one (or more) deliverable(s) identified against a specific drop-dead date is (are) missed, then we know we are late.

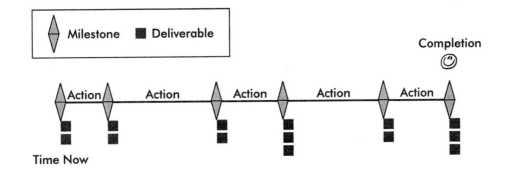

Figure 8.3 3-D Schedule

 A 3-D schedule helps identify when we are in trouble, while there is still time to do something about it.

Adding detail to the DBS and the 3-D schedule can be done in several ways, depending on the preference of the project manager and the team, as well as the size and complexity of the project. One option is to use RACI+ charts.

8.8   RACI+ Charts

RACI+ charts have been around in various forms for many years. The idea behind the original ones was to identify the roles of participants in each element of a project.

As we manage SMART projects using deliverables, the RACI+ charts will be closely linked to them. The acronym RACI stands for:

- Responsibility
- Action
- Coordination
- Information.

The "+" has been added because it often makes sense to add more information to one of these charts. (A sample RACI+ chart can be seen in Chapter 13.)

Building a 3-D Schedule

1. Obtain consensus answers to the three questions.

2. Identify the deliverables that are the last ones to be delivered (project completion).

3. Identify the action that will produce these deliverables. It may be a partial activity, such as *complete commissioning* or *finish training*.

4. Identify the deliverables needed to allow the action item to be completed.

5. Repeat Items 3 and 4 until the deliverables identified in Step 4 are currently in hand.

6. Add PLO duration estimates for each action item.

7. Add all of the durations to get an overall PLO estimate of project duration.

8. Typically, you will find that you should have started the project several months ago if you wished to compete by the target end date.

9. Adjust the processes and action items by making appropriate changes to the implementation plan, such as fast tracking, scope reductions, overtime, and so on, until the shortest practical and believable schedule has been achieved.

10. If you still need more time, eat crow, and get the completion date deferred!

11. Read Section 8.9 before completing this exercise.

For small projects, where the activities are well understood, and the roles of the team members are very easily comprehended (perhaps because the team members have previously worked together or because the project is *routine*), there may be little benefit in using RACI+ charts. If the project is small, one RACI+ chart for the whole project may be appropriate.

As can be seen from Figure 14.8.3 (see Chapter 14), the chart includes the following information:

■ list of activities (these should each produce a deliverable or mini-deliverable)

■ simple bar chart showing when the activity is expected to happen

■ list of people involved and their roles (more on this in a moment)

- other information, as required. I like to show budget, actual costs, and work hours; I plan and track these separately, as work hours are volatile.

The role of each participant will be denoted by one of the four letters: R, A, C, or I. Whoever is responsible for an activity—and it should only be one person—will, by implication, also have action, need to coordinate, and keep people informed of what is going on. Anyone with action will have to coordinate and keep people informed. All those who need to coordinate or be coordinated with will also need to trade information. If the chart is completed and distributed to all the people who have roles in delivery of that part of the project represented by the RACI+ chart, then everyone knows what is expected of him. The RACI+ chart becomes an effective communications road map for the project, addressing the main needs of a communications plan, while also identifying who has to do what in order to stay on track.

8.9   PLO Estimates and How to Use Them

I invented the term *PLO estimate*; you will recall that I named these types of estimates as such because they are estimates of perfect, likely, and outrageous outcomes. They are all about obtaining better information on estimated costs, effort, and durations. When we quote or are quoted estimates, they tend to be single-point ones, because all too often ranges are not acceptable. Who will get a project approved if we say it is going to cost between $3 million and $10 million? Even narrower ranges leave the recipient of the information nervous! (We will deal with this in greater detail in Chapter 9.)

For now, and for the purposes of developing a project charter, let us consider the advantages of using PLO estimates. First, they give us a range of likely outcomes; the bigger the range, the more uncertain the item being estimated, or the more nervous the person providing the information. Either way, it is useful information. Let me explain.

Consider two deliverables that will each take an estimated ten workdays to complete. Which one will you spend time managing? The correct answer is, "I do not know!" Now consider the same two deliverables but with PLO estimates.

One has an estimate of nine, ten, and twelve workdays (perfect, likely, and outrageous estimates, respectively). The other deliverable has a range of four, ten, and thirty-two workdays. It is pretty clear now which activity you or I would manage—the second one, because it is more volatile.

Not only do we know where to focus our limited time and energy for best effect now, but we can also start to take some action. If we ask the team member who provided the information what is likely to cause the overrun, we can determine what can be done to eliminate or mitigate the risk. Similarly, we can ask what circumstances will lead to the perfect estimate and take action, when possible, to nurture the opportunity.

Another useful feature of this approach is that close PLO estimates, where you know the risks are high, can help you flush out unjustified optimism in the estimate!

The range estimates produced this way are good input for further analysis (for example, using Monte Carlo simulations) of the risks. (This is covered in detail in the next chapter.)

Range estimating is not new. PERT and other techniques using pessimistic, likely, and optimistic estimates have been around for nearly half a century. I deliberately renamed the ranges for two reasons. First, the PERT mindset will normally give you a static or conservative range. We are after the range that includes at least a part of the *tails* in the estimate range. Second, I want the idea to stick and be used more than it is in industry today, because PLO estimates are so much richer in information than single-point ones.

 PLO (range) estimating provides significant additional information that helps us understand where risk and uncertainty affect our estimate of time, resources, or money required to deliver a project.

Collecting this information—and most of the other information that we need to put our project charter together—requires working with the whole team. This means that we need to have a series of effective and relatively short meetings, which the project manager or some other person will chair and facilitate.

8.10 Process Issues Around Facilitation

Planning meetings set the tone for the project, as well as for subsequent meetings. It is therefore important to manage these meetings well so that they not only are effective, but also are seen to be so! Here are a few things to consider:

- Be prepared for the meeting: talk to participants ahead of time, and make sure that they are aligned with the objectives of the session.

Don't Park Your Brain Outside

- Have a clear agenda: let participants know what is important and what needs to be accomplished.
- Have a positive attitude: it *is* contagious if it is genuine!
- Make sure that the right people are present or are at least fairly represented.
- Be inclusive: ensure that everyone has an opportunity to participate.
- Validate what is being said: make sure that we are communicating precisely and that there are no misunderstandings.
- Do not criticize or discard ideas: put them in a parking lot if necessary; identify and recognize differences—it's OK to have different ideas; in fact, it's good to have a choice!
- When there are differences, ensure that we have consensus (or a dictatorial decision, if you really do know what is best) before moving on.
- Confirm what was decided, and make sure that there is acceptance of the outcome of the meeting before breaking up the meeting itself.
- Record the results, and distribute them to all participants and anyone else who needs to know the outcome.

 Following a few simple steps in facilitating a meeting generates better results than leaving the facilitation process to chance.

8.11 Planning for Success Through Use of Contingency and Allowance for Learning Curves

The amount of contingency that you wish to allocate for a project is typically measured in terms of elapsed time and cost. The elapsed time extends the planned end date to provide float. Costs capture expected procurement overruns and additional or extended use of resources—especially people. The contingency amounts are usually multiples of five; it is common to see contingency amounts calculated as 5 percent, 10 percent, 15 percent, and 20 percent of the base estimate or original elapsed schedule time. There is very little science and even less logic behind these estimates, which is why so many projects are late and over budget. SMART project managers will apply some science to this estimate and provide another important option: a risk mitigation plan. (The science behind the plan is described in the next chapter in more detail.) What we need is some understanding of what the results give us, and how they help us round out an intelligent and complete project charter. Specifically, we need the following: target dates for deliverables, based on an agreed and appropriate probability of success; budget with a realistic and properly assessed probability of being adequate; and risk mitigation plans for all of the significant challenges and uncertainties that we are likely to encounter on the project.

By following the SMART approach to risk identification, assessment, and mitigation, we end up with the following information:

- range of outcomes for budget and scheduled completion date for the project
- probabilities associated with these ranges
- clarity with regard to what risks and uncertainties create these ranges and how they can be *tightened up* by replanning (risk mitigation steps)
- classification of risks in a risk matrix (probability, impact, and degree of control possible)
- when risks are *live* and how the project plan responds to those risks
- alternative plans, in the event of a risk occurrence (more significant risks only)
- risk register, summarizing the earlier-mentioned information in an accessible form.

Armed with these data, we can now put together an informed risk management plan, and, based on that plan, set target completion dates and budgets as well as resource requirements for each. These plans will be based on the willingness of the project sponsor to take specific risks. This in turn will be linked to the program risk management plan that will reflect how risk and contingency will be managed over a suite of projects that constitute a program.

 Informed risk mitigation and management requires appropriate information to support decision-making and planning.

8.11.1 Setting Project Targets

The target date and budget for a deliverable will likely not be the number you first thought. As we saw in Chapter 6, the likely estimate is typically a lot less than likely! Think about it: If we have to guess at what effort it takes to do something, we generally think of what it takes at close to ideal conditions. Even if we are less optimistic, the potential for doing better is clearly limited. The potential for doing worse is essentially limitless. So, our best guess is going to be at the optimistic end of the full spectrum of potential outcomes!

When we set targets for delivery dates and budgets, we need to bear this in mind. We should set realistic targets with an appropriate probability for success. We can set these individually for each deliverable. We can do so for the entire project. Or we can (as I would recommend) set them for both, balancing the need for success on individual deliverables (some are more urgent than others) against the expectations for the overall project. The same type of balance—between projects and an entire program—should be achieved in program management of a suite of projects.

 Within a project and between projects, planning for and balancing risk and mitigation options will help achieve realistic and intelligent plans; it will also help in managing the expectations of stakeholders.

8.11.2 Confirming the Adequacy of Budget, Schedule, and Scope

If we have established a project end date, and it is based on an adequate risk assessment, we will have a probability of success assigned to this end date. The same holds true for budgets, work effort, and other variables. If one of the risk mitigation plans is to reduce scope in the event that budgets or schedules are likely to overrun, then we need also to understand what an orderly retreat looks like. We need to classify the elements in the DBS under the following categories (or their equivalents):

- Must have: these components are essential to the success of the project.
- Should have: these should be included for completeness, but we could live without them if forced by circumstances.
- Would be nice: these are icing on the cake. We will be really happy if we get these, too!

Adequacy of budgets, schedule, and scope are based on the perception of the beholder. We need to be sure that the stakeholders for the project are aligned with the expected results, and be aware of how these may change over time as risks occur and are addressed. We need to manage everyone's expectations at the outset and as the project progresses.

Remember, it is better to eat crow when it is young and tender than when it is old and tough! If we are aware of potential risks, the project sponsor should be made aware of them and allowed to make an informed decision regarding their investment in the project and its execution plan. If the risk assessment suggests that the project should be canceled, it is better to do so before you invest any money.

 Keep everyone informed about risk—and that means you know what is going on.

8.11.3 The Nature of Risk Mitigation Plans

The very nature of risk mitigation is compromise. We trade risk against the cost and time required to address the consequences. In developing risk mitigation plans, we introduce different and new risks into the project. For example, if we add money to the budget or time to the schedule, we may render the project uneconomical, or we may miss a market window. If we introduce mitigation steps, we may change the specifics of the project or introduce a new risk. A feasible example may be to increase staffing, but it increases the risk of miscommunication, adds to coordination problems, and may reduce productivity.

 Balance of objectives with reality is important in determining the best risk mitigation strategy.

Chapter 9

RISK ASSESSMENT AND MANAGEMENT

What is the completion date for your current project? How much will it cost? How many work hours will you expend? Write down your answers for these three questions, then compare them with the schedule, budget, and allocated personnel for your project. Are they the same? If yes, do you believe them? If no, why are they different?

Where am I heading with this? Hang on a moment longer. I will first introduce you to the *Idaho test*, Idaho being a compression of "I do it at home." We do smart things at home; then we go to work, park the car, and *park the brain outside* before we check in for the day. If we forget to park the brain before we start work, there is a good chance that we will be asked to switch it off and take it out before it causes any trouble. The Idaho test is one that helps identify opportunities for smarter thinking at work. Try answering the following questions (again): How long does it take you to commute to work? How much gas do you use (if you drive), or how many calories do you burn (if you are self-powered)? Probably you have answered these questions with a range—fifteen to twenty minutes, about half a gallon of gas, or how the blazes should I know how many calories I burn!

Now compare these answers to the first set of answers. Do you have single-point answers for the completion date and cost of your project? Most of us do, and they do not pass the Idaho test. At home, we understand that even with stable everyday things, there is some variation and uncertainty. When it comes to projects that typically involve lots more people, have never been done before, and are far less predictable and of much longer duration, we have an amazing inclination toward precision in our estimating! It simply does not make sense; we set impossible or (worse) irrational expectations for success. We must understand the risks involved in our projects and how to deal with them. Some, we can manage; some, we cannot. We need to manage those that we can and adjust client expectations for those that we cannot. Also ensure that everyone understands and acknowledges the uncertainty associated with the outcome of our project.

 Projects are uncertain. They all have inherent risks and, therefore, are somewhat unpredictable. We should not deny this but should work with the realities of risk and uncertainty.

9.1 Options for Risk Analysis: Concept and How to Simplify Tools

Risk analysis means many different things to different people. *Risk*, as a word, means different things, depending on our individual perspectives; yet, some definition is required to get us going.

9.1.1 Risk, Uncertainty, and Chance

The three terms in the heading are often mingled. The definitions I use are not universal; they are presented here so that we can follow the rest of this chapter with some consistency.

Risk is the (usually unknown, at least in magnitude or timing) event or factor that leads to a changed or different outcome.

Uncertainty is the range of outcomes that are possible, given the existence of risk.

Chance is uninfluenced possibility of a change in expected outcome.

Let's try these terms in a sentence: When you play a game of *chance*, the *risk* of losing is high because of the high degree of *uncertainty* of the outcome.

Risk analysis helps us identify the elements that can increase the uncertainty of the outcome of a project. What we want to do is avoid or reduce the chance of failure.

 Not conducting risk analysis may leave too much of the project to chance.

9.1.2 What Is Risk Analysis?

First, what risk analysis is *not* is producing lots of charts, statistics, evaluations, and analytical data. It *is* about understanding what needs attention. In Section B of this book, we identified the need to keep our eye on the ball. There are lots of balls in the air for any project at any time; risk analysis helps identify which balls to watch. It also helps eliminate or mitigate risks, making the performance and outcome of our project more predictable.

  Risk analysis helps make projects more predictable.

Predicting a project's outcome is based on finding the most volatile parts of the project and stabilizing them by doing something about the risk that leads to uncertain outcomes. It's that simple. The tools we will briefly discuss in this chapter will help us find the risks, and then we can look at the different ways of dealing with them.

  First we need to identify project risks; then we can start doing something about them.

9.1.3 Basic Steps for Risk Analysis

The three phases of risk analysis are 1) identify the potential risks, 2) assess their impact, and 3) develop strategy and tactics for dealing with them. Remember, as we go through the steps, to choose the level of detail you may need to assess and manage risk on your project. The process will be anything from a brief mental exercise to one of some complexity.

  Do not get carried away with risk analysis. Like all tools, it has limitations, and the real value is in what you learn from the exercise. Only keep going until you stop learning!

Identifying risks. This step is a combination of brainstorming with the team, using checklists (if you have them), and talking to experts. There is no magic formula. Do not rely on checklists alone, as they will not tell you what the team may know. Use at least two of the techniques; over time, you will develop your own checklists to help in the future. When you have a list of possible risks, you are ready for the next step.

✹ Do not rely on just one way to identify risks.

Assessing risks. The first step in assessing risks is to determine the probability of occurrence, which can be as simple as *high* or *low*. If you need more granularity, use it. A common way of doing this is to use ranges of probabilities. For example, you may assign the risks to groups such as $< P_{10}$ (probability of less than 10 percent) or $P_{11}–P_{20}$ (probability of 11 to 20 percent), and so on.

Then assess the impact on the project, should the risk occur. This may range from low to high or be assigned to more detailed classifications.

If we use a simple classification, we end up with a two-by-two matrix that looks like the one in Figure 9.1.3.1.

More sophisticated risk-assessment matrices can be developed; many larger corporations have them. Some of these are specific to certain types of risk, such as health and safety. An example of such a risk matrix is shown in Figure 9.1.3.2.

Once we have effectively prioritized the risks, we can then try to quantify their impact. The simplest way of doing this is guessing at the likelihood of the risk event occurring (e.g., 70 percent probability), then estimating the likely impact on schedule, cost, or other factor (e.g., increase schedule by about three days). More sophisticated techniques include use of the Monte Carlo risk analysis (described later). Such techniques require a degree of analysis or assessment.

 Risk analysis tools help us understand the mechanics and behavior of risk on our project. The trick is to avoid overanalyzing risk. After all, any analysis is going to have to be based in part on best guesses of the future, so it will have limited accuracy.

One of the easiest ways to begin risk assessment in any particular element of a project is to consider the range of outcomes that may be associated with a particular deliverable. The outcomes most commonly used are cost, work effort required, elapsed time, and acceptability of the end product. The first three are usually readily quantifiable. The acceptability issue is a bit more difficult.

For the first three, using a range of outcomes based on a PLO (perfect, likely, and outrageous) estimate is usually a good start to the process of understanding the risks involved.

Don't Park Your Brain Outside

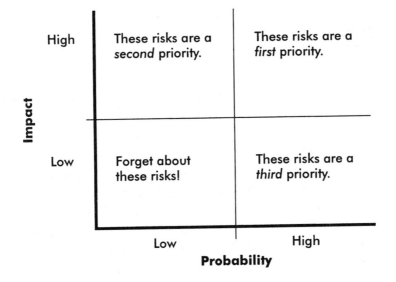

Figure 9.1.3.1 Simple Risk Assessment Matrix

Dealing with (or managing?) risks. I am not sure that we manage risks; we would be overstating what really can be done. However, it is possible to influence the likely impact of some risks, hedge against others, and so on. If we remain realistic about the process of *risk management*, we need to ensure that the worst (unacceptable risk events) do not occur. We accomplish this primarily through avoidance, although other options are possible. High-impact risks need careful management and close monitoring. Senior management and others in a project sponsorship role must be aware of these risks and agree to the risk management plan. They may be held legally (even criminally) responsible for the outcome. Moderate and low risks need to be evaluated and appropriate plans put into place to address them. (These are discussed in more detail later in this chapter.)

 Effective and timely communication of potential risk to project sponsors is an important part of risk management.

9.1.4 Objectives of Risk Analysis: Results

When I talk about results in the context of risk analysis, I do not mean lots of pretty charts and confusing statistics. What is important here is that there is a rational and acceptable plan for dealing with the risks associated with a project. The useful result of risk analysis is a *plan* to

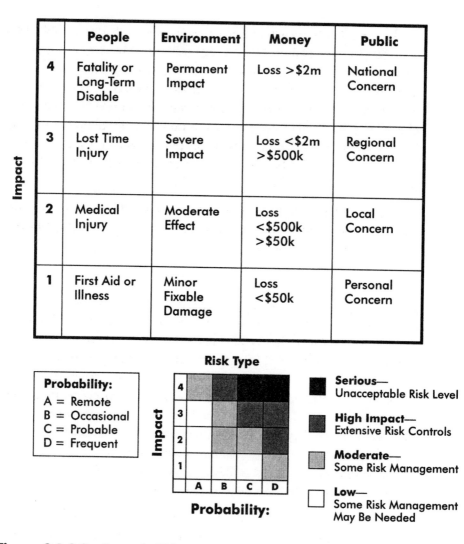

	People	Environment	Money	Public
4	Fatality or Long-Term Disable	Permanent Impact	Loss >$2m	National Concern
3	Lost Time Injury	Severe Impact	Loss <$2m >$500k	Regional Concern
2	Medical Injury	Moderate Effect	Loss <$500k >$50k	Local Concern
1	First Aid or Illness	Minor Fixable Damage	Loss <$50k	Personal Concern

Impact

Risk Type

Probability:
A = Remote
B = Occasional
C = Probable
D = Frequent

Impact

4				
3				
2				
1				
	A	B	C	D

Probability:

■ **Serious—** Unacceptable Risk Level

■ **High Impact—** Extensive Risk Controls

▨ **Moderate—** Some Risk Management

□ **Low—** Some Risk Management May Be Needed

Figure 9.1.3.2 Example Risk Matrix

manage the identified risks—and we should have identified the most important risks, leaving little or nothing to chance. Remember the definitions at the beginning of this chapter!

 The key result of risk analysis is a plan to mitigate the impact of things that can go wrong on the project.

Don't Park Your Brain Outside

We can think of risks in four main categories, as shown in Table 9.1.4.

Success in risk analysis is being able to identify the potential causes of problems in the execution and successful delivery of the project. Over time, as you develop lists of possible risks, these lists can help others as checklists for future projects. However, remember the risk of only using checklists: people will leave their brains outside. Checklists should either have a few random blank lines to get people thinking again, or they should be used *after* brainstorming or another information-gathering process.

 Checklists of potential risks and their likely outcomes, used judiciously, can be a useful resource to accelerate the risk analysis process.

Sorting risks into categories ranging from the most to the least important is the next step. It may be followed by some more sophisticated analysis to determine the contingencies, impacts, and other quantifiable implications of different risks and strategies for managing them. One of the things that we are trying to do in developing a risk management plan is manage the expectations of the stakeholders, especially the project sponsors. If sponsors are unaware of the risks that they are taking with a particular project, they will, arguably, be justified in thinking that they do not exist, or, worse, that the project manager knew (or should have known) about them but did not discuss them at the right time. All of this is bad risk management, to say nothing of unprofessional!

 Finding and reporting risks (and how to deal with them) before we commit to a project makes it easier to manage the project and the expectations of the stakeholders.

What we want is a better plan that considers the risks involved and the range of likely outcomes. Its success is best measured by the level of confidence that the sponsors and project team have in the resulting plan for implementation of the project as a whole. Now, measuring confidence levels is not that easy! Project approval with a range of acceptable to brilliant outcomes is not a bad deliverable for determining success.

Risk Category	Risk Type	Sample Critical Factors	
Business Risk	Market	What Will Change? Price Sensitivity? Competitive Products? Market Window?	Who Are the Customers? Volume Sensitivity? Distribution? Half-Life of Product?
	Financing	Source of Funds? Sensitivity to Overruns?	Stability of Business? Cash Flow Available?
	Shareholder	Perceived Value? Sustainability?	Interest in Project?
Technological Risk	Robustness	Established and Proven? Track Record?	Cost of Failure? Warranties?
	Complexity	In-House Expertise? Reliance on Other Organizations?	Special Training?
	Ownership	Intellectual Property? License Agreements? Reliance on Others?	Own Technology? Spin-off Ownership?
Social Risk	Environmental	Environmental Damage: Long and Short Term? Health Issues? Studies Required?	Unknowns? Permits?
	Socioeconomic	Jobs Created or Lost? Local Competition? Special Interest Groups?	Local Benefits? Unions?
	Political	Government Support? Tax Breaks/Problems?	Opposition to Project?
Project Delivery Risk	Duration	Longer-than-Usual Projects? Corporate Changes Expected during Life of Project?	Very Fast?
	Size	Large Project for Organization? Impact of Project on Business?	High Profile? Impact of Failure?
	Complexity	Number of Partners and Stakeholders Large? Organization Capabilities?	In-House Expertise?
	Definition and Volatility	Scope Clear? Client Knows What She Wants?	Likely to Change? Clear Definition of Success?

Table 9.1.4 Risk Types and Considerations

We had these monitors specially made when we discovered
that there was a risk of a schedule delay.

9.1.5 The Basic Toolkit

The analytical tools that we need for effective risk assessment are
briefly described in the following sections. In particular, Monte Carlo
simulations are described in some detail, as this tool is increasingly
being used. For the rest of the process, keeping it simple will gain
clarity, ease of use, and better plans. The loss is in alleged accuracy
of the risk models that you may use, but then we are dealing with
such soft information that this is no real practical loss.

9.2 Sensitivity Analysis

The purpose of sensitivity analysis is to provide a sense of which variable in a project will most likely influence the success of the project.
The use of sensitivity analysis tools can be quite sophisticated. What I
describe is a simplified version of sensitivity analysis, using two different
approaches to the issue to get quite different views of the risk problem.

9.2.1 Sensitivity of Financial Model

Building a financial model of the project is the first step. Some models are very complex, and financial modeling goes beyond the scope of this book. At any rate, any project that will have a significant impact on the sponsor corporation should have some sort of model, however simple, to determine whether project investment is sound. Often, these models will be set up on spreadsheets. Typically, they will be used to forecast future outcomes of the project investment, measured in terms of revenue, savings, or some other quantified benefit. We change one variable at a time and see how each change affects the outcome of the project. As you increase and decrease the variable, the outcome will change. We want to assess the relative change. The faster it changes per unit of increase or decrease of the variable, the more sensitive the project is to changes in that variable. This simple concept used correctly will help us find the variables that need attention when planning and managing the project, the ones that will have the biggest impact on our success—or otherwise.

Let's try a simple example. The project is to develop a new product that can be added to a conventional photocopier to turn it into a computer printer. The new product is based on an existing technology platform that is part of another product line in the organization. The market for the product is the home office, where studies have shown that 60 percent of the target customers would be interested in reducing space needs for office equipment and eliminating the need to keep two different toner cartridges. The financial model suggests that the return on investment for development of this new idea into a commercial opportunity is viable under the following conditions:

- The market share for this company is 20 percent.
- The cost of development and the capital tied up in manufacturing does not exceed $5 million.
- The product can be developed and tested in six months.
- Component costs can be kept down to $2.70 or less per unit.
- The labor cost for manufacture is less than $24 per unit.

The sensitivity analysis reveals that the return on investment is very sensitive to manufacture labor costs and market share. It is significantly less sensitive to the other factors.

We are now told that the market share may be eroded if the competition's product is available to the public—estimated in eight to ten months—before our product is ready. Armed with this information, we can see that it's important to have our product out in less than eight months, but faster than six months may make little difference to the value. We can also provide guidance to the designers, informing them that manufacturing effort should be minimized, which can be done (within practical limits) at the expense of using slightly more costly components. This in turn tells us that the designers should be talking to manufacturing and to the suppliers of the more difficult-to-assemble components.

 Sensitivity analysis sensitizes us to the real needs of the project and to whom we need to turn in order to develop a better result.

9.2.2 Sensitivity of Risk Model

The concept behind this type of model is similar to the financial model. The difference is that we look at what could go wrong and assess the impact of that event on the project. For example, what if the supplier of a key component fails to deliver or is declared bankrupt? If the impact can be assessed using the financial model, this may be reflected in a change in price to purchase from another supplier or in the time delay resulting from redesign. If the likely delay is a high risk, then we may consider developing two prototypes, using the alternative component; thus, we have a backup for the eventuality of a failure of this type. If, on the other hand, we see the risk as slight and the impact as minimal, we may elect to do nothing unless the event occurs. In such a case, we will at least know what we have to do, and our response time will be much smaller, further mitigating the effect of the event.

9.3 Tornado Diagrams

Once we have completed a sensitivity analysis, it is sometimes useful to present the results in a user-friendly way, such as a tornado diagram. (It has its name because it looks like a tornado.) We simply list the tested variables or risks that could occur in descending order of likely impact. Alongside the list, we draw a bar, centered on a vertical line, the *neutral axis*. The lines extend from either side to reflect any negative and positive impact that the variable or risk may have on the project. The longer the line, the greater the variability (see Figure 9.3).

Figure 9.3 illustrates the results of a series of sensitivity analyses, where each variable was altered by a set amount determined in a number of ways. One common approach is to increase and decrease the variable to a preset expectation at a fixed probability of occurrence. For example, we may set the ranges for a variable at 5 percent probability (P_5) and 95 percent probability (P_{95}). The neutral axis

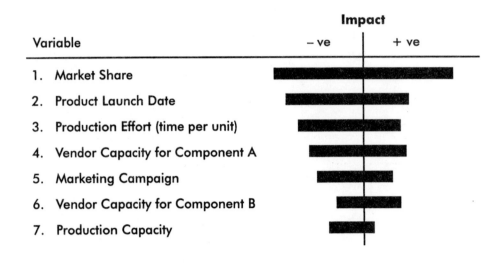

Figure 9.3 Example Tornado Diagram

would not necessarily represent the 50 percent (P_{50}) probability point, as the distribution may be skewed one way or the other. We can readily see how this fits well with the SMART concept of working with PLO ranges; we simply substitute any numerical probability with our perfect and outrageous estimates. I believe that this approach is more honest, as we rarely have empirical evidence to support any true statistical analysis that we may use to justify claiming that a particular outcome has a specific and precise probability of success.

9.4   Influence Diagrams

An influence diagram pictorially presents relationships between different parts of a project and how individual risks may influence the project overall. This tool helps us understand the way that one risk event may ripple through a project. Figure 9.4 shows a simple influence diagram for a simple project, illustrating how such a diagram may be built. The mathematical modeling behind it can be quite complex and will be used to work out the estimated quantified impact that a particular risk impacting one part of the project will have on other parts. I will not even try to present any detailed calculations; my purpose is simply to illustrate how the tool works. For most projects, should we even bother using this tool, all we need is the picture to help us map out how risks may affect our project.

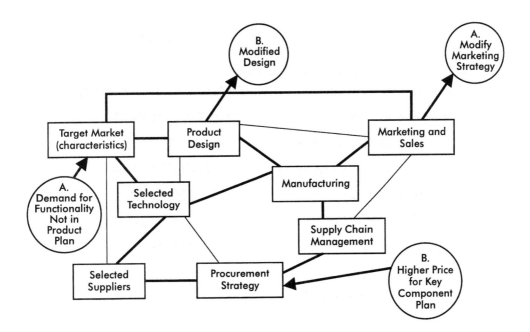

Figure 9.4 Simplified Risk Influence Diagram

Figure 9.4 shows connected project elements in rectangular boxes; the lines linking the boxes show relationships between the components. The ovals represent risks that will primarily impact the project element to which they are connected. The *ripple effect* of the risk can then be followed by tracing the impact from one element to the next.

There are several ways to embellish the diagram in Figure 9.4. For example, we could add a factor (number) to each of the lines linking project elements—the higher the number, the stronger the link between these components. Currently, the diagram simply represents the strength of the relationship through the thickness of the line linking the elements. Another way of adding to the utility (and the complexity) of the diagram is to add the impact of a risk event in terms of time or cost.

Figure 9.4's value derives from identifying the relationships between the project elements and how a risk event may affect each of these elements. For those projects where use of such a diagram is warranted, the greatest value is in understanding the relationships between the various project elements. After that, the return on effort diminishes rapidly unless the project is particularly complex with significant risks. Sophisticated tools exist to develop this type of model, yet only the largest projects can justify their use with today's technology.

Shhh! With luck, he's having nightmares about the project.
Then, when he wakes, we can ask him what risks we need to consider.

 Gain an understanding of how risk events might ripple through different parts of a project.

9.5   Decision Tree Analysis

The idea behind decision tree analysis is to determine the impact or likelihood of a particular decision. Its application in uncertain or ill-defined projects is obvious when we think about it. These projects are fraught with decisions, and people do not like to make decisions or guess their likelihood in advance.

Use of the decision tree analysis technique is illustrated briefly in the next few paragraphs. There are many books that are far more scientific than I am in presenting the finer points of the technique; I recommend them for details if the following is not enough for your needs. Figure 9.5 shows a simple decision tree for a small project: developing a new toy.

Many classic practitioners of decision tree analysis will fall off their chairs when they see the chart in Figure 9.5. I have taken some liberties, as I wanted to show how we could adapt the original idea to show common project options. There are three things I want to demonstrate here: 1) how to use the basic tool, 2) how to bend the tool to serve our purposes, and 3) how to take full advantage of what the results tell us.

Be open-minded and flexible in how you use this (and almost any) tool. It is there to help us understand what is going on, or likely to go on, with our project.

The classical approach to decision trees is to identify the decisions (shown in boxes in Figure 9.5) and the probability of their outcomes. I have shown binary decisions (yes-or-no answers), but there can be several possible outcomes. Add to each outcome a percentage representing the expectation that a particular outcome will occur; the percentages should always total 100 percent for each decision. When this is done, we can then add the next decision until we reach the logical outcome of that particular chain of decisions. If we do the math (multiply the probability percentages), we end up with the probability of a particular outcome at the end of each line.

In Figure 9.5, I have shown three possible outcomes: 1) Known Target Market, 2) New Ideas Needed, and 3) Develop New Toy (where we started!)? The probability of each outcome is as follows:

- Known Target Market: Two paths lead to two boxes showing the same outcome (one way to represent this). The paths are made up of the following probabilities: 1) 80% x 40% (= 32%) and 2) 80% x 60% x 90% (= 43.2%) for a total of 75.2%.
- New Ideas Needed: Two paths lead to one box (see earlier example for the other way to show this). The paths comprise the following probabilities: 80% x 60% x 10% (4.8%) and 20% x 30% (= 6%) for a total of 10.8%.
- Start again, or Develop New Toy?, has one path leading to it with the following probabilities: 20% x 70% = 14%.

If you add up all the outcomes, you should end with 100 percent: 75.2% + 10.8% + 14% = 100%.

The first point in using this tool is to get a sense of the likelihood of particular outcomes for a project.

Now for the second point: bending the tool. I have already started on this (in Figure 9.5) by using one box to represent the outcome of more than one path. I also have reversed arrows so that they do not all flow from left to right. In the end, we use diagrams to simplify, so bend the rules to give you the easiest-to-understand picture. This may be dictated by corporate standards; e.g., always go from left to right, or always show a separate box for each possible outcome. It makes sense to be consistent, as you do not waste time trying to understand the diagram.

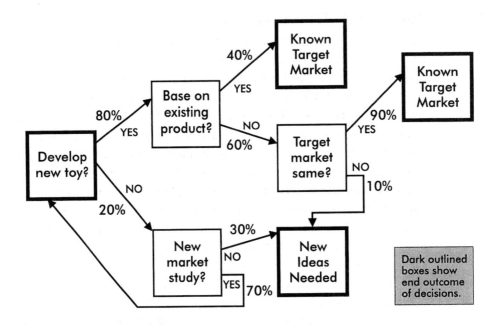

Figure 9.5 Decision Tree

The tool clarifies what may happen as a result of key decisions on the project. Ensure that the tool is easy for you (so you can explain it) and for the person(s) who also need the resulting information (so they can follow the logic and understand the outcomes and significance).

Finally, what do we learn from this exercise? First, there is a big chance that we will decide to stick with a known market. Next, if we do not stick with a known market, we are more likely to re-ask the original question (14 percent) rather than come up with a new idea (10.8 percent). Overall, this presents a risk-averse picture, which may tell us something about the corporate culture, or at least the view of that culture held by the person(s) building the chart. One word of caution: Do not take the percentages as gospel; they represent only an indicator of relative likelihood. The numbers tend to look more precise than they really are because of the effect of multiplying several of them together as you travel along a particular path.

 Cautious guesswork, experience in use of this tool, and a bit of sensitivity can help us understand the risk culture of the project team, client, and other decision-makers.

9.6   Monte Carlo Risk Simulations

Named after the famous casino city, Monte Carlo simulations offer a useful and, nowadays, accessible means for developing a risk profile of a project's quantifiable aspects. In SMART Project Management, we use ranges of estimates to determine the likely outcomes for a deliverable in terms of elapsed time, effort (work hours), and cost (money). These PLO estimates can be used as the basis for developing a picture of many possible outcomes of the project using Monte Carlo simulation. This technique develops a series of simulated outcomes, based on random outcomes within the ranges defined by a PLO estimate. In other words, each elapsed time duration (or effort or cost estimate) for each deliverable is altered within the PLO range, using a random number to create one possible outcome for that item. The sum of all of these outcomes for the whole project is then calculated, giving one possible combination of random outcomes for the overall project. The exercise is then repeated, generating more outcomes, until a statistically significant population of possible project results has been generated. The set of outcomes is theoretically an indicator of how the project is likely to behave in the future. The theory is undoubtedly sound. The challenge is found in that we only do a project once, so people are intuitively nervous of the process. In the following sections, we will look at results of Monte Carlo simulation, how they can be manipulated, and how to use them constructively to help your project become a success.

 Monte Carlo simulations are based on statistics. Although the results of these simulations are useful, treat the data with caution.

9.6.1 Presenting Monte Carlo Risk Simulation Results

To understand the results, we should first look at the input needed for a Monte Carlo simulation; then we will see how this input is used to generate the result.

Input data are required for a Monte Carlo simulation. In essence, input is in the form of a numerical model, containing a number of elements that can vary within a specified range. For most projects, these models are typically one of the following:

- financial model (such as forecast cash flow over the project life)
- critical path method (CPM) schedule, 3-D schedule, or other timeline
- estimate (cost or work hours).

The information required for each variable is the likely value, the upper and lower bounds, and the expected distribution of the variable within the range. For example, we may have three deliverables with different *profiles* for their likely cost (see Table 9.6.1).

Collecting or creating the data needed for a Monte Carlo simulation is a small step beyond what we normally do when we estimate. Adding the perfect and outrageous estimates to our single-point likely estimate is no big deal, and this process gives us so much more insight into the risks associated with our plan.

Software packages such as Crystal Ball, @Risk, @Risk for Projects, Risk+, or some top-end CPM packages such as Primavera Project Planner will perform the analysis for you. The process is simple; the software generates a series of random results from within the defined range of outcomes in the model. These project results are represented as a distribution of possible outcomes for the project.

 Today, the accessibility and ease of use of risk analysis software—especially Monte Carlo simulation packages—make this analysis tool an easy and powerful option to consider in the project planning process.

The Monte Carlo simulation result can be presented in several different ways. A common way is to show the outcome as a cumulative probability curve, which plots the probability of something happening on the vertical axis and the event on the horizontal axis. Typically, we need to read the horizontal axis such that the event is an upper-limit example of what the probability represents. This is best understood with an example; let's look at one outcome from a Monte Carlo simulation. Figure 9.6.1 shows the cost estimate range for a construction project.

In the example featured in Figure 9.6.1, a developer had asked a design/build company to estimate the cost of a Class B building on the outskirts of a large city. There were many unknowns, including the exact site, size of building, and what the scope would include. As a result, there was a range of possible cost outcomes. Each component was evaluated, and a range of outcomes was identified (our PLO estimates) for each. The factors that affected the outcomes were also noted. This second step is useful if you want to track these. As they are eliminated—through design decisions, final selection of market, product image, and so on—the ranges can be reduced and the simulation rerun with updated ranges reflecting the reduced uncertainty.

Deliverable	Cost Estimates			Distribution	What It Looks Like	What This Means
	Perfect	Likely	Outrageous			
Typical Deliverable	10	15	25	Triangular	10 15 25	This is my recommended default distribution, if you do not know how the deliverable will behave. (See also Section 9.6.2 on lying and cheating.)
Normal Deliverable	12	15	20	Normal	12 15 20	This deliverable can be expected to vary within the specified range and in a normal distribution. It will most frequently be close to the likely forecast.
Special Deliverable	8	10	20	Rectangular	8 10 20	The chances are the same that the deliverable will cost any amount within the specified range.

Table 9.6.1   Example Ranges and Distributions for Use in Monte Carlo Simulations

The results show that the *tails* of the analysis range from about $6 million to over $22 million. Clearly, nobody will go ahead with that range of costs, unless even the most expensive is still going to produce a reasonable return on investment. However, this analysis is being done at a very early stage in the development of the project. With a 70 percent confidence level (we ignore the 15 percent of results at each tail), we are working with a range of $10.7 million to $14.4 million—a far more rational range! If the project is worth continuing, provided its cost is within the range, then we proceed. If not, or if the risk still seems too high, we will need to work on reducing the risks associated with the larger PLO ranges. In our example in Figure 9.6.1, this was achieved by focusing on one site, tying down the footprint of the building, and setting a cost maximum for the external cladding, which eliminated some of the more expensive options being considered. With this done, the market study was revisited, and the viability of the project was reassessed.

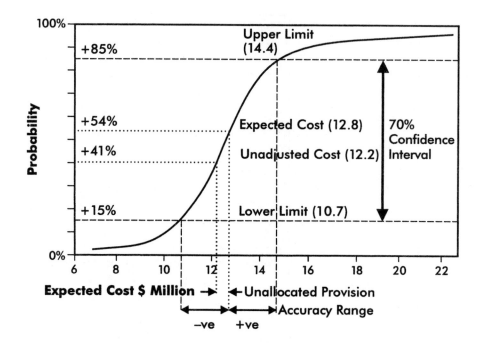

Figure 9.6.1 Sample Output from a Monte Carlo Simulation for a Proposed Mid-Rise Office Building at Conceptual State

 Don't be surprised if the project for which you have just run a simulation looks riskier than you first thought.

What else can we get out of an analysis like this? From Figure 9.6.1, we can see that there is (about) a 41 percent probability that we will complete the project for the likely or unadjusted cost; the probability increases to (about) a 54 percent chance if we add a 5 percent contingency. The unadjusted cost is simply the sum of all of the likely estimates. We can also determine the probability of completing the project for any amount from $6 million (almost no chance) to $22 million (probably can do it for this amount or less!). These figures suggest that there is a very large range of outcomes for virtually all of the individual elements in the estimate, or at least for the largest elements.

In this example, we can also see that the likely estimate has a less-than-likely (i.e., less than 50 percent probability) of success! In fact, this is not unusual. My observation of practice in industry shows the following ranges of outcomes for the probability associated with the likely estimate in Monte Carlo simulations:

- construction projects (tangible outcome, established technology, well-understood practices)—between 30 and 55 percent probability of completing the project for the likely cost or less
- mineral exploration and environmentally or politically sensitive projects (full of hard-to-identify and diverse stakeholders)—between 10 and 40 percent probability of completing the project for the likely cost or less
- software, corporate reorganization, and cost-reduction projects (typically poorly defined, hard to estimate, often new technology involved, rapidly evolving practices)—between 15 and 30 percent probability of completing the project for the likely cost or less
- research and development, new product development, and pharmaceutical projects (going where no one has gone before)—between 5 and 25 percent probability of completing the project for the likely cost or less.

We can quickly see that the likely estimates are invariably optimistic. *Likely* is a misnomer! We have an unlimited capacity to exceed budgets and schedules but only limited scope to improve on them. The odds are against us from the outset!

Evidence suggests that we overrun original budgets and schedules, which usually are based on single-point estimates. The chance of delivering a project to such an estimate is less than 50 percent; Monte Carlo simulations help expose such critical risks. The significance is that a single-point estimate will invariably be an optimistic one. If not, it has a built-in and therefore hidden and unquantified contingency. Unquantified contingencies simply muddy the waters and lead to games that are routinely played from project office to boardroom when selecting projects and setting budgets and targets for team and individual performance. (We will look at this in a bit more detail in the next section.)

 Using ranges to estimate time, cost, and effort helps uncover real base costs and establish a rational basis for determining contingencies.

That's about the most scientific way I've seen of working out
how much contingency to allow.

9.6.2 Lying and Cheating with Monte Carlo—and Why It Is Important to Know This Stuff

Monte Carlo analysis simulation is based on estimates—remember that estimates are defined in most good dictionaries as guesses. They may be informed guesses, but guesses they remain! Thus, we are dealing with soft data (as opposed to hard accounting) information. The range in our PLO estimates will also be based on subjective interpretation of what perfect and outrageous might mean. Now, on top of this, we have added a guess about how the forecast we have just made behaves; i.e., we are guessing (in most cases) at the statistical distribution of outcomes between the perfect and outrageous estimates. We feed this soft information into a computer program, and the software spits out figures and charts that are reported to several decimal places! The graphs are drawn with thin precise-looking lines. *Don't be fooled!* These are still soft data, and we need to recognize them as such.

 Monte Carlo risk simulations are based on estimates that, by their very nature, are approximate. Be very wary of any implications of too much accuracy in the results.

Assumption	Specific Example	Impact on Results
Range of PLO Estimate	Narrow Range	Steepens the "S" Curve
	Broad Range	Flattens the "S" Curve
Relative Position of *Likely* Estimate Within Range	Close to Perfect Estimate	Moves Curve to the Left
	Close to the Middle (halfway between Perfect and Outrageous)	Moves Curve toward Center
	Close to Outrageous Estimate	Moves Curve to the Right
Distribution of PLO Estimate Range	Rectangular Distribution	Straightens Curve
	Triangular Distribution	Recommended Default if You Do Not Know How a Range Really Behaves
	Normal or Log Normal Distribution	Steepens Curve Relative to Triangular Distribution

Table 9.6.2 Impact of Assumptions on Monte Carlo Result

Once we can overcome the initial sense of having precise information in either the Monte Carlo simulation model or the results, we can move to understanding how the assumptions we make will affect the outcome of the simulation. We make three types of assumptions when using this tool (see Table 9.6.2), together with the impact of each assumption on the outcome of the simulation. References to the "S" curve in Table 9.6.2 represent the cumulative distribution of probabilities (also see Figure 9.6.2).

The somewhat messy picture in Figure 9.6.2 shows us that there is a family of curves representing possible outcomes of a Monte Carlo simulation, depending on the assumptions we made in setting up the model. We also see that it is possible to manipulate the outcome by changing the assumptions. Listed are a few guidelines that may help you manage the use of this tool and get at least some degree of consistency in the results. As you will see, there is some conservatism in the guidelines; this is because it is usually more realistic to be pessimistic than optimistic when assessing project outcomes!

■ The range of your estimates should be based on a consistent set of ends; for example, set perfect at the outcome—under perfect conditions that you might expect to happen once in every hundred projects—then use the same probability for outrageous.

Too much information!

- Position the likely estimate where you would position a single-point estimate. Often, it is easier to estimate the likely first, then go for the perfect and outrageous.
- Unless you know the likely behavior of the estimate element (the expected distribution of outcomes between the perfect and the outrageous), use a triangular distribution. It is a simple distribution that looks like what it is—a guess in the absence of a better choice. As a test, challenge any distribution that is not your default and note the reason why it is different to provide a useful record of your understanding of the project in the event that it is challenged at a later date.

Using these guidelines will help you avoid pitfalls associated with using Monte Carlo simulation, especially if it forms the basis of target negotiations with contractors for incentives or bonuses!

 Using some simple guidelines to set up a Monte Carlo simulation will help keep the results consistent across simulations and avoid the more common misuses of the tool.

Don't Park Your Brain Outside

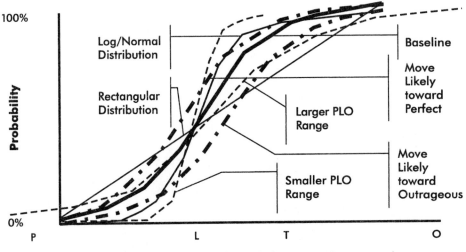

Figure 9.6.2 Impact of Decisions on Output of Monte Carlo Simulation: Cumulative Probability Curve

9.6.3 Using the Results of Monte Carlo Simulations to Help Your Project

Now that we know how to be cautious with the tool, add one more tip to your collection: using a highlighter, draw a broad line over the printout of the cumulative probability curve. This will remind you that we have really only got an approximate result, based on a set of assumptions. (The curve will look like that shown in Figure 9.6.3.)

We can now realistically extract information from the analysis that will give us a type of statement similar to the following examples:

- "There's about a 50 percent chance that we will complete the project before the end of June next year."
- "If you want this project completed for $42 million, there is a 15 to 20 percent chance that we will be successful."
- "With a contingency of 10 percent on this base budget of $420,000, we increase the chance of success from about 60 percent to about 90 percent."
- "Based on a target schedule of ten months, there is a one in five chance (20 percent) that we will need a time extension."

I know what I'm doing—so I don't need a plan to build a canoe.

These types of statements are now based on somewhat rigorous and realistic analyses of the estimate data and how these data are perceived in terms of accuracy or reliability. We use this information and these types of statements to begin managing the project stakeholders' expectations. This is the first important outcome of this type of analysis, but there are others.

 The results of a Monte Carlo simulation can be used to help manage stakeholder expectations by reflecting the real uncertainty of the project's outcomes.

9.7   Risk Analysis Results and How to Use Them

The best reason for doing any kind of risk analysis is to get a better idea of what can go wrong on a project and how to head off potential problems before they cause us too much grief. In a way, it is a proactive form of crisis management. We all have crises on our projects. If we define a crisis as an unforeseen event for which we have no immediate response, then we can eliminate 80 percent of all crises to which we may be exposed through a bit of risk analysis. How? Simply by using the tools to expose potential risks, thinking

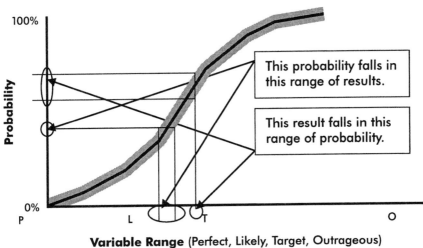

Variable Range (Perfect, Likely, Target, Outrageous)

Figure 9.6.3 Monte Carlo Output Marked for *Reality*

about how we may address them, and then putting some sort of contingency plan in place. Following are steps for putting risk analysis to use:

1. Identify possible sources and causes of risk: brainstorm, use PLO estimates as signposts, develop checklists of common risks, ask experts, and so on.
2. Assess the risk by determining the impact and probability of occurrence.
3. Determine whether you can do anything about the risk; is it controllable or not?
4. Determine what you will do to mitigate each important controllable risk. Build the solution into your plan.
5. List risks you plan to ignore and ensure that stakeholders buy into this approach.
6. Do the same for uncontrollable risks and consider your options in terms of adding time, money, or a *Plan B* for your project.
7. Reassess the schedule, budget, and resource plan in the light of the risk mitigation and contingency plan.
8. Allocate contingency to the critical parts of the budget and schedule.

Take another look at your revised plan to make sure that you have not added new risks in the process, and that you have the right balance between the risk you are taking and the value or potential return of the project.

Following a few simple steps at the outset of the project to identify and plan for risk will significantly improve your chance of success.

There are a number of ways that we can manage risk. The next section looks at the basic available options.

9.8   Risk Management Options

There is no magic to managing risk; the principles are very simple. Once we have identified potential risks and ranked them in terms of likelihood of occurrence and impact on the project, we need to decide what to do about them.

The following sections explore the more common risk mitigation strategies. Not all of them apply in every situation.

9.8.1   Ignore the Risk

In some cases, it makes sense to ignore a risk; this should be the remote risk that typically has little or no impact on the project. It is all too easy to identify endless improbable or low-impact risks that simply muddy the waters. If you ignore any significant risks (perhaps a remote one that would have a big impact on the project, such as the project manager being struck by lightning), ensure that they are listed. Also be sure that the project stakeholders—or at least the project sponsor—is informed of your decision.

 It's OK to ignore risks, but make sure that everyone is willing to live with the consequences of doing so.

9.8.2   Insure the Risk

Buying specific insurance is a way of spreading risk. It is important to ensure that the premium is worth paying; under certain circumstances, it pays to self-insure. (See also Section 9.8.4.) When purchasing insurance for your project, consider the following types and be aware of the limitations of each policy. My experience is that insurers are in the business of collecting premiums in preference to paying out. Because of prevalent fraud, perhaps this is not surprising. Common types of project insurance include the following:

- third party, accident, fire, and theft (normal liabilities for damage to third parties and loss due to accident, fire, and theft)
- professional liability (covers errors and omissions in the event of someone suing you because of them)
- key person insurance (covers the cost of replacing key personnel lost to illness or death—and, in some cases, other causes). As this usually does not cover loss due to someone leaving, we need to consider golden handcuffs or other incentives to stay with the project until it is done or the key person is no longer critical to the project's success.

 Buying insurance is a simple and effective way to mitigate certain risks. To do this well, we need to be sure that we know both what the insurance covers and what it does not. The latter remains an exposure to the project.

9.8.3 Purchase a Bond

Bonds are a form of insurance; the most common bonds are:
- Bid bond: covers the risk of a bidder defaulting on her bid. Typically, this type of bond will cover the cost of going to the next-highest compliant bidder.
- Performance bond: covers the failure of a contractor to perform. Typically, the surety that issued the bond will retain another contractor to complete the work under the contract, in the event that the bonded contractor fails to perform under the terms of the contract.
- Payment bond: covers the cost of paying for a contractor's sub-contractors, labor, and materials in the event that they were paid in a progress payment, but the contractor went into receivership or experienced other specific financial troubles and failed to pay its suppliers with the money intended for that purpose.

All bonds are hard to call. If there is a failure covered by the bond, there is usually—in my experience—a significant delay and often a significant battle with the contractor and the surety that issued the bond before there is any positive action. This is not surprising when you think about it. The contractor is the surety's regular client, and they will both lose if the bond is invoked. In most cases, bonds provide a nice warm feeling to the customer—a feeling paid for by the customer. The real value only exists if you have picked the wrong contractor in the first place!

Bonds are a traditional way of dealing with certain types of risk. They are rightly falling into disuse with more enlightened clients. They have questionable value in today's litigious and fast-paced world because they take time to invoke.

9.8.4 Add Time, Money, or a *Plan B* as a Contingency

Contingency is one of the most popular forms of project risk management. However, contingencies are normally determined by applying a politically correct percentage to the number that first came to your mind! All too often, this is identifiable by looking at the contingency percentage: if it is divisible by five, it is probably a guess!

A more intelligent means of adding contingencies is to do so as a way of increasing the probability of success. This can be determined from a Monte Carlo simulation with some degree of science and accuracy. It also serves a nefarious purpose: it gets the customer involved in the crime! If you guess at a contingency amount, and it is wrong, it is your guess and, therefore, your fault! If, however, you discuss probabilities of success, the client identifies an acceptable probability of success and you set the contingency based on that probability (using the Monte Carlo simulation to support your number), then the client was part of the decision process and will own the outcome. If the client prefers to pick a budget or completion date, you can link this to a probability of success, and advise the client accordingly.

Sometimes the best contingency for a project is in knowing what you will do if something goes wrong. For example, if something is likely to be late, ensure that team members have other things to do while waiting for that particular deliverable. Or, if some purchased item is likely to become really expensive, have an alternate in mind.

 It's foolish to throw money and time at a project in the hope that it will fix all future problems. A bit of science and care in setting and allocating contingency goes a long way toward improving the probability of success and ownership of the outcome by the client.

Don't Park Your Brain Outside

Contingency plans to deal with likely events and provide preplanned *work-around* options for delays, loss of resources, or other challenges are a very powerful part of any effective risk management plan.

9.8.5 Avoid or Eliminate the Risk

Some risks can be removed from a project. We can fall back on established technology instead of risking innovation. We may decide to contract out some work to specialists instead of trying to develop in-house expertise on this project. We may change the project location to where there is likely to be less resistance from third-party stakeholders.

Avoiding or eliminating risk can take many forms from changes in specifications and scope to doing a quite different project in order to achieve the same result. Creativity plays a big part in developing and understanding the options under this heading.

 Some risks are simply not worth taking; these we should eliminate by redefining the project—or else the project may not be worth doing.

9.8.6 Contract the Risk to Others

Another favorite—and another sinkhole for money: If you add a clause into your contract that makes your contractor responsible for a specific risk, the contractor will, in some way, add money to the price to cover that risk. This is so ingrained that contractors are unaware of the premiums they charge, which include the cost of the following:

- more expensive project manager
- more overhead in administering the contract and *papering the file*
- fees for lawyers and other specialists to look for defense mechanisms or prepare claims
- premiums charged by subcontractors and suppliers to whom the risks have been passed by the contractor
- contingencies in excess of those normally added.

Before adding such clauses to a contract, consider the following:

- Are you willing to pay any premium?

- What would really happen if the risk occurred and the contractor refused to respond in accordance with how you interpreted the contract?
- Who really has control over the risk?
- Would your contingency for the risk be larger or smaller than the premium likely to be charged by the contractor?

Typically, if managed well, the risks to pass on to a contractor are those that are rightfully his. They include performance and delivery of what he is supposed to produce, such as risk associated with obtaining the required resources and materials.

 Contracting out risk is more expensive than most people realize—and the benefits may be illusive.

9.8.7 Share the Risk with Others

Alliances, partnerships, joint ventures, channel marketing deals, and other risk-sharing business relationships have been around for a long time. Their use in projects is growing as risk increases. These approaches can be used to mitigate conventional project risk, but they also can be used to reduce business risk such as sustainability, competition, speed to market, and access to key resources and expertise.

 In today's fast and volatile world, risk sharing on an equitable basis is often a good business decision.

9.8.8 Cancel the Project

This is one of the most underrated options! At least it seems to be one that is appropriate but not used in all too many instances. If we do not consider and present this option, we will continue to complete projects that never should have started. Such projects include those spawned by a senior executive's whim that are fundamentally flawed from a business, technical, or social perspective, and that have too high a risk profile for the potential return to the business.

 Consider canceling the project rather than spending good money after bad. Make sure that canceling the project is not a career-limiting option!

Chapter 10

ORGANIZATIONS FOR PROJECTS

The questions that start this chapter may make you feel uncomfortable when writing or voicing answers to them! If that is so, just think about the answers as we work through them.

■ How effective is the corporate organization in which you work today?
  ◆ What gets in the way of doing a really good job?
  ◆ Is your boss always logical and organized?
  ◆ Do corporate politics get in the way of achieving excellence?
■ What would you do to improve the organization?
  ◆ Restructure it?
  ◆ Give people more (or less) authority to act independently?
  ◆ Improve communications?
  ◆ Give clearer directions on intent rather than process?
■ Why would you do this?
  ◆ Consider your personal objectives and those of the business.

At this point, you are probably thinking of something that is linked fairly directly to effectiveness of communication, rather than authority or responsibility. If I'm right, you've come to an interesting observation: Organizations are really all about communication, although they often reflect responsibility and authority. If you got stuck on turf issues, power plays, and politics as being ills you would try to cure, consider how the world might look if we truly had *open* and *effective* communication.

Communication is key to effective organizations. As such, we must have organizations that allow us to communicate effectively.

Let's try a few more questions:

- Do you work in a large or small organization?
- If it is a small one, how formal is it?
- If it is a large one, when was it last reorganized?
- When is it going to be changed again?
- What are we after here?

Most of us who have worked in small organizations know that they tend to be informal, collegial even; communication is wherever it needs to be. As companies grow in size, the perceived need for structure increases. As we become structured, we develop organization charts with all of the little boxes, turf issues, hierarchical aggravations, and politics that go with them. Worse yet, as we get into these organizations, we spend more and more time trying to manage them only to find that there is probably a better way. Then we reorganize to accommodate the latest thinking. However, the process is expensive and time consuming, and often the results are questionable!

 If we lose sight of what organizations are really all about—effective communication—the organization is likely to get in the way of what it is there to serve.

No, that's not the only thing that's wrong. Reorganization also creates discomfort and anxiety. It can decrease efficiency. Along the way it is bound to be demoralizing for someone, too. To manage our projects effectively, we need to rise above the detail of corporate organizations—be they hierarchical, matrix, or anything else. We need to develop a project team structure that works for us and will not be negatively affected by the parent organization.

 A good organization for a project does not fight the corporate structure, but works with it and sometimes in spite of it.

As many projects today involve more than one organization, we probably have to be concerned about at least one other *parent* organization.

Chances are that it will have different ideas on project organizations and how they work. It will also have different cultures. Quite likely, it will have a different language as well.

The SMART solution is quite simple. We will develop an independent organization for our project and build appropriate bridges to the companies and other organizations with which we need to have a working relationship. Think of your project team as a tribe. (We will learn more about tribalism and how to use it later; refer also to Chapter 12.) This sounds easy. Now let's look at what we need to do.

 We are accustomed to belonging to tribes—we belong to at least two: the family tribe and the workplace tribe. Each has its own culture. We can harness this tribal *instinct*, found in all of us, to build a project tribe to which we'd like to belong.

In this chapter, we will explore organizational issues that can either help us or get in the way of making the best possible progress on our projects. I would not hope to offer a solution to every problem that we face in making projects happen from an organizational point of view. Instead, I offer a few tips that, I hope, will help you find a way around the biggest barriers to effectiveness, allowing you to harness the best of the available opportunities for success. Specifically, we need to look at the following areas:

- How do we work with conventional corporate organizations, such as hierarchical or matrix management structures?
- What are the seven magic ingredients for effective teams, and how do we get them to work for us?
- How do we manage the prime purpose of organizations: communication?
- Should we use a glossary of keywords and three-letter acronyms?
- What is more important: structure or flexibility?
- What are interorganizational needs, and how do we address them?
- How can we use RACI+ charts to help with communication?
- How do we get started with tribalism?
- How do we use meetings, memos, and other tools to manage our project organization?
- What about procedures manuals and their role?

Let's take each of these in turn.

> ## The Boss and the Coffee Maker
>
> A few years ago, I had the privilege of working with a near bankrupt and failing construction company. I was brought in to try and turn it around. We had generally a great team of committed but somewhat demoralized people. But, I could not get to the real issues. I felt that everyone was telling me what I wanted to hear rather than what was really going on. I was new and clearly a threat, as we would have to lay off a number of people fairly quickly. Nobody wanted to talk to the boss.
>
> One morning (I was often in early), I decided to make the coffee. The room was a bit dirty, so, while the coffee was brewing, I cleaned it, washing mugs and wiping surfaces. As I did this, others wandered in, and they started to chat to each other and me. I learned more about the problems of the company in that next hour than I had learned in the previous week. I also learned that it is easier to talk to the person cleaning the coffee room than it is to talk to the boss. I should have known!

10.1 Working with Conventional Corporate Organizations: Hierarchical versus Matrix Management Structures

Most of us have worked in corporate organizations that more or less resemble hierarchical or matrix structures. Just as a reminder, hierarchical structures are typically focused on function. They are pyramid(ish)-shaped, with the board at the top. The CEO reports to the board, and vice presidents report to the CEO. Typically, vice presidents are responsible for a specific aspect of the business: finance and accounting, marketing and sales, production or operations, and so on. Reporting to them are department heads, who have more specific responsibilities. This is a vertically aligned structure; it is easy to understand and arguably suits organizations with repetitive businesses.

In matrix organizations, we add a horizontal component, which is task or project oriented. The teams that work on a project are drawn from the vertical, functional parts of the organization on a temporary or semipermanent basis. Their home for purposes of performance reviews, pay, and promotion will normally remain with the functional unit, but their work will be for the horizontal unit—the project. We can explore weak versus strong matrices: In weak ones, the function dominates, and in strong ones, the project dominates. We can look at hybrid organizations and those that do not fit either of these molds. In the end, we need to consider whether or not they matter to successful project management.

Well, they do, and they don't.

The organizational structure of the parent organization matters because it will affect how we manage the project team. It does not matter if we manage the team well. What we need to do is discover how to manage project teams *in spite of* the corporate organization. In other words, we need to set up our project team as independently as possible of the corporate organization, given the practical constraints of doing this.

 Uncoupling the project organization from the corporate one helps provide the project team with independence to respond to dynamic project needs. It can also allow the team to develop its own culture, resulting in higher performance levels.

To understand these practical constraints, we need to first know what they are. In a book of this size, we can realistically look at only a few; the following sections feature the big ones (in my opinion).

Organization Policy

Watch this one. Half the time, *corporate policy* is used as an excuse, a way of maintaining control, or the status quo. If there is a genuine policy that inhibits what I will propose below, then tell me about it, because you have a potentially serious problem: The organization's policies may get in the way of survival of the business.

Management Style

Managers who require a lot of control over their staff are not uncommon. It is this type of manager that typically will react negatively to what I say. There are two groups under this heading that will likely affect our approach to managing projects: functional managers and project managers. It is the former that needs to be worked with from a project team's point of view. They may feel threatened or exposed by the SMART approach to putting project teams together.

Politics

Corporate politics is alive and well in any organization. Some of us enjoy playing with politics, while the rest of us find it annoying, counterproductive, childish, or all three and maybe even more! Whatever we feel, we still have to deal with politics. On SMART projects—and with SMART Management generally—we primarily try to work politics out of our system as much as possible. (I will show you how to do this in a moment.) This is why we begin talking about tribalism in this chapter.

That's How We've Always Done It

This certainly does not apply in your organization! But for those who have to deal with the problem, we will discuss it. Some organizations attach blame to failure. This makes doing things the way that they have always been done the only safe option. Because we do not get into trouble for doing things the same old way—even if it results in failure—we are on a safe road. We are also heading for eventual extinction. Without innovation, we stagnate, and the competition takes over. Innovation requires that we do something different, which means that we cannot do things the way we always have and still survive. Try this argument on people who object to doing things differently.

 The SMART approach to project management normally deals with the most common barriers to team effectiveness and independence.

So what does this mean for us as people who need to organize a project team within our organization? The first thing we need to do is make our project team as independent of the organization as possible. We need to add to this a working environment that allows the team to be effective. (This latter piece is addressed more fully in Chapter 12.) Let's look at the seven things we need to consider when building teams fast and effectively. Oh, and we should do this independently of the corporate organizational structure.

 There are seven factors that positively affect the performance of a team. These factors both require for the team and support a degree of independence from the corporate culture.

10.2   The Seven Magic Ingredients for Effective Teams and How We Get Them to Work for Us

How do we work independently of the corporate structure with our project team? We need the following—in addition to the seven magic team ingredients; a way of:

- bridging the gap between our responsibilities and our authority
- getting people to want to work on our project

- maintaining the team's independence without upsetting the corporate *system*
- ensuring that the team stays *plugged in* to the organization: effective communication and good working relationships.

The first item has been around for a long time and is often referred to as the *authority gap*. Good project managers have learned to deal with it in different ways, depending on their personalities. Some use persuasion; others use coercion. Positive enforcers work best in most circumstances. When corporate morale is low, this is often a challenge! To a large extent, doing what is laid out below (and in Chapter 12) will address most of these concerns, because we create an environment in which people will want to work.

Which brings us to the second point: Where do *we* want to work? Try the following list for some of the more important aspects of a good place to work:

- Your efforts are recognized and achievements rewarded (and it does not have to be anything costly—a handwritten note from the boss or a "thank you" is often enough).
- It is safe to have and present nontraditional (wacky, even) ideas and, generally, to think out of the box.
- Initiative and creativity are good things!
- We have the freedom to do as much as practical in our own way—given realistic limitations due to a need for consistency, compliance to standards, and the resulting efficiency.
- The people with whom we work are pleasant (at best) and courteous (if we do not like them). Most of us like to work with people with whom we can connect at a *human* level, as opposed to a purely business or functional one.
- Challenging work and a place that is fun add to the appeal.

If we want to work on one particular project, we will be more inclined to give it time over others that have fewer of the characteristics identified and on which we are therefore less likely to want to work. Now, if we see that this is largely true for ourselves, it is quite likely that, within the normal bounds of human variety, our team members will respond in the same way. This gives us some ideas about how to get people to want to work on our project.

Maintaining the team's independence and not upsetting the parent organization in the process requires that we remain sensitive to what is important to most organizations. Here are some common characteristics of organizations with which I've worked:

- The more successful you are, the less people will (or can) criticize how you do things: so be successful.

- Consistency is valued more than compliance with policy: so be consistent.
- It is acceptable to do atypical things, if they are blessed by someone further up the food chain: so get approval ahead of time if what you propose is truly radical.
- If what you do does not negatively affect the rest of the organization, and you can prove this, then it is probably OK to do it if you are willing to take the consequences (including credit).
- The chances are good that nobody else knows your job as well as you do; therefore, base your arguments on the results (deliverables), not on how you get there. It is tough to argue with results! And if you know your job, it will be tough arguing with you about that, too!

 It is quite easy to establish your independence as a team if you set about it in a thoughtful way and work within the practical bounds set by your organization's culture.

Now let us look quickly at the seven ingredients for a successful team, in order of application:

1. Open communication: This implies effective communication, a high degree of honesty, and no hidden agendas.

2. Ownership of your work: This is about being allowed to do things your way. Most professionals are willing to learn, but do not like to be taught what they already know or know better. It is also all about buying-in to project plans including schedule, sequencing, methodology, effort required, and adequacy of budgets.

3. Propensity to take risk: We need to go beyond what we have always done. Most organizations are risk averse. We need controlled anarchy in the form of creativity and not being hidebound in our thinking and actions. The control you need comes from not being an anarchist in isolation. You need concurrence of others on the team. We are also interested in having a *safe* work environment where we do not punish failure, but celebrate what we learn. Making the same mistake again is not so forgivable; therefore, we must learn as we go.

4. Creativity: We all know what this is. Interestingly, it seems that we have lost most of its related skills by the time we leave high school. Also, those of us who go on to college may have lost any remaining vestiges of creativity! (Do not get upset yet—please. Read Chapter 12 first!) Creativity takes many forms and is more important to some than to others. We need to create opportunities for it. Some retraining may also be useful.

5. Fun: Remember those days when you got home from work so excited about what was going on that you wanted to get back as soon as possible? In this context, what happened on those (probably all-too-rare) days is fun. It's not about wild parties; it's about a rewarding and satisfying workplace.

6. Tribalism: Anthropologists and primitive cultures have known about this all along; it is the rest of us who can use the idea in the workplace to build *esprit de corps*. We need to develop a special culture and sense of belonging for our project team.

7. Trust: It is ethereal and magnificent when it happens. We need trust to enable much of the best business practices that we see in the management of successful projects. Thus, we need to learn to trust and value the contribution of all project participants.

We will explore each of these in more detail in Chapter 12. We need to be aware that these ingredients are important to the fast formation of highly efficient project teams.

 The magic of effective teams lies in a sense of belonging to a group that will succeed in all that it undertakes and looks after its own.

10.3   The Purpose of Organizations: Communication

Earlier we identified the purpose of organizations as providing a road map for communication. In the more Dickensian organizations, this is also linked to power and control. Hierarchical structures, protocols of who can talk to whom, and departmental turf arguments are all symptoms of this type of older-style organization. At one time, they served a useful purpose, and to some extent they still do—primarily to keep things *stable* and as close to how the people at the top can understand them. This works in companies with highly repetitive businesses and stable product lines that are not likely or expected to change. If you are reading this book with interest, this is probably not the type of organization for which you work! Or at least it should not be, because you are involved in the business of managing change to improve shareholder value.

 Project-oriented companies need a flexible and dynamic organizational model to be responsive to ongoing changes in the market, workplace, technology, and elsewhere.

The best organizations today keep trying to restructure to accommodate change and respond to market and other conditions. We see *corporate reorganization* on a large or small scale almost annually. What is going on? Some theorists suggest that a nature-based model is better than the structured and artificial models that we try to establish through our attempts at formal reorganization. Others suggest that regular restructuring is healthy, while others simply do not see the reason for all the fuss.

 Today, continuous corporate reorganization and *churn* seems inevitable in fast-paced organizations. Projects cannot afford the time and energy needed to continuously change, so they need a dynamic and flexible organizational model.

I am going to add to this pool of ideas yet another one: the concept of a dynamic organization, one that constantly changes to suit the situation but does so in a predictable and manageable way. Specifically, this is the type of organization we need for projects. The reason is simple: On projects, we have a transient team, and we need to change our jobs and roles as we move from one phase of a project to the next. Let me introduce the idea of a *target organization*. The concept came from an earlier model that used the analogy of an onion. At the core, we had the core team, and the more transient the team member, the further out that person was. Since then, Ken Hanley, a former student and now a colleague, has made a wonderful presentation on small and large targets. His point was that normal project management behaviors were aimed toward making project objectives a small target, which left the project manager a big target. He indicated that it should be the other way around. Part of this encompasses the issue of what and how we communicate on projects, so I unashamedly stole his target idea and applied it to my analogy for how project organizations work well.

Figure 10.3 shows this target organization. The concept is simple. There are very few people who are involved in a project from inception to completion. They comprise the core team, a subset of the project team. They intimately know the project and its objectives, having developed the ideas and the execution plan—at least at a high level. They can normally communicate very efficiently because they share the same language, ideas, and context for the project. They need to precisely communicate the intent of the project to the project team, which requires time and

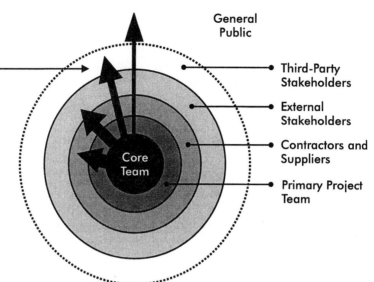

Arrows represent communication on the project. The longer the arrow, the more care and precision required; the broader the arrow, the greater the amount of information needed.

General Public

Third-Party Stakeholders

External Stakeholders

Contractors and Suppliers

Primary Project Team

Core Team

Figure 10.3 Target Organization Model

patience. The core team should also share its culture with the project team as it builds, creating a common language and addressing other tribal issues (see also Chapter 12). Communication between these two layers of the project team will improve over time. The critical stage is early, as the team sets its direction for management of the project, which is why we use RACI+ charts in developing the project plan at the working level.

 The core team sets the primary targets for the project. It must communicate these to all other parts of the project organization.

If we must communicate, one of the challenges is to know what needs to be communicated and when. We also need to avoid information overload. It is important that information is not stale but accurate and timely.

 The right people need to know the right stuff at the right time.

To manage this, we need to establish communication channels and ensure that the people at each end know who is to communicate with whom. Also, both ends of the channel must take responsibility for ensuring that the required communication takes place; this is where the RACI+ charts enter the picture (see Chapter 8). As deliverables become *live*, because action is required on them, the RACI+ chart tells us who needs to communicate with whom and at what level of detail. By keeping the RACI+ charts current, we keep an up-to-date road map of this information in front of all team members so that they know what to do and expect.

 RACI+ charts provide a current road map for project communication to all participants.

One of the important outcomes of using this approach is that the recipient of a project deliverable is put in touch with the person responsible for its delivery. In this way, the recipient can work with the producer to define (or negotiate) what the deliverable should look like in order for it to be acceptable to the recipient. Acceptance often does not happen well on projects, as the expectations of the receiver are not met and additional work is required, causing churn, delays, additional costs, and bad feelings. How often do we see specifications that the person producing the specified item does not fully understand, a report with a critical component missing, or a deliverable that the person producing it thinks is finished but the person receiving it thinks is incomplete? All too often, I suspect.

 A good communications road map reduces project churn by facilitating alignment of project team members' expectations of each other.

 If we look at the organization of a project in terms of managing effective communication among team members, the layout of our project team changes significantly.

10.4   Use of a Glossary of Keywords and Three-Letter Acronyms

If we are going to communicate, a road map is not enough; we need to have a genuinely common language. Some cultures seem to love three-letter acronyms (TLAs). For example, "We need to upgrade the TOBs on the RMFs if the W3P's are to operate without going NBG on us in front of the COO!" may mean something to the person saying it, but it probably means nothing to you or me. Or, worse, it does mean something, but not what the speaker intended, and we do not question our interpretation. For example, you may be congratulating yourself on understanding COO because it means chief operating officer. But maybe it means commanding officer (outgoing), corporate operations office, or cognitive organ opening (eye?). If we use a lot of jargon, TLAs, technical terms, or specialist words, we need to build a reference dictionary. These special words will have specific meaning in the project tribe. These specific meanings serve two purposes. The first is to clarify communication; the second is to reinforce the tribal culture for the project team. (Credit goes here to Mike O'Neil of KPMG who suggested developing a project lexicon to define keywords for the team.)

 Language is important to all teams because it allows us to communicate effectively. Specifically, effective communication requires trust. We are more likely to trust someone who is part of our tribe than an outsider, especially one who speaks a *foreign* language.

In addition to a lexicon, you might consider developing a thesaurus. The purpose of a thesaurus in this context is twofold. First, it helps one recognize and validate other people's languages. We are not saying that your word is wrong and ours is right; rather, we are saying that this is the word we will use for clarity. The second purpose is to help people who work further out in the target organization to become sensitized to specific words and their meanings, and to be able to translate from their own language to that of the project language.

One simple example is the word *deliverable*. When I was working with a large management-consulting firm to introduce SMART materials, I had one meaning for this word while the firm's team had another. I meant deliverables as what we produce to deliver a successful project for the client (specifications, design, prototype product, and so on). The team meant the deliverables required to support delivery of the project (specifications, work breakdown structure, schedule, budget, project charter, and so on). The fact that some of the examples—such as specifications—were the same for both of us meant that it took some time to track down the problem and clarify our intents. Actually, the fact that our discussions were going around in circles for a while helped us identify the problem!

The TLA Company

Sad but true, most of us do not need to be told what TLA means. It is a three-letter acronym for three-letter acronyms. A while back, TLA and the explanation of its meaning prompted a funny line in one of my presentations.

In those days, I was presenting an early version of SMART Management to a company in Ottawa, Canada. The company name was itself a TLA, so I should have been warned. However, I put in my humorous line about TLAs, and I did not get a reaction—not even a crack of a smile, just a few bored nods. Curious, I probed a bit, asking if everyone already knew what TLA represented.

"Yes," they replied. "In fact, we even have an OTD."

I had to ask. "What is an OTD?"

"It's an online TLA directory!"

The company had so many TLAs, it could take years to learn all of them. I still get confused in meetings with this company after years of working with it. I need a glossary of terms to save me from interrupting all the time at meetings!

There are several symptoms to tell you if you are communicating effectively or not. Many of these symptoms are hard to spot until we are sensitized to them, because we generally work on the assumption that we are effective communicators and understand what others are saying. Nonetheless, here are some:

- What the other person is saying is right but a bit off the mark.
- They are saying really stupid stuff.
- We keep repeating the same thing, only slower and louder, but they still do not understand.
- They look more puzzled each time I try to clarify.
- Those two think that they are agreeing (or disagreeing), but I *know* that they are saying something different (or the same thing).

 Become aware of the symptoms of miscommunication, and check to see if you and others truly understand what is being said.

Often, it is not enough to leave communication to chance. A little bit of active listening helps ensure that we do not communicate erroneously. Active listening requires feedback to the person trying to communicate with you. (I was first made aware of this when I took a parent effectiveness training course.)

We think we understand, but all we do is interpret, using our own filters and judgments. Interestingly, most people appreciate the time taken for active listening. It tells the speaker that you are listening. It confirms that you understand. If you misunderstand, that person has a chance to correct what you have misunderstood and can do it before any damage is done. Another of my interesting observations is that people do not get upset, bothered, or critical if you feedback an incorrect interpretation of what they are trying to say. This is so important that in the military it is often required that you repeat back a command to confirm that you have at least heard it.

 Do not leave communication to chance. It is a two-way street. Use a closed feedback loop to ensure that you understood.

10.5   Structure versus Flexibility

Where are we then? We have seen that we need to have our *own* organization for an effective project team. The team is ever changing as specialists come and go, contractors are hired or finish their work, regulators approve or intervene in the work, and so on. In the changing team, we need to establish effective communication, or we end up with waste, stress, mistakes, and—ultimately—failure.

So, how do we manage all of this? Do we need to have lots of structure in our project organization, or should it be really flexible? What we need is a balance between the two. Structure brings clarity of roles; we know where we fit. There is little ambiguity—something that makes many of us uncomfortable—*but* structure brings inflexibility.

On the other hand, flexibility brings the capability to respond quickly, and it enables creativity. We work in a dynamic and an exciting environment, are more empowered, and have more professional freedom—*but* this verges on anarchy if we are not careful. Flexibility makes things harder to control.

Young Mike's Problem

Dad was in the kitchen making coffee when Mike ran in crying. He'd been playing with Johnny next door. His little red face spoke volumes.

Dad says, "Mikey, you're hurt."

"No, I'm upset, because Johnny called me a bad name!"

"You're upset because you don't like being called bad names. They're rude and hurtful."

"No, Dad, silly. I'm upset because I couldn't think of a worse one to call him!"

 Effective project organizations balance the need for structure and control with the needs for creativity and responsiveness.

The real question is how do we achieve this balance? Here are some general guidelines; the specifics of how you implement them will depend on the particular circumstances of the project and the team:

■ Determine the nature of the project.

   ◆ Impact: How much will this project affect the sponsor organization? The bigger the impact, the greater the demand will be for control and, therefore, structure.

   ◆ Complexity: The more different disciplines and other organizations involved in the project, the more you need to be responsive to the different cultures, language, perceptions, and biases of the groups. This will affect the discipline you put around the need for a project lexicon and managing communication.

   ◆ Uncertainty: This dimension has to do with how predictable the project is. Structure will not help with unpredictable projects, but flexibility will, as there are many potential twists and turns on the way to completion. Here also, continued and effective communication is particularly important. If you have a large (high-impact) and uncertain project, then you may be better off changing the sponsor organization's culture to reflect a more flexible, less-structured approach. The chances are good that the organization is already that way, or it would not be tackling a large and volatile project!

- ◆ Beauty: Everyone likes to work on a beautiful project. (That is the definition of a beautiful project.) Ugly projects will require more attention to the needs and preferences of the team, rather than the needs of the project. If people do not want to work on a project, then at least they should have some say in how it may be run. This will lead you to a more flexible approach in most cases. Interestingly, the default option for this type of project is to be highly structured, as high staff turnover will be best accommodated with such an approach.

■ Understand the need for integration; I mean the need for cross-functional and cross-organizational participation and activity. The greater the need for this, the harder it's going to be to use a structured approach, but the greater is the need to manage communication, so things do not fall between the many gaps and cracks that will inevitably be there.

■ Look at the way in which the project work packages can be bundled. The greater the independence of individual components, the easier it is to introduce a structured approach to the organization. This is also affected by the need for interaction, created by the contracting strategy adopted. Stipulated price and lump-sum contracts lend themselves to hands-off and structure while target cost, evergreen, cost-plus, and alliance arrangements require more sharing of information and thus are harder to formalize through project organizational structure.

 There are many factors that will affect your choice of organization. Equally, the way you organize the project team will impact significantly on how you can manage the delivery process.

10.6   Interorganization Needs

Projects rarely happen in isolation. They often involve more than one organization through alliances, contracts, client-supplier, and other relationships.

The organizational needs common to all of these relationships are primarily connected to how we communicate and who has what authority. Many of these issues are dictated by the way that the relationship between organizations is established. If this has been done by contract, then we need to know what the contractual relationship is and what is required of each party. Ideally, the contracting strategy is set based on the optimal way of organizing the project. Unfortunately, this rarely happens, because purchasing and legal departments get involved in the wrong way or policy is sacrosanct. Good project managers head these issues off at the pass. They identify a contracting strategy as part of the project charter, and link it to the organizational approach for managing the team.

The relationship between organizations involved in a project is one that must, of necessity, span cultures. Even if the difference between the two (or more) cultures is slight, it will manifest itself in many ways, including misunderstandings, mistrust, and requirements of one group that seem strange or even run counter to the style or expectations of the other. The best way to address the problem is to establish a common—but different—culture for the team; this has been successfully achieved in different ways. It is common practice to have physically separate space for the team, away from any of the organizations contributing staff to the team. Another practice is to develop a unique style for the team (its own logo and business cards, a dress code, an employment benefit unique to the team, and so on). Yet another way is to put the team in a position that unites them against a common *enemy*.

 An important part of building a team that consists of participants from different organizations is to have the team unite in a common cause.

The most obvious common cause for the team must be success of the project. If we have done all the right things in developing our project plan and in subsequent management of the stakeholders' expectations, then we've already addressed this. We've identified common ground, resolved conflicting requirements, and kept all stakeholders informed as the project evolved. These steps, in and of themselves, go a long way toward address the differing needs of the participating organizations.

 Focus on shared objectives and address differences at the outset; then maintain good communications to keep stakeholders aligned.

Finally, just to make sure that this point is clear, if the contributing organizations have specific expectations for how to set up a project organization, address them up-front. Start with clarity about the project. Lead the proponents through the argument that how we get there does not matter if we are successful, on time, and within budget. Then pick the best ideas from each, add a unique team flavor, and go. This process has worked for me repeatedly over the years, and I have seen it work for others.

 Differences in organizations' project management delivery styles are best dealt with by plotting a course that is independent of them all.

10.7 Using RACI+ Charts to Help with Communication

Earlier, we looked at the idea of using RACI+ charts to enhance communication; now I want to cover the few remaining points related to this idea. RACI+ charts are developed in a rolling plan, typically looking four to eight weeks ahead. Each week, we lose the last week, and add another week of detail on the far end. As deliverables become live, we plan their delivery in detail, identifying who needs to be involved in doing what to stay on target. Usually, we only do this to replace someone who is going to precipitously leave our team. Also, we reaffirm our plans on an ongoing basis. Every week, as we look ahead, we reset expectations and ensure that the right people are involved in the detailed planning, and that everyone knows what needs to be done by whom.

Working with the RACI+ charts should be efficient and take only a few minutes at each progress meeting, if people come to the meeting properly prepared.

 RACI+ charts provide a tool and a focus for regular detailed planning and related communication.

Finally, knowing what is on the RACI+ chart, we know that the map for communications is laid out.

10.8 More on Tribalism

We will deal with the more interesting details of tribalism in Chapter 12. I just want to point out that much of what we have addressed in this chapter relates to the tribalism phenomenon. Tribes are about unique culture, language, costume, having your own village, hierarchy, sense of belonging, and defense against any common enemy.

No doubt you have spotted these ingredients in the earlier parts of this chapter—that's it for now.

10.9   Meetings, Memos, and Other Tools

This is a tedious subject. We hate to go to meetings. Memos are OK (at best) to write but a pain to receive. Minutes of meetings are a nuisance and particularly boring to read. After all, we've been there, done that! So why waste time on this stuff? Well, efficient meetings can and do help serve a number of purposes. Memos and other tools can also be used constructively. We will deal with the administrative side of these in Chapter 14. Now, we need to look at the organizational issues around these tools that help us communicate.

Part of successful project teams' cultures is the expectation that any form of communication will be addressed with respect. In other words, we come to meetings prepared. That in turn means that we have an agenda for each meeting, and we stick to it. We read and respond to memos, E-mail, and other communication (return phone calls, say hello in the hallway when others greet us, and so on), or, if we decide not to do so, we need to be consistent and manage expectations around this. Either way, we need to respond to any mission-critical communication.

 An important part of a successful team's culture is effective communication, which requires sending, receiving, and responding to messages.

10.10   Procedures Manuals and Their Role

Project procedures manuals conjure for me a picture of fat binders on shelves. I struggle to recall when I have actually seen them used. Their mere presence usually means that someone has at least thought through the procedures for the project, or maybe they were copied from a previous project. That too has some significance, because it hints at some tradition and ingrained procedures that have evolved over time. In a classical world, this type of procedures manual is useful, as well as on large projects where we want to be sure that process is followed. Because it is the most efficient way to provide project management quality assurance, use of traditional procedures manuals still has value.

Another useful application of such manuals lies in capturing good practice and experience. If we have done similar projects, then presumably we have learned from them. Templates for plans, checklists, and other such tools for transferring knowledge and experience or for speeding up planning and other activities is also useful.

The SMART approach to procedures manuals is to minimize them. It is much more effective, it seems, to train the whole team in project management. Done efficiently, the training uses the real project on which you are working to develop examples, exercises, and so on. By the end of a two-day training session, all of the team members will know about the process you use to plan and manage the project, and they will have participated in the development of the real plan.

Time-efficient training for the project team is a good supplement to procedures manuals. Unless you sleep through the training, you will learn more about how the project is going to be planned and managed in two days than you will in many months of having the procedures manual on your shelf. If the training is available, a few cheat sheets with the more important elements of how you manage the project (tools, processes, and competencies) will serve you better than a detailed procedures manual.

From the organizational perspective, procedures manuals should embody the tribal culture of your team. In this context, words and descriptions that are brief, effective, to the point, and easy are good. Long, awkward, rambling, and tedious are not too good!

 If you want to have a procedures manual as a reflection of the project, try identifying with the words that will describe the end product. They will give you a good start in setting the level of detail that you really want.

10.11   The Project Office (or Program Management Office)

The project office should be a resource to the project team. It should *not* be the project management Gestapo! The functions of a project management office (PMO) and a program management office (also PMO!) are essentially the same. In a program, added roles include interproject coordination, management of shared resources, and a central service to all projects for common functions such as scheduling support, estimating, purchasing, contract administration, and so on. This is worthwhile where doing so is cost efficient through better use of resources or through the benefits of synergy, bulk purchase, and consistency.

The similarity between a project and a program management office lies in the fact that large projects are often managed as a program of smaller projects. This is usually discernible from the assignment of responsibilities, how the project (or program) is organized, the work packaged, and even how the deliverables breakdown structure is set up.

The role of the PMO will typically include the common services identified earlier, as well as specific functions, such as stewarding to the project procedures, training of team members (anything from project management to safety and risk management), and progress reporting. Data acquisition, sharing learning, developing and enhancing project management tools, and developing and maintaining checklists, templates, and other standards and support materials is also part of the work commonly seen in a PMO.

 The role of the PMO must be positive and supportive of the projects. It should not be a regulatory or bureaucratic one, as this will quickly disconnect the PMO from the project and its team.

A final thought about the PMO: If it is for a program, consider making the project managers part of the PMO, as they should have say in how it is run. They should own it, as well as the services it provides to them.

 The project managers and their teams need to have a stake in the PMO for it to be most effective.

Chapter 11

CONTRACTS AND CONTRACTING OPTIONS

Projects that involve more than one organization also involve contracts that create the business relationship between companies and set who will do what. Try the following questions in relation to the project on which you are now working and the contracts with which you work:

- Are outside companies or departments in your own organization involved with your project? (If no, you may want to skip this chapter for now!)
- If yes, do you have a contract with these companies? If no, you are mistaken; we'll see why soon.
- If yes, do you know the contract terms?
- If you do not know the contract terms, how do you know when you (or they) are violating them, or if you are being treated fairly by the other organization?
- Did you have any say in the terms and conditions of the contract?
- Were you involved in selecting the contractor?
- Does your contract have exculpatory clauses in it? Is it a fair contract for both parties?

In order to manage their work effectively, project managers require information about and involvement in the contracts that affect their projects. To accomplish this, we need to understand how contracts come together and how to manage them to avoid disputes and litigation. Better yet, we should know how to manage them to get the best deal for both parties to the contract. To understand the business of contracting and what the options are, we will explore the following topics in this chapter:

- Conventional contracts: What are the most common types of contracts and when should we use them?
- Cost of exculpatory clauses: There is a cost associated with asking another party to take certain risks. We need to know what that cost is.
- Attitude and its role in contracting success: We and our contracts have *attitude*. This affects how we work with others. It needs some thought up-front because it has an impact later on.
- Drivers for change in contracting approaches: The world in which we operate continues to change, demanding better and faster solutions. Contracting is slow to change, so we should know what needs to happen to meet today's business imperatives.
- Strategic and project alliances, channels, and other deals: Innovations in contracting approaches are emerging or reemerging. We look at a few of these new approaches.
- An interim model: If we decide to make changes and cannot wait for our organization to catch up, what can we do? We will look at some options.
- Nontraditional contracting arrangements: What will come next in contracting is hard to guess, but some interesting things are starting to happen. Here is a peek at just a few.
- Issues: Buildability, concurrent engineering, and value engineering: These and other ways of adding value are closely linked to how we contract out work and even to what we contract out.
- Incentives and what works: Incentive schemes, as well as penalties for nonperformance, have been around a long time. What really works, and what gets in the way of project success? Here we will look at a few ideas in this fascinating arena.
- Contracting framework: When we award contracts, we need to have in place a working framework for bidding, award, administration, and closeout. We will look at this, including some of the things that we can do to improve how we manage contracts in our project or program.
- Disputes and dispute resolution: In the end we will likely have a number of things go wrong. If we cannot resolve problems, we will have a dispute. Here we cover the basics of how disputes are resolved.

Contract Types > Scope V	Stipulated Price or Lump Sum	Unit Rate	Cost Plus
Implement to Design or Specification (Specs)	Fixed price, based on full specs and drawings.	Variable price, based on unit rates and variable quantities of product- or service-defined scope; incomplete details.	Actual cost (usually audited) of contractor plus a fixed or percentage fee for a defined scope.
Design and Implement	Fixed price, based on performance specs and general order-of-magnitude scope.	Variable price, based on unit rates and variable quantities of product or service base on outline scope and performance specs.	Variable final price, based on contractor's audited cost plus fixed or percentage fee, based on approximate scope and performance intent.
Finance, Design, and Implement	As above, but also provide financing for the project. This usually means that the project itself delivers a tangible product that can be used as collateral against which the money is advanced.		
Finance, Design, Implement, Then Operate	As above, but also operate the resulting facility for a specified time and usually with specific guarantees on minimum revenues from the client.		

Table 11.1   Contract Types

 This chapter provides an introduction to contracting issues. It is a huge field, and a little knowledge can be a dangerous thing. The focus is on the not-so-legal and not-so-technical aspects. For more information on these areas, refer to the bibliography.

11.1   Conventional Contracts

There are three basic types of contracts, and they encompass a range of different scopes (see Table 11.1). The examples in Table 11.1 are indicators only and generic in nature. Corporate policy, industry practice, and requirements of the investor or lender will influence the specifics of how each type of contract is used.

Are you sure that's what the contract says?

The appropriate use of traditional contract types is based largely on the completeness of the information for the bidder(s) at tender time and the extent to which the client wishes to take specific risks. In this context, we can look at risk in two ways: performance and cost. Normally, the contractor retains performance risk. The exception to this situation occurs when the client interferes with the methodology by action or by specification. When this happens, unless the contract specifically states otherwise, the owner takes on the performance risk.

 Contract risk comes in two forms: cost risk and performance risk.

The cost risk is generally assigned by the type of contract that is selected (see Figure 11.1.1).

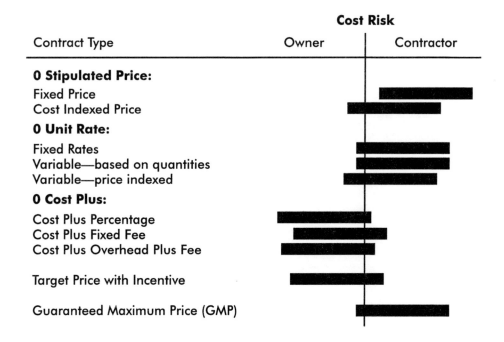

Cost Risk

Contract Type	Owner	Contractor
0 Stipulated Price:		
Fixed Price		
Cost Indexed Price		
0 Unit Rate:		
Fixed Rates		
Variable—based on quantities		
Variable—price indexed		
0 Cost Plus:		
Cost Plus Percentage		
Cost Plus Fixed Fee		
Cost Plus Overhead Plus Fee		
Target Price with Incentive		
Guaranteed Maximum Price (GMP)		

Figure 11.1.1   Cost Risk Allocation by Contract Type

Performance risk normally resides with the contractor, unless the client interferes.

 Cost risk is dependent on the type of contract you select.

Risk assignment is a very significant part of contracting out work. Another view of the risks being taken and how they may be addressed is shown in Figure 11.1.2, where we look at different commonly assigned risks in contracts and how associated risks are typically assigned to the owner or contractor.

We can readily see from a review of Figure 11.1.2 that the choice of formal contract type will influence the distribution of risk. What Figure 11.1.2 shows is not definitive, as the specific wording of clauses will shift the risk. Therefore, when we select a specific contracting strategy, we need to consider where we want the risks to lie. We should also give serious thought to mixing different types of contracts, as this subsequently requires significantly more complex administration.

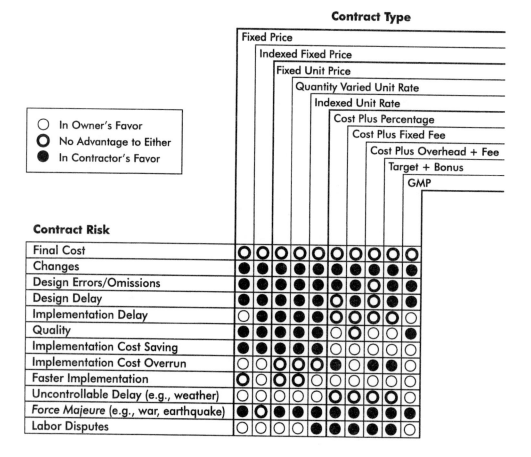

Figure 11.1.2 Common Risk Apportionment in Contracts

 When picking a contracting strategy, we should decide which risks we want to carry and which we will assign to the contractor.

Here's another thought on contract types: The type of contract that we ultimately end up with will also depend on the timing of the award. I am not talking about the legal form, but the effective type. Let me explain. If we were to award a stipulated price contract with inadequate scope and content definition, we would inevitably end up with numerous changes to the contract, which would be managed through change orders. These in turn would be processed for payment, based on actual costs plus a reasonable overhead and profit.

I'm checking the contract.
It doesn't say whether this is a risk or a crisis!

Effectively, you now have a cost-plus contract. If only it stopped there. A good contractor, who has bid on this work or negotiated it with you, will have spotted the shortfall of definition at the outset, and he will have structured his pricing to maximize his return.

 An effective type of contract, from an operational as opposed to a legal point of view, will depend to a large extent on the completeness of the contract scope and requirements information at the time of award.

We can see the same thing happening, only the other way around, when we look at using a unit rate or cost-plus contract with complete scope definition and clear specifications. If this is the case, nothing will change, and the original estimate will be close to the final price. In other words, we really have a fixed-price contract, for all intents and purposes. The choice of contracting strategy in the world of traditional contracts needs to be governed by where we want to see risks assigned and the completeness of definition for the work we are contracting out.

Assigning risks through contract clauses has been done forever. The problem is that we do not know the true cost of reassigning these risks.

Another way of assigning risk in contracts is through exculpatory clauses.

11.2   Cost of Exculpatory Clauses

Exculpatory clauses assign risk—often, inappropriate risk—to a contractor. The types of risk that are commonly assigned include:

- penalty for delays (such as liquidated damages)
- accountability for someone else's design being compliant with governing codes of practice
- responsibility for the meaning and interpretation of someone else's report, on which the contractor must rely for bidding purposes
- risk associated with others' actions, resulting in additional cost to the contractor or delays to the work
- cost associated with delays caused by other contractors
- almost anybody's errors and omissions!

If a contractor takes risks, where does the money to cover the risks come from? The contractor must be able to cover the cost of risks for which she is responsible. The money comes from somewhere; in a worst-case scenario, it comes from bankruptcy. Assuming, however, that the contractor is making money, then the money to cover risk comes from its only source of revenue: customers. But how much is the premium charged by the contractor? Until recently, we had no idea. If you were to ask most contractors what they added to their bids, they would tell you that they add nothing, especially if the work has been tendered on a competitive-price basis. In my days of managing a contracting business, I also would have replied in a similar fashion. After all, if we added money to the bid price, we would not get the work, would we? The idiot who did not add any risk contingency would get the work—but we are not idiots. Contractors add risk premiums in numerous and different ways. We put better (and more expensive) project managers on the riskier projects. We hire lawyers, add administrative staff, fluff up contingencies, and adjust our prices to reflect inefficiencies and *normal* losses. Then, if we have subcontractors, we pass on risk to them too. Subcontractors are not fools either.

The burning question is: "What does this cost?" How much money is spent on these types of activities, resources, and other risk-related costs? In the end, what is all of this worth to the client who eventually pays for it? I was curious. One of my graduate students, Mohammed Khan, studied this problem with me. In summary, here is what we found, based on a cross-Canada survey involving contractors, owners, and consultants in the construction industry in 1997–98.

In responding to the questionnaire, contractors reported additional costs or premiums that averaged between 9 percent (in a buyer's market) and 19 percent (in a seller's market), related to five frequently found exculpatory clauses in construction contracts. These specific results are not necessarily generalizable to other parts of the world or other industries. They do, however, offer an indication of what we are paying to get the nice warm feeling that someone else will take the fall! The value of this nice warm feeling was also part of the study.

 There is a real cost associated with the use of exculpatory clauses. It is not easy to determine but can potentially be very high.

We wanted to assess the utility of these clauses. What were they worth to the people who put them into contracts? In short, the answer was that they were essentially worthless. If we stop and think about it, this makes sense. What happens if we have a risk event that triggers one of these clauses? The first likely reaction is that the contractor tries to justify why the clause does not apply in this instance. If he does not react this way, it is likely because he has enough money in the pot (from other items for which the client is paying) that he doesn't mind paying for the risk. Once the more likely sequence is triggered, we will have a dispute. If we settle the dispute in the contractor's favor, we have not taken advantage of the clause, so why did we have it in the first place? If we do not settle, then we continue down the path to litigation. Once we are in litigation, everyone is a loser. If we settle out of court, see earlier. If we do not concede, we will have lost a lot of time and money in the process, which often exceeds the cost of a settlement. It is not difficult to see why there is little perceived value in the clauses!

 There is little perceived value in the use of exculpatory clauses.

The real mystery is that despite this, we continue to use the clauses!

We need to be very careful how we manage risk with exculpatory clauses.

11.3 Attitude and Its Role in Contracting Success

One of the interesting things we do (or not, perhaps) is consider the message we send with our bid documents. Some documents are quite aggressive; the examples in the sidebar, Some Wilder Weasel Clauses, provide a flavor of what we see in weasel (exculpatory) clauses. Other messages along similar lines are sent with words such as *shall* and *must* liberally dotted throughout the contract. Severe cautions to bidders also send messages that say *beware* to the bidder. Language also has a *tone* to it that, I'm sure, influences how people perceive the risks in a contract. This also must influence the way in which we respond to and price the bid.

Think how you would react to the wording of the contracts you put out. It is possible that the *attitude* implicit in your bid documents will add risk money to the bids.

On more concrete ground, there is significant evidence to suggest that pricing and staffing—especially defensive staffing—are affected by who will manage the contract for the buyer. As a contractor, I always added a lump of money to my bid if I knew that the contract administrator or project manager for the client was awkward in dealings. I also would assign the project to one of my better project managers. In the more extreme cases, I would add staff to ensure that we could fill the file with appropriate defensive paperwork. And, where necessary, we would start a claims file before we started the work! I also know that this was not unusual practice. Another piece of corroborating evidence is that our subcontractors often asked if we had assigned a project manager (and other key personnel) to the job *before* they submitted a bid. I can think of just one reason why they would do this. I was first alerted to the problem when I came across the Sine factor. (See the sidebar. I have changed the name to protect the guilty!)

 Attitude and reputation can also affect how people will price work for you. The amounts involved can be quite significant.

The impact on contracts and their cost, how the contractor performs, and when the project is likely to be completed does not stop at the bid stage. It carries through the whole life of the contract.

There are as many ways of managing contracts as there are people who manage them. The relationship between the contracting parties depends to a large extent on the people involved in the management of that particular contract. It seems that most *attitudes* attract a response.

- On a large construction project in Vancouver, a contract administrator earned a reputation for cutting all contractor change orders, extras, and claims by 30 percent. Guess what? Within a short period of time, contractors were adding that amount to their requests for extra payment, so he could negotiate it down. Everyone ended up happy!
- On another project, a series of changes took one part of the work through four significant changes, costing the contractor several hundred thousand dollars and about six months of delay.

The Sine Factor

Shortly after I arrived in Canada, I was working for a firm of consulting engineers. I was asked to review a series of bids from contractors on a large mining project. Generally, the bids were about 5 percent higher than we had anticipated, given the market conditions and the pricing by more or less the same contractors on another recent similar project. I was unsure how we were going to deliver the bad news to the client, so I consulted with the project manager.

He was not only not surprised, but he also actually recognized the cause. "That is the Sine factor," he said.

Unsure how trigonometry fit into estimating the cost of a large capital project, I asked him to explain.

"Simple, really. George Sine is the designated project manager. Everyone knows he's difficult to work with, so most contractors add a Sine factor—usually about 5 percent. The client knows this but feels that George saves them about the same amount in claims, so it all comes out in the wash!"

The last change brought everything back to how it had originally been designed and specified! The owner refused to pay for anything, saying that the contractor, in the end, only did what was specified in the original contract and was therefore not entitled to any additional payment. Unfortunately, the project had to be completed by a certain date, and the owner acknowledged that the changes caused delays. The cost of accelerating the completion of the project was very high, all things considered—unless you added the cost of the changes, that is.

■ During the development of a venture capital-funded software product, another company was interested in acquiring the technology that was being developed. The investors wanted to cash in, but, at the assessed value of the technology (and the whole company, come to that), they would not see the return for which they hoped. Their solution was to stop supporting the development of the product and offer to fund it out of another of their venture capital funds. This invoked a *ratchet clause* that increased the investors' percentage holding in the company from a minority position to a significant majority one. They had read the management team well: It would honor its commitment to the staff and meet payroll even if it cost them their stake in the company. The investors, however, misread the position of one of the key people who left the organization when it was sold. She found the unethical behavior of the investors abhorrent and took with her some of the unique knowledge needed to successfully complete the software development. This probably cost her a potential stock buy-out worth over $2.4 million. The buyer never got the project completed. More important, however, the staff members got paid, and they got jobs in the buyer's organization. The investors never got paid, because the payment was based on completion of the project. Touché!

■ On a large film and arts festival project, one of the larger sponsors withdrew support at the eleventh hour. It wanted a larger profile and demanded a series of specific forms of recognition before it would reinstate funding. The sponsor got what it requested; the money was paid out, and the festival went on to be a success. Unfortunately, the sponsor never specified the size of the lettering to be used on the banners, leaflets, and other material. I believe the festival had at least one different sponsor the following year.

These examples do not tell us what was going on behind the scenes. But, likely there were face-saving exercises, acceptable and unacceptable expenses, politics, and more to be considered and actively going on. Above all, I suspect there was a breakdown in communication—maybe more than one breakdown. There were misaligned expectations and probably some hidden agendas.

 People have interesting ways of responding to how we administer contracts. It is probably more of a people-relations issue than one of legal rights and wrongs.

Legal-based solutions to contracts seem to be drawn out and costly to all parties. This option remains, however, and we will look at dispute resolution in more detail later. For now, let's just consider the value of good relations and a constructive attitude toward contract administration. Is this a better way of managing? I think that it is.

11.4   Drivers for Change in Contracting Approaches

If relationships are what contract administration is largely about, what is it that makes this more true today than ever before? Consider the following changes in how we have done business over the past twenty or so years. In looking at these, think about how little seems to have changed in our approach to contracting. Also consider how we need to rely on other companies more and more to get our own business done.

- The half-life of most technology-based products is half what it used to be. New market opportunities are coming at us faster, and they demand faster response time.

- To stay competitive, we now outsource many things that we used to do in-house. We need to specialize more, as the knowledge base to maintain competitiveness continues to grow and efficiencies are needed in every aspect of our business.

- We keep redefining and narrowing what we mean by *core business*. We need to understand our entire business more than ever before. Cross-functional teams add power to our business through synergy.

- The time available to bring products to market is much shorter than it used to be. Responsiveness is a critical skill—the larger the organization, the harder this is to achieve.

- Markets are global and much more fickle than ever before. Thus, we need to address continuous change.

- Regulation is more intense, whether national or international and whether it deals with the environment, mergers and acquisitions, product licensing, or a myriad of other aspects that may influence our projects. We need knowledgeable contractors to help us stay out of trouble.

- The shift toward more knowledge work should be pretty clear to almost everyone. Contractors are smarter than ever; so are their customers.

- This shift has helped increase the spread between the richer and poorer segments of the population in Western countries, as well as in many others. Labor management is becoming a shared responsibility between contractor and client.

This is far from a complete list of changes, but just this snippet shows us that we need to consider several growing needs.

To address time to market and sustainable relationships with contractors and suppliers that are important to our business, we should revisit the way in which we have traditionally selected our project partners. Faster appointment cycles, negotiating instead of bidding competitively on price, working with the same people, sharing development of new technologies, and even sharing of resources are serious options. For example, one large Japanese auto manufacturer owns the major equipment in some of its key suppliers' factories. This is because the specialist equipment is expensive and needs to be modified in close collaboration with designers as car models change and improvements are introduced. This type of integration between companies linked by their supply chains saves precious time in responding to market demands.

Another automobile maker has done away with most of the paperwork in bill paying. It does not try to match purchase requisitions with purchase orders, then with receiving notices and stock lists, before lining all of them up with the invoice and approval for payment from elsewhere in the organization. It just receives and pays the bills. The trick is that, from time to time, and on a random basis, the company will check an invoice. If it is in any way incorrect, it gets rid of that supplier! Simple and, it seems, effective. The maker believes that it saves more on payroll than it costs in fraud.

To what is all this leading? In today's project environment, we need to reconsider all of the more traditional ways of doing business. Specifically, we need some or all of the following:

- Faster ways of contracting to speed up time to market, which includes negotiating rather than bidding, working with trust-based contracts, and accelerating change-order processes.
- More flexible terms to respond to continuous change on projects; moving away from fixed to variable price contracts is one way of doing this, provided there is enough work to justify the additional administration that may be involved.
- Different ways to make pricing competitive; lowest bid is no longer good enough. Better cost reduction opportunities can be found in joint solutions to problems, working with the contractor, eliminating learning curves by working with the same people over a series of projects, and continuity of work so marketing and other costs can be reduced.
- Closer ties with suppliers and contractors as more mission-critical components are outsourced. This is achieved through evergreen contracts, strategic alliances, and partnering agreements.
- Built-in flexibility to respond to changing market conditions and shifting project priorities. Here again, longer-term relationships based on quality of service and people relationships win—usually hands down—over more traditional and *formal* contracting forms.
- Independent of the type of project or contract, improved communication is important in a global marketplace. Competition in this environment is tied to appropriate sourcing of materials and services. We need to know what is important in what we are contracting. Is it price (materials, labor) or is it innovation, technology, or quality? We tend to get stuck on price! And is price not often a symptom of efficiency, productivity, innovation, and so on?

- If regulatory compliance is important, *local knowledge* in the area by your contractors is worth a significant amount to you.
- If what we are contracting is knowledge work, we need to treat the contractor's staff appropriately. This often includes sharing of proprietary information, involvement in the decision processes, and participation as partners, not as in a master-servant relationship.
- If we are buying based on low cost of labor, then other considerations probably have more to do with corporate strategy and policy than anything else. Pay equity and reasonable reward for work are important elements. In most cultures, input from the people who do the detailed work can often generate innovation, leading to better ways of doing things, improved competitiveness, and more job satisfaction for the workforce.

 Overall, contracting today needs to consider delivering a balanced and equitable package that takes into account business, technical, and social or societal issues. We need to think more *out of the box* to be competitive today.

One of the ways we are tackling this *new* type of contract is through strategic alliances and partnering arrangements.

11.5   Strategic and Project Alliances, Channels, and Other Deals

We should probably start with a definition of these terms. The terms *partnership* and *alliance* are often used interchangeably. I will be a bit more specific, so we are all on the same page as we work through this next part.

Alliance: A working relationship, which may be based on a contractually binding agreement, that has the primary purpose of achieving business objectives for all parties to that agreement. Although these business objectives may not be the same, they do need to be aligned with each other.

Strategic Alliance: An alliance with long-term objectives that span more than one project.

Project Alliance: An alliance that has been established for the duration of one project, usually with specific goals to be achieved.

Partnering (or Partnerships): An alliance that has actual or implicit shared risks and rewards. The terms *partner* and *partnership* have specific legal significance in common law jurisdictions. All partners are liable for the outcomes of actions of any one of the others.

Channel Agreements: An agreement to market a product in conjunction with your own. Examples would be the sale of preloaded software with a computer, sale of doors preinstalled with hardware (hinges and door lock), and sale of a car with a specific manufacturer's sound system.

Each of these relationships has in common a more than usually close relationship between the participants. At least, the relationship should be close for the full value to be realized by all, and "all" includes the customer of the alliance or other relationship. The client's benefit lies in enhanced quality, lower cost, or other value that can be achieved through synergies between the participating organizations.

 The value in innovative contracting ultimately translates to competitive advantage to the buyer and greater value to the buyer's customer.

One of the challenges found in many organizations is making the connection between how we procure services and how we sell what we produce. The connection lies in the competitive advantage that we gain from our relationships with contractors and suppliers. If the relationship is constructive, as opposed to antagonistic, we are more likely to reap the benefits of shared resources and ideas. The tradeoff is with real or perceived price value from the supplier. If all we are buying is a commodity, then we should use a price-competitive process to procure what we need. If we are buying more than that or are buying something different, we should use a value-competitive process.

 Commodities should be purchased based on best unit price. Just about everything else should be acquired based on value.

Most of what we need to purchase on projects falls into the second category. We buy consulting services, designs, manufactured items, software, information, and other knowledge-based items that are also value based. Even some of the commodity items are more than just commodities in our project environment, as we are also buying timely delivery, warranties on quality, and consistency or reliability of supply.

In many cases, buying based just on price is pennywise and pound-foolish. So we need to look at alliances and other working relationships where synergy and competitive advantage can grow out of the business relationship.

Many alliance-type relationships contain strange bedfellows—at least at first glance. We routinely see competing utilities, oil and gas companies, software vendors, contractors, consultants, and others getting together to develop new technologies, standards, proposals to clients, and other business tools that they may then use in the businesses that normally compete with each other. Why? Because they need the product of the project to survive, but they cannot develop the project on their own for a variety of reasons. One of the prime drivers for alliances is risk sharing; another driver is to gain a competitive edge that may not otherwise be attainable.

 Prime drivers for alliance formation include risk sharing and the need for a competitive edge.

11.6   An Interim Model

So where do we start if we are accustomed to a much more traditional approach to contracting? What most companies need is a stepping stone (or even a series of them) to help move from a traditional, legalistic, and confrontational approach to one that allows us to gain some of the benefits of the newer contracting approaches. The interim model outlined in the following sections is just one way to help us make a transition.

The following steps for selecting a contracting strategy represent the first part of the interim model. Preparing the contract documents, bidding and awarding, and finally contract administration follow. At each phase, we will look at the steps and what we are trying to achieve, which will help you to modify this framework more easily to suit your own working environment.

11.6.1   Contracting Strategy

The purpose of this step is to establish the best approach to contracting for the project. Each project is different; therefore, we should expect to review the contracting strategy afresh each time, even if it appears to be a trivial or tedious process.

Don't Park Your Brain Outside

When reviewing the contracting strategy, here are some of the more important questions to ask:

- What are we really buying (commodity or not)?
- How critical is this item to the success of the project, and how critical is the project to our business?
- Which policies in our organization must be followed in contracting and procurement? To what extent will they adversely affect our choice of contracting strategy?
- What does our priority triangle look like; what is more important: quality and scope, cost, or time?
- How can we package the work to make best use of the skills of available contractors and suppliers?
- Which work packages rely on others to be completed or in progress with respect to their own progress?
- Where will one contractor likely interfere with another?

The answers to these questions help define the scope of any one work package, and how to contract for the work in order to make best use of the available resources, whether our own or those of contractors, subcontractors, or suppliers.

For example, a city may have a large plan to develop its public transportation infrastructure. Because of rapid population growth, the decision has been made to accelerate construction of a significant number of bridges, overpasses, and intersection improvements, and to expand the light-rail rapid-transit system. A different approach to contracting needs to be considered, as the work is not normally done by the city's engineering department, and the required financing is more than would normally be expended on this type of infrastructure in the time planned for the project. There are endless options, so the one outlined here is not necessarily the right one, but it illustrates how the project could be addressed. Particularly note the steps as we go through this example.

Let's first look at some of the things that the city needs to acquire or consider in order to be successful with this project:

- Find a means for financing the project.
- Import expertise to do what it normally does not.
- Manage a much larger than normal volume of capital expenditure—and demobilize the resources when the project is done.
- Consider the impact of higher demand on construction and design resources from the private sector.
- Consider processes to select the right participants, especially if the approach that will be used is nontraditional.

- Do the work in half the normal time for this type of development, requiring significant acceleration of conventional processes from funding through approvals, public participation, planning, design, and construction to commissioning and operation.
- Use appropriate care and due diligence in selecting the many possible contractors and suppliers, because stakeholder involvement in the project will be significant.

 The first step in developing a contracting strategy is to determine what you need for project success, and identify what needs to be—or can be—outsourced to obtain the best mix of resources.

Following this first step in the process of formulating a contracting strategy, we look at how to best provide these needs. It would seem logical to do the following:
- Finance the project.
- Retain on a temporary basis the key resources needed to manage and deliver the project.
- Develop the internal infrastructure to handle the added rate of expenditure for the project and all of the controls and audit requirements.
- Plan the work to smooth the workload of the industries that may be affected for several reasons, not least of which is the cost of the project in a seller's market.
- Develop a tender or contractor selection process that allows the participants to deliver competitive bids meeting city procedures and protocols—or change those project guidelines.
- Package the work to streamline project delivery and allow for faster completion.
- Address the political and social issues related to the successful delivery of such a large project. Some of these issues may even be created or modified by the selected solution.

 The second step in developing a sound contracting strategy is to develop a list of potential generic solutions to effective outsourcing for all required goods and services.

We now have a general list of items to provide and can consider the available options for contracting strategies, addressing the most critical concerns first. If there are conflicts in the needs, they should be resolved

Don't Park Your Brain Outside

before making a contracting strategy choice. For example, there may be a conflict between the city's policies and the best solution for delivery of the project. Specifically, there may be no formal policy for a lease option or a public/private partnership. Perhaps normal policy dictates that different companies provide the design and construction; if so, acceleration of the work would be easier if the design and construction were awarded to a single entity—perhaps a consortium of designer and contractor. Often the key to optimizing the solution may be found in the project charter, where the priority triangle and the mission will help determine where the priorities lie, and an appropriate recommendation or action can be worked out using these as guidelines.

 The third step in developing a contracting strategy is to develop a balanced approach to delivery of the required goods and services, taking into consideration all relevant factors.

Once we have some clarity regarding the requirements for project success, we need to consider the options for packaging the work. In the example of the city's transportation infrastructure expansion, we may consider options such as single-source turnkey package for all financing, design, construction, and operation of all facilities, or the contractor may be compensated through annual payments over a specified period. The source of revenue may be taxes, tolls, service agreements for operating the facilities, or balloon payments from grants made by other government agencies (e.g., federal funding). Clearly, a business case needs to be made.

Financing may be separated from the rest of the project, but design and construction may be combined into one package. The advantages of potential collaboration between designers and contractors needs to be assessed against the real or perceived risk associated with control and verification of quality.

Because of the size of the project, the work may be broken down by major phases and types of work. For example, each bridge, interchange, and road or rail section may be a separate contract. Continuity of work and simplicity of administration needs to be evaluated against the risk associated with single sourcing, larger contracts, and the ability of local contractors to be involved.

The design and construction of each package of work may be combined or separated. We need to consider the relative advantages of fast tracking the work, design/build synergies, and contract risks.

The supply of major components (such as steelwork, rails, rapid transit rolling stock, and concrete) may be contracted separately and provided as needed to each of the installation contractors or to the project as a whole. The amount of required coordination and administration needs to be evaluated against the potential cost savings resulting from bulk purchases.

There are many other options that we could consider. For this example, however, we will assume that these are the best and main choices.

In developing the options for a contracting strategy, it is often best to consider what needs to be done and how to package the work to gain the best commercial and operational advantages before considering the type of contract to use. Once the work has been packaged into pieces that can be awarded to suppliers, we need to consider the contract form.

Organizational issues should be considered at this stage as well. The additional work required above normal workloads needs to be identified and assigned. For large projects, such as our city example, there will be a significant impact on the organization for the duration of the project. One option for the city would be to establish a project management office (PMO) for the duration of the project. The PMO could be staffed by both permanent city employees and contract employees retained for the duration of the project. A mix such as this can cause problems and frictions during the life of the project, because pay and other real or apparent inequities bubble to the surface over time. (Care in managing these differences is important and is touched on in Chapter 12.)

11.6.2 Contract Documentation

The main elements of a contract are listed in the following paragraphs and in Table 11.6.2. Depending on the situation and what is being contracted, content will vary. Table 11.6.2 is not intended to be definitive, but merely illustrative. Once again, you may find that my use of words differs from yours. It is the components themselves that are important.

The contract documents need to be based on the type of contract we want to use (see Section 11.1). Once we have selected the type of contract, we should consider the specific commercial and other terms. Earlier, we looked at the impact of risk apportionment; many of the clauses in a contract deal with the assignment of specific risks to one party or another. As a general guideline, it is best to leave the risk for a contract element with the party best placed to manage or absorb it, as that is where the risk premium is likely to be the lowest.

Contract Document Component	Function	Usage
Bid Documents	Provide a basis on which contractors or suppliers can tender for the work and the owner can compare like bids.	Any contracts awarded, based on some form of competition between prospective contractors and suppliers.
Agreement	The legal instrument that forms the basis of the contract. This typically will include reference to all other parts of the final contract.	The foundation of all contracts. This is the part that the parties usually sign.
Commercial Terms	Set out the business deal. Typically includes key components describing payment, changes, timing, and dispute resolution.	Essential to all contracts. They should be as consistent as possible across all contracts on a project, as administration becomes much easier if this is the case.
Specifications	Provide description of what is to be provided under the terms of the contract.	Describe the scope of the work to be done and the standards of materials and workmanship sometimes couched in terms of expected performance of the end result.
Drawings	Graphically illustrate what is to be provided under the terms of a contract.	Common on capital projects; unusual in many other situations such as software, corporate reorganizations, and so on. May include storyboards for an advertising campaign, prototype screens for a new software system, or an organization chart for a corporate reorganization.
Addenda	Document changes prior to finalization of the contract.	Usually used during the bid process if there is a change during the tender period.
Supplementary or Special Conditions	Additional terms and conditions that are specific to a particular project.	Often used if a *standard* contract is used, to modify terms and conditions for a specific case.

Table 11.6.2 Contract Elements

Contract documents should be assembled with care. Often the different components are prepared by different people and based on previous contracts. This leads to internally inconsistent documents that are awkward to manage afterward. Time taken in careful preparation and review of contract documents usually gets repaid many times in saved time on disputes and misunderstandings. The trouble is you cannot really prove this!

It pays to have consistent and well-thought-out contract documents.

11.6.3 Bid and Award Process

Under this banner we will look at two main types of contract award: negotiated contracts and competitively bid contracts. Why should we pick one approach over the other? If we work in an environment where we are spending someone else's money, we are usually (and rightly) held accountable for how we spend it. Many projects are managed in just such a work situation. The safest way to manage a project in these circumstances is to competitively tender all of the work. That way we can demonstrate that the work was awarded to the most competitive contractor in all cases, and we are safe from criticism. Unfortunately, this is not always true.

 The safest way to award work to contractors is to tender it competitively—because that is the way we have always done it. Often, though, it is not the cheapest or best solution.

There are many situations where selecting the lowest bidder can result in a higher final cost than other selection methods. Some of these situations include the following:

- Poor contract documentation creates opportunities to increase the price through change orders after award.
- Use of multiple contractors who are inadequately coordinated by the owner may result in delays and associated extra charges.
- Bidder makes a mistake—the reason it is the lowest bid—and seeks every opportunity to recover losses through claims. Even if unsuccessful, the process of defending can be costly and unproductive.
- Rivalries that flare between contractors forced to work together on the project, because they were awarded the work, leads to expensive disruption and delay.
- The lowest bid contractor completes the work late, and the owner loses revenues that cannot be recovered.
- The contractor is bankrupted by the project.

Again, lowest bid is attractive, but it is often not the lowest final cost. What we need is a mechanism to assess the lowest future final price, using one contractor rather than another. How do we do this?

Unfortunately, you will not find a definitive answer in this book, but I will offer one story that gave me a clue to locating cost savings and explains why this section of the book addresses bidding and negotiation under the same heading.

Bringing a contractor on board is not a simple process. If you are truly buying a commodity—and service, performance, cooperation, and other factors are unimportant—then choose based on price. Otherwise, carefully consider your contractor selection process.

The story in the sidebar, Proud to Be Cheap!, is about construction of a manufacturing facility. I have repeated the experience many times in other industries, including software systems implementation, providing consulting services to oil and gas companies (for both upstream—exploration—and downstream—refining and processing projects). I have used a *soft* contractor selection process on pharmaceutical projects, too, and I have experienced nothing in its use that suggests I should do anything different in the future. But there is a catch: The contractor selection process that I suggest does create a commitment to the process that makes you want to try harder as a buyer to be successful.

Regardless of the industry or the goods or services you are about to procure, consider negotiating with a preferred supplier. The analogy is that we would not hire the cheapest employee out of a set of candidates, so why do we hire the cheapest contractor? Is a contractor not another employee (or group of employees) who will help us deliver a project?

Selection of the right contractor for negotiations is probably more of an art than a science, but there are a few things we can do to help us get it right. Consider suggestions in the following paragraphs.

Obtain references. Because most people will offer names of people who will say nice things, ask specifically for references from a contractor's last four projects. She is then forced to give you names of clients who will respond based on recent performance rather than relationships. Ask the referee about both strengths and weaknesses. I tend to be suspicious about contractors and other people who are absolutely perfect—not that there are no perfect people; simply that they tend to be rare!

Look at the track record with respect to what you need to have done by the contractor; also consider creativity. Balance the two. Only track record and no creativity will give you what the competition has! Only creativity and no track record may give you a contractor who may not understand the problem.

> ## Proud to Be Cheap!
>
> A Canadian car manufacturer was given a mandate by its head office in Japan: Reduce the cost of manufacturing one particular model by 25 percent over five years. It did not take the executives long to figure that they could not do so without the full cooperation of their entire supply chain. As a contractor that built manufacturing facilities for it and its subsidiaries, we were clearly in the manufacturer's supply chain. Along with everyone else, we were asked to do our bit. All we had to do to keep the car manufacturer's account was build at 5 percent lower cost each year for the next five years.
>
> After much thought, we suggested that the next project be built on a design/build basis. We encouraged the company to bid competitively with its regular engineering design consultants as one bidder and with us, their regular contractor, as the other. We were building its facilities at about $130 per square foot at the time. The two bidders would be asked to assemble their teams and prepare a bid for the next project. The company agreed. We were pretty certain that the consultant's team would be assembled after the design had been worked, and the contractor would be selected by competitive bids. We were right! We approached the project differently. We negotiated with our preferred design team and subcontractors, selecting creative people and team players ahead of those that we thought could, under normal bid conditions, deliver the cheapest work. The deal was structured around each party being paid a fair price, but the competitive edge would come through a team approach to design and construction.
>
> Not only did we make a much larger profit on the next project, but we also built it for just $85 per square foot and in about 20 percent less time that we would normally have taken. Our contractors were delighted and so was our client. They were happy to negotiate the next projects and were an excellent reference for us.

Meet the people who will do the work. I look for good communication skills, especially listening; I also look for openness and leadership. If you are a regular buyer of the commodity you need, consider the reputation of both the organization and the people who will work on your project. If you are not a regular buyer, it may not be possible to directly assess the reputation of the supplier, so ask your contacts in the industry.

If we elect to negotiate with a contractor, we need to pick that contractor. Selecting a contractor or supplier is analogous to recruiting a new (and temporary?) hire. Take up references. Have a clear job description. Be objective in your selection process.

If we have the right contractor, we need to make him part of our team. This notion is important in the negotiation process. Let me explain. If we use conventional bidding logic, we're trying to reduce cost by attacking the contractor or supplier's profit margins. What we should be doing is attacking the cost of doing the work. Crudely, there are three parts to this cost (see Figure 11.6.3).

We can see clearly from Figure 11.6.3 that the potential for savings is much greater by working on the creative rather than the normal solution. Other factors, such as both buyer and seller having some commitment to success and the opportunity for working as a more effective team, also can contribute to a greater potential for success.

If we are going to look for cost savings, the areas of inefficiency in our own administration of contracts and in the contractor's approach to work are richer fields than the thin seam of the contractor's profit margin.

The normal tender process has a number of features that should be in place:

- complete set of bid documents that are internally consistent and clearly and unambiguously state what is being procured
- basis on which the bids will be evaluated—price, speed of delivery, quality, ability to cooperate with others on the project, expertise of key personnel, and any other criteria—with their relative weighting
- list of bidders or a set of qualifying criteria for an open bid
- commercial terms and conditions
- compliance and alternatives (what happens to bids that do not exactly comply with the set terms and whether alternatives will be considered; if alternatives are to be considered, the basis on which they will be assessed)
- clear times for tender closing
- process for addressing bidders' queries so that all questions and answers are available to all bidders. (Sometimes a bidders' meeting at the start of the tender period is worth considering. It gives all participants a chance to start with the same information and have the more obvious questions answered. If you do have such a meeting, document it and issue minutes to all who took part.)
- bid evaluation process reflecting all of the above and as objective and auditable as possible
- complete, clean, and simple tender process leading to the best results in bidding for outsourced work.

The contract does not say, "Build a ship," but it does
tell us to follow the client's instructions.

Bidding work requires effort and cost on the part of a bidder. Too large a list of bidders means that we are wasting the time and resources of those who are least likely to succeed. Prequalifying bidders is an obvious and common tool used to reduce this wastage.

 In the interests of all, it pays to prequalify bidders and not waste the time of those who are unlikely to succeed.

11.6.4 Contract Administration

We will now consider the main components of good contract administration, specifically looking at what we try to achieve in any good contract management practice. (The subtle changes required for addressing a new model are covered in Section 11.7.)

Contract administration is easiest if there are no changes and if the relationship with the contractor is good. This tells us that there are

Don't Park Your Brain Outside

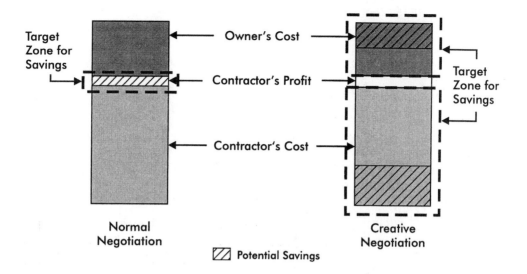

Figure 11.6.3 Mining the Right Seam for Cost Reduction

three things with which we need to be concerned: 1) good routine administration, 2) management of contract changes, and 3) maintaining good working relationships with the contractor (and if you are the contractor—good relationships with the client!).

Routine contract administration has the same elements whether you are the client or the contractor, and they all deal with contract compliance:

- Make sure that work and materials are being delivered as expected (quality and schedule). This is most easily achieved if we have defined everything in terms of deliverables.
- Ensure that the contractor gets paid. Again, a deliverables-based approach makes this straightforward, but services are harder to pay for and measure.
- Make sure that adequate records indicating progress and changes are maintained. These records will typically be in the form of change orders, reports, correspondence, minutes of meetings, and diaries.
- Communicate on a regular basis to be sure that work is being adequately coordinated, and that both the client and the contractor are happy with what is happening. Regular meetings and use of RACI+ charts to help people stay in touch with the right people will make this process easier.

What is left then is the need to manage changes and good working relationships. Changes are usually managed through a change-order process. Generally such processes require the following steps:

1. Identify the change.
2. Advise the other party of the change.
3. Provide an estimate of the time, cost, scope, and quality impacts of the change.
4. Agree to proceed with implementing the change.
5. Issue a change order that amends the contract to reflect what has been agreed.
6. Do the work and get paid, or cancel the work and credit the contract price.

 Change management on contracts is a simple process, if both parties to the contract can agree on what is different and equitably address the impact of that difference.

If we administer the contract well and manage changes, we will likely maintain good relations between the contractor and the owner. But we must not leave this important piece of the puzzle to chance. Friction between contracting parties is all too common; much of it can be laid at the feet of unmet expectations. We need to continuously manage the expectations of the other party to the contract. Where is this effort best focused? In the areas where things most often go awry, such as:

■ disagreement on the impact of a change
■ schedule slippage
■ delayed payment
■ quality of workmanship or materials below client expectations
■ interpretation of the contract. (This is a common one that has an important legal significance. The responsibility for clarity of a contract rests with the party that drafted the document. If there is ambiguity, most courts in common law jurisdictions will hold the contract party that was responsible for authorship of the contract liable for the consequences of ambiguity.)

If we focus on the things that are most likely to go wrong and we are flexible when resolving differences, relationships are much easier to manage. The time spent on managing relationships is usually more pleasant than the time spent in disputes—I suspect that it is less time consuming, too.

If we manage expectations of the other party to our contracts, we will normally be successful in managing the relationship.

11.6.5 Project Completion and Closeout

We sign *on* to delivery of a project at the start of a contract; we need to sign *off* when it has been delivered at the end. Typically, not everything has gone to plan, and most contracts are therefore a bit awkward to complete. Some deficiencies never seem to get fixed; some changes remain unresolved. Schedule has been impacted—often the impact is still under discussion by the end of the contract.

Making a fresh start toward the end of the contract helps bring the project to closure. Specifically, I like to treat the completion of a project as its own little project. If necessary, this may include redefining the end of the project if it looks like we cannot readily get to the end as originally defined. Redefining the end of a project is accomplished by the following, when appropriate (meaning that not all of these apply in each case):

- Delete—and get or give credit for what is deleted—those items that are more readily completed by others or no longer need to be completed. This may include something that was painted the wrong color, a data entry screen with an extra field, an item for which redundant help information was required, detailed documentation that has been superseded by a change in technology, and so on.
- Review the list of deficiencies and eliminate those that are issues of compliance with original specifications but do not materially affect the performance of the product.
- Define the completion of the contract in terms of what each party still needs to deliver, and develop a schedule for completion that is realistic under the circumstances.
- Provide incentives for completion of specific segments of the contract.
- Announce a completion date and invite lots of people to the party to celebrate it. It is amazing how this focuses attention.

 Set up project and contract completion as a new project to finish the old one—then celebrate success.

11.7 Nontraditional Contracting Arrangements

As we continue to seek better ways to do business, new and innovative ways of contracting are emerging. These new approaches do not have many standards; even the terminology is inconsistent. Following are some of the more interesting arrangements—some newer than others and some that have been around in specific industries for a long time.

11.7.1 Strategic Alliances and Partnerships

Now quite well known as a concept, these arrangements are intended to achieve better working relationships and long-term synergies that come from established working relationships. If we were to differentiate between partnerships and strategic alliances, here is one way: Partnerships, in the true sense of the word, have legal significance. A partner can commit the resources and liability of other partners because they are part of the same legal entity. Many wise corporate lawyers look sideways at the term and prefer to work with less fraught terms, such as strategic alliance. If nothing else, it is vague!

There are two types of *strategic alliance*. One is project specific, usually on a large project. Strictly, this is more of a project alliance than a strategic one. The other is a longer-term arrangement to share resources, technology, or other business assets. These arrangements are intended to be mutually beneficial. Each party brings something to the table that is of value to the other, and between them they can gain some business advantage. If any of those elements are missing, we do not really have a strategic alliance.

 Strategic alliances create opportunities for all members that would not exist if each worked separately.

Other elements of a strategic alliance can include contractual commitments to deliver specific things; exchange of resources such as employees, knowledge, products, and market intelligence; and a common set of business objectives that must be met for the alliance to survive.

While strategic alliances typically span several projects and perhaps several businesses, project alliances are established for the purpose of delivering a specific project. It is not unheard of that such an alliance will survive the project and over time become a strategic one.

The benefits of strategic alliances come in the form of synergies and development of relationships between people in different organizations, leading to competitive edges through reduced learning curves, trust, shared information, creativity, and more.

11.7.2 Joint Ventures

A joint venture is a legal entity created by two or more businesses; it is normally separate from its parents. Ownership may be split evenly, or it may be weighted in favor of one or more parties. The purpose of a joint venture is to establish a separate business unit to address specific market needs that none of the parent organizations wishes—or is necessarily able—to tackle on their own. Reasons for joint-venture arrangements vary; some of the more common ones include sharing business risks, developing new markets or products, expanding capabilities, and dealing with specific restrictions to business such as union affiliations, regulatory compliance, or local ownership.

11.7.3 Gainshare Contracts

Gainshare contracts have many different labels and flavors. The idea is simple. If the contractor can do something cheaper than was expected, it shares in the resulting gain. This type of contract has been called *target cost*, *guaranteed maximum price*, *shared savings*, and more. Each label carries a slightly different connotation, depending on industry, location, and a few other variables; therefore, be careful when you hear the terms used—not everyone may be talking about the same thing!

The model comes out of the North Sea; it was used on a number of oil and gas recovery projects, sometimes with quite spectacular results. The principle is quite simple: a base target for cost and schedule are set for the project. Performance that is better than target leads to savings that are shared between the contractor(s) and the client. Overruns are also split, usually in the same ratio. The objective is to get all participants working at whatever it takes to deliver at lower cost and faster. (In concept, this is what Figure 11.7.3 shows.) We try to reduce owner management costs and contractor costs by working more closely and with more of an open-book policy.

Figure 11.7.3 helps us work through an example. Let's assume that we have three contractors working on a project for the owner. Each of the four parties has estimated its cost, and the total cost works out at $11 million at a 50 percent probability of success. (See range estimating in Chapter 10.) The components of this total are made up of the following:

Owner cost	$1,000,000
Contractor A	$5,000,000
Contractor B	$3,500,000
Contractor C	$1,500,000

The contractors, as part of the gainshare plan, will risk all of their profits and possibly part of the overhead contribution in exchange for sharing in the potential upside, if the project can be completed for less than the target cost.

In Figure 11.7.3, we can see the target cost, which would represent the cost of $10 million identified by the contractors. The overruns and savings will be shared at 60 percent to the owner and 40 percent to the contractor (shown generically as X% in Figure 11.7.3). Any cost over the target is paid 40 percent by the contractors and 60 percent by the owner. When the cost to the contractor reaches the amount predetermined to be the overhead portion of their fee, he stops paying. This is to prevent contractors from risking too much and going bankrupt on the project. Contractors that fail financially can only delay and damage a project.

If on the other hand there are savings below the target cost, then 40 percent of these savings go to the contractors. All parties influence costs and savings; as a result, the risks are shared. It is possible for contractors to share overruns and savings on an equal footing or in some proportion to reflect risk or portion of the original value of the project in which they participate. Typically, these ratios are set before work begins.

In our example, the split of savings would be 50 percent, 35 percent, and 15 percent to contractors A, B, and C, respectively, if this were based on the original value of their contracts. It is possible to set up the three contracts on this project independently. The rationale behind putting the gainshare portion in one pool is to encourage the contractors to reassign work if it can be done better by one contractor rather than another.

Here is another concept. In our example project, assume that the anticipated total cost of the project is $12 million, including contractor's overhead and reasonable profit, as well as the owner's direct cost. This becomes the pool of money available to the project team (owner and three contractors). The money can be split into two components: *Teflon* and *sticky* money. Teflon money is what the team spends on subcontractors, equipment, labor, and materials; it flows through the system without sticking to anyone. The sticky money is left; it is split 60/40 between the owner and contractors. The contractors' portion is then divided in a predetermined ratio between them.

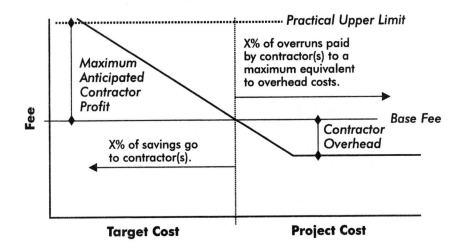

Figure 11.7.3 Gainshare Model for Contractor Fee (Cost-Plus Contract)

 The gainshare contract model is intended to encourage team members to share ideas and solutions for a common good. Done well and with the right team environment, it can lead to substantial cost and schedule savings.

11.7.4 Edge-to-Edge Teams

The edge-to-edge deal is for contractors; the idea is that each contractor in a consortium takes her own risks and rewards. The relationship requires a significant degree of trust, as the entire team's success at the tender stage is based on collaboration and agreed margins for all. It only takes one greedy participant to eliminate the competitive edge of the group. Often one contractor will take the lead role in the team and contract with the owner. The other contractors (typically specialists) will develop their portions of the bid at their own expense and coordinate with the lead contractor. By combining skills and resources from the tender stage onward, the contractors develop a competing bid, based on efficiencies generated through collaboration and assignment of work to the best organization to do it competitively.

Edge-to-edge contract arrangements allow a consortium of contractors to work in their own areas of expertise and take the risks and rewards associated with their own work.

11.7.5 Trust-Based Contracts

This is probably the most interesting deal; it is essentially the *handshake* contract of old. The agreement to work together is based on trust and personal relationships. It really goes further and relies on mutual confidence in the ethics and competence of partner individuals and firms. Each example that I have seen has been different. I have such an arrangement with a large consulting firm. We bid on work together, are currently doing a couple of projects—one where my organization is the lead and one where it is the lead—and we have no formal agreement to collaborate. Most of my clients have no formal contract with my company. If we do not meet each other's expectations, we will probably stop doing business. As long as both parties are benefiting from the relationship, we continue to work together and share the rewards of the relationship. No contract means no safety net. The advantage is that we must keep working on the relationship and understand each other's needs—or we both have a long way to fall!

Under common law, even undocumented agreements like this create an implicit legal contract. Enforcing it is difficult, as the terms and conditions are hard to prove. The disadvantage is that as a result both parties are exposed. The advantage is that they are less likely to resort to litigation to resolve differences and are encouraged to continue working on the relationships needed for good business.

 Trust-based contracts encourage cooperation and flexibility by both parties. This is in part because these contracts are difficult to enforce through the courts.

11.8 Issues: Buildability, Concurrent Design, Value Design

Contracts do serve the purpose of providing a legal framework within which to do business. This is not enough for today's projects, however, as we need every competitive edge we can gain. Good contracts in this day and age will at least consider the need for greater collaboration between parties to address issues such as time to market, easier implementation as a result of input from the implementers, and a mechanism to help identify opportunities to be more competitive.

Buildability is designing a product (building, car, computer, software package, and so on) so that it can be built more cost effectively without compromising the integrity of the design or the functionality of the end product. The people who will build the end product are often not consulted in the process of designing it. As a result, potential savings in construction or manufacture are lost. To capture this expertise, we need to contract with the builder before the design is complete.

 Buildability is the art of designing products and components with their production in mind. Typically, the expertise for this resides with the people who build rather than with those who design. The process is to bring together the two areas of expertise before the design is complete.

If we do this, we can take advantage of concurrent design (also referred to more narrowly as concurrent engineering). Concurrent design is about fast-tracking design and implementation, so the expertise of the implementers is brought to bear on the design. For example, a good telephone handset manufacturer will involve the supplier of plastic molds and other components in design of the parts that it will supply. This way, the overall design will accommodate any cost advantages that can be gained as a result of easier manufacture of components by suppliers, as well as assembly sequencing and timing.

 Involving suppliers and others further down the supply chain in the overall design of a product will help identify opportunities to save time and money and improve the product.

Value design is most simply described as "asking *why*." Like all good four-year-olds, we should innocently ask why we do anything in our business or on our projects, such as scope and specifications of the end product. If we do not get a good answer, we should consider doing without the item, process, or other deliverable. On one large project, this process led to identification of over $10 million dollars worth of unnecessary instrumentation, piping, pumps, and other materials. For one utility, the construction of its service buildings (as many as thirty each year) was reduced by 20 percent by eliminating items that were there because "they were always done that way."

Let others look at our business with innocent eyes, and ask why we do what we do. What is unnecessary or adds little or no value may surprise us.

11.9   Incentives and What Works

Incentive clauses in contracts are intended to provide the contractor with an incentive to meet or exceed specific performance criteria. They may be related to schedule, cost, safety, or quality. Such clauses need to be treated with caution, as they can become greater problems in administration than they are worth. If the incentive is significant, the contractor will work hard at protecting his interests. All events that may impede the contractor's chance of success will become a point for potential conflict. This is doubly true if the incentive clause is balanced with a penalty for underperforming.

Thus, if we want an effective incentive, we need to put a few things in place. Consider the list that follows when adding incentive or bonus-and-penalty clauses to a contract:

- The target must be achievable and easily measured. If this is not so, then the contractor will be placed in a position where any and all impediments will be seen as reasons to claim for delays or other causes that will increase his chances of success.

- If the contract circumstances are volatile (lots of indeterminate components, such as an incomplete design or high potential for change), then any incentive targets must be easy to change to suit modified circumstances. The formulas for such change should be defined at the outset; if they cannot, then incentive clauses may be inappropriate.

- If there is a penalty for nonperformance, it should be limited to a ceiling that the contractor can afford. Penalties are dangerous instruments in contracts, as they create confrontation. Such confrontation is more likely to be triggered if the contractor's entire business is exposed.

 Handle incentive clauses and bonus-and-penalty clauses with care. They can quickly become the primary focus of the client and the contractor, dominating the contract.

Whatever incentive scheme we use, it will likely be more successful if:

- It is really simple to understand.
- Incentives are based on producing deliverables.
- Priorities are aligned with those identified in the project charter and on the priority triangle.
- We reward behaviors that contribute to project success.
- All participants in the work benefit in the rewards.

 Incentive schemes need to be aligned with project objectives and the overall approach to delivery.

11.10   Contracting Framework

What have we got so far? We have identified that there are different types of contracts for work that can be packaged in different ways. We can modify the scope of contracts to include everything from financing through operation of a facility, system, or other project product after it has been built. We can see that there are certain basic and necessary steps in selecting our contractor and in administering a contract. A few common threads drift through the picture.

We need to carefully plan our contracting strategy. It will have a significant impact on the outcome of a project if there is a significant amount of work to be outsourced. Our relationship with our contractors will also affect the outcome of the project. We need to manage expectations of both parties. Trust is an important element in this process; the cost associated with risk can be significant and will likely increase as trust decreases.

Following is a list of what we should consider at each step of building a SMART approach to contracting:

- Contracting strategy: Pick the best types of contracts to be used and the appropriate scope of work, balancing the needs generated by:
    - expertise available within your project team or organization
    - completeness of definition of what you want
    - risks that you want to take and those that you are prepared to pay others to take
    - relationships that you wish to have with your contractors—anything from involved to hands off.

There is no *right* contracting strategy, but following a careful process, reviewing how you will arrange your contracts, will lead to better commercial and technical arrangements with your contractors and should result in a better product.

- Contractor selection: Pick the contractor who will best serve your needs for the project. Corporate policy and existing business relationships may influence part of your decision. Within these bounds, consider the following:
  - ◆ the match of what you need from the contractor and her track record
  - ◆ the people who were proposed by the contractor
  - ◆ your level of trust in the contractor
  - ◆ commercial terms offered.

 Do not leave choice of contractor to chance. If you plan on having several contractors on the project, you are building a team. Consider more than just price in this process.

- Risk management: Managing risk in contracts is done to a large extent by assigning specific risks to the contractor. This practice has been around for so long that the risk premiums associated with it are deeply ingrained in the pricing structures of contractors and their risk-mitigation behaviors. As a buyer, consider the risk premium. After all, most people do not buy insurance without knowing the premium, so why buy contracting insurance without knowing? In order to determine the cost of assigning risk to contractors, consider the following process:
  - ◆ Select the best type of contract for the situation (see Section 11.1).
  - ◆ Identify the risk-assigning clauses in your contract.
  - ◆ Ask the contractors to price these clauses separately. In other words, take out all clauses that give the contractor risk exposure, and then ask the contractor to price each of them separately, should you elect to include the clauses.
  - ◆ Determine the price you are willing to pay for inclusion of each clause.
  - ◆ When the bids come in, use only those clauses that are priced at or below what you are willing to pay for them. Exclude the

Risk-Assigning Clause	Owner Price	Contractor A Price	Owner Price	Contractor B Price
Base Bid with No Risk	N/A	$14,000,000	N/A	$13,500,000
1. Liquidated Damages for Delays	$200,000	$250,000	$200,000	$100,000
2. Design Compliance with Codes/Contractor's Responsibility	$50,000	$0	$50,000	$10,000
3. Consequential Damages for Product Failure	$2,000,000	$700,000	$2,000,000	$1,500,000
4. Owner Delay of Contractor's Work/No Penalty	$100,000	$400,000	$100,000	$100,000
5. No Limit to Owner-Requested Changes	$20,000	$100,000	$20,000	$40,000
Total Lowest Cost Option		$15,070,000		$15,230,000
Owner's Contingency (owner's price for retained risks)		$320,000		$20,000
Value of Contract as Awarded		$14,750,000		N/A

Table 11.10.1   Risk Premium-Based Contract Pricing

other clauses, but, for bid comparison purposes, add in your price for the clauses you did not include.

◆ Contract for the best risk combination resulting from this analysis. A simple sample analysis is shown in Table 11.10.1.

From Table 11.10.1, we can see that Contractor A's bid, when combined with risk pricing by the owner, represents the best deal. The Owner retains her own contingency to cover the risks in clauses 1, 4, and 5, while the contract includes risks 2 and 3 and the base (risk-free) bid is adjusted to include the contractor's risk premium.

As part of the process, it is advisable to have a lawyer review the legal implications of adding and deleting specific clauses, especially if one clause relies on another for its efficacy.

The contract was for a paperweight,
but the scale on the drawing was wrong.

 There is more to managing risk than just assigning it to someone else. Consider the impact of the premium on your project.

- Administration: Contract administration should be simple, if we have the right type of contract in place and the project plan is reasonable. The key is to manage all stakeholders' expectations, ensuring that they are aligned and stay that way. The biggest part of effective contract administration is keeping communications channels open and ensuring that decisions are kept objective and reasonable.

 Fair and open dealing in administration of contracts is the biggest single factor in success in this area.

- Audit: Many projects are subject to audit; thus, all key decisions and actions need to be well documented. Depending on the size and complexity of the project, this can be a simple case of maintaining a professional diary of events to much more detailed record-keeping, filing systems, and reporting. The key is to know what to record and what to ignore. Typically, if an event, decision, or action meets one or more of the following criteria, it should be recorded:

Don't Park Your Brain Outside

- Someone's money is being spent in a way not clearly laid out in the approved project plan.
- There is a material change to scope, schedule, budget, or quality of the project as a result of the event or leading to the event.
- A lay person may not understand the rationale being employed.
- What is being done does not follow normal industry practices.
- There is significant risk in the process.
- There are dissenters to the chosen course of action.
- Someone is nervous about what is being decided, planned, or done.

 Audit of a project should be able to track decisions and actions, together with the contemporary thinking.

11.11   Disputes

Contract disputes are common; in North America, they are the second largest source of litigation (after personal injury suits). If we consider what a dispute really is, we can start to understand the phenomenon better. A contractual dispute typically arises over a difference of opinion regarding the intent of a contract. It is simple really. If we can find a way of reducing or eliminating such differences of opinion, we can dispose of the dispute issue. Let's look at how we can minimize contract disputes, and then we'll look at how to resolve those that still occur despite our best efforts.

Many contract disputes can be identified before they actually occur; we call these latent disputes. The idea is most easily illustrated with an example (see sidebar, It's Pretty Clear to Me!). In the example, observe how each party understood one thing that was—from his point of view—a natural interpretation of what the contract and bid documents said—and there was little reason why he should have doubted his interpretation of the wording.

The nature of the story in the sidebar, It's Pretty Clear to Me!, is far from uncommon, although it is a bit more spectacular than many others. We routinely see differences of opinion on what is meant by the wording in a contract. Following are more examples:

Design Project: "The designer shall include rework of the design following review by the client." How many times must the designer

It's Pretty Clear to Me!

A company wanted to build an addition to its manufacturing facility. Because of recent trouble with power shortages, it wanted to include the supply and installation of an emergency power generator. This addition had not been confirmed at the time of bid, so the following words were added: "The Bidder shall provide a separate price in its bid for the supply and installation of the emergency power generator."

The successful bidder was awarded the contract for about $20 million. Shortly after the award, the company found a generator that it thought could be purchased for significantly less than the $2 million quoted as the separate price in the bid for the work. Therefore, it issued a credit change order for $2 million, reducing the contract price from $20 million to $18 million. Then the fun began.

The contractor expressed surprise at the request of a credit, as the $2 million had been a separate price and was not included in the base bid. The owner was shocked, as it thought that the bid included the $2 million—the instructions to the bidders were pretty clear.

Eventually, an arbitrator was selected, and the dispute was put to him. His first point was that the $2 million was for supply and installation, and the owner wanted to credit for supply only—the contractor was still expected (by the owner) to install the unit.

The problem was getting worse now, as the breakdown between supply and installation was not defined in the bid. Eventually, the problem was resolved. The contractor was paid extra for the installation, and the owner purchased and paid for the generator. The arbitrator's decision was based on the fact that the owner created ambiguity in its bid documents; therefore, the owner was liable.

redesign within the set fee? Typically, this is an open issue for the client, but the designer priced only one rerun of the design.

Software System Implementation: "The contractor shall include full system documentation." Is this user documentation, technical documentation, or both? Is it separate from any source code? Is the documentation what is provided by the system vendors, or is it supplementary information? Is it in hard copy or online?

Business Process Improvement: "The price shall include all services to complete the assignment." The options here are numerous, too.

Asking either or both parties to a contract if they understand the terms and conditions will probably solicit both an affirmative answer and a "Do-you-think-I'm-nuts?" look! We need to find a better way of identifying the problem.

One useful tool is to ask the buyer and seller in an agreement who has the risk under each clause. Use a scale from +5 (all the risk with the buyer) to –5 (all the risk with the seller). If the buyer and seller's numbers are close, there is probably some agreement as to what the clause might mean, but check it out anyway! If the numbers are far apart, you likely will have a latent dispute.

 Use of a *mine detector* to ferret out potential disputes before you sign a contract can save a lot of subsequent grief and will undoubtedly eliminate disputes. The resolution of a potential dispute is much easier before the contract is signed.

11.12 Dispute Resolution

If we do have a dispute, it is invariably best to resolve it as quickly as possible and at the level in the organization closest to the occurrence. We also want to resolve it before positions become firmly entrenched. The classical options for dispute resolution include those in Table 11.11; the list starts with the worst.

The moral is simple: avoid disputes if you can. Resolve as quickly as possible those that you cannot avoid. If you have to go beyond negotiation, start with the options at the bottom of Table 11.11!

 Avoid disputes if possible. If not possible, then negotiate. If that fails, mediate. If that fails, you should reconsider your options before spending a lot more time and money in the process—everyone loses from this point on.

That wraps up the business of contracting work out to others for our project. Now let's look in the next chapter at how we make an effective team out of the disparate members we have assembled— including our contractors and suppliers.

Resolution Method	Who Has Control	Comments
Litigation	The courts—neither party ends up with any real control over the outcome.	Expensive, slow, stressful, and the lawyers win! Your dirty laundry ends up in the public domain.
Mini-Trials	Similar to litigation.	Privatized version of public litigation—may be marginally cheaper; usually a bit faster.
Arbitration	The parties get to select their judge—can be a panel of three judges, where each party picks one, and the two appointees pick the third.	An arbitrator, selected beforehand or appointed by mutual agreement, acts as judge and jury. The arbitrator's decision is normally legally binding to both parties. Usually cheaper and faster than the above—unless someone appeals the decision through the court system! Nonbinding arbitration is also an option.
Dispute Resolution Board	The parties get to pick the decision-makers. Depending on the contract terms, the parties can challenge the decisions.	A panel of industry experts assesses each claim as it occurs and provides a ruling. These rulings may be binding on the parties, or they may be an interim solution that can be challenged, usually after the contract has been completed. Lower cost of resolution; fast decisions—may only be temporary relief, though evidence suggests that decisions are rarely challenged in the end.
Mediation	Parties have control over the decisions they make; a good mediator—an impartial facilitator for the discussion—retains control over the process.	The track record for this type of dispute resolution is excellent with a high success rate. This option does not preclude other approaches if it fails—generally fast and affordable.
Negotiation	Complete control by the disputing parties.	Cheapest and, if done right, fastest way of resolving a difference.

Table 11.11 Dispute Resolution Options

Chapter 12

TEAMWORK

Have you ever worked with a dysfunctional team? How about with a really effective team? What were the differences? Did team-building exercises play an important and effective part in getting your team members to work together? Or were they seen as a bit of a joke? What role did the team leader play? Was this leadership role different from or part of a facilitating role? If the leader had a different personality or management style, would the team have been different?

Whatever your experience, following are some elements that will be familiar to you, and some that will be (or perhaps should have been) on your list of things that make teams really effective. We will explore each in turn in this chapter as we work through the process of how to build a truly effective project team.

In Chapter 5, we looked at how we arrived at the SMART approach to regenerative work environments. In Chapter 10, we explored some broader organizational issues related to how projects and programs work. Now we can build on this to see in detail how to develop high-performance project teams. Specifically, we will work through the steps of implementing the seven elements of highly effective regenerative teams.

In the following sections, we will work through the steps of getting teams to work well. The sequence is one that I have found most effective, but don't feel that you have to follow it exactly—I don't. It is important to be flexible when working with teams. Several of the pieces described in the next sections will happen concurrently. It is important that we pace the team's development to suit its people and style.

It is worth taking a bit of time to develop your team. Effective teams recover this time and effort invested many times over.

12.1   Open Communication

Just a reminder: This is all about minimizing hidden agendas and sharing information on a project. Beginning the process of developing a culture of openness is best done through leadership and example. Here are a few approaches to try, many of which will work at the project kickoff meeting.

The kickoff meeting starts the project; on most of my projects, it's the first planning session that brings the core team together. It's worth preparing carefully for this meeting; you will need an agenda. In my own agendas, I include a brief description of what we want to achieve during the meeting. Then we know at the end of the meeting that we've had a useful session. It is also useful to review the agenda with all of the participants before the meeting. I use it as an opportunity to meet with all of them before the real meeting, when we'll start getting everyone aligned and a sense of how they will respond to being part of the team.

The first meeting of the team and how you manage it helps to set the tone for the rest of the project. This meeting is too important to leave to chance.

If any members of the team have some ideas on how to build the project plan, I find it useful to learn what they are and offer encouragement or alternative options, as appropriate. I also like to get a sense of what, if anything, team members would like to get out of the project. If you go out on an intelligence mission like this, it is wise to be prepared to explain what you are seeking. It's an opportunity to lead by example. If you are looking for a promotion, to build your reputation, or for a whopping great bonus, why not tell people that? They may be more inclined to share their aspirations with you. The risk is that they may think you a fool. First, this risk is small. Second, if they do look at you sideways, tell them why you are doing what you are doing. If team members don't know what you want, then they're less likely to deliver it! If they do know and don't think that you'll get it, at least they can manage your expectations from the outset!

If we want to manage expectations successfully, it pays to start doing so from the outset. To manage expectations, including our own, we need to let others know what they are, and everyone should be allowed to respond to those expectations. After all, is this not what open communication is all about?

Either at the first meeting or during the planning phase of the project, we need to work with the team to encourage open communication. Following are other ways of doing this:

- When building the deliverables breakdown structure (DBS), point out that anything not included in the DBS will not be part of the project. If someone has an agenda item that is not addressed by the DBS, it should come out.

- Make a point of asking each team member to identify things that she or others might want to see in the project or as a consequence of doing or completing it. I have often been surprised by what comes out—both good and bad!

- Ask the team to identify what others may need, which have not been considered or included in the project plan.

- Consider asking about other stakeholders, such as those not immediately connected to the project. There may be people or organizations that could contribute to—or interfere with—the project and who could also benefit from it.

- The more we learn about others on the larger project team, the more we may find in the way of expertise, experience, and background that could contribute to the better, faster, or safer delivery of the project. Just think how often you have *not* been asked anything (or worse, how many times you've contributed and been ignored) in a project-planning or problem-solving meeting. Now multiply that by the size of your project team!

- Use techniques to encourage people to communicate. Consider using suggestion boxes, yellow stickies for people to write ideas, a facilitator for planning sessions, or any other tools that may help people open up.

- Avoid criticism of ideas and contributions. They slow or stop the process of opening up communication.

There are many ways to encourage open communication. It needs to be nurtured. It is also the easiest of the seven team-effectiveness elements to get to work for you. Do not expect too much at the beginning, though.

12.2   Ownership of Your Work

The idea of ownership is not quite the same as *empowerment*. For a start, the latter word has been worn thin by hollow use in too many situations. Ownership is all about both having control of your work and the ability to influence the larger work plan. It is, in many ways, the antithesis of micromanagement. How do we achieve ownership for our team as a whole and for the members individually?

The answer lies in balance. We need to balance the needs of the individual against those of the team, and the needs of the team with the project. In our planning process, we are smart if we align the project with the needs of the corporation. In doing so, we involve senior management in the direction of the project, as well as in commitment to the plan and associated risks. This is the start of the ownership process. A senior manager who has committed to a plan and its inherent risk will have some sense of ownership in that plan. If the team was involved in the planning, then it also will have ownership of the plan.

Ownership begins with involvement.

Involvement at the outset is clearly not an option for many project participants; this is where we need balance. We are balancing involvement with what is practical, which implies a certain amount of negotiation. We cannot negotiate plans with latecomers if the plan is complete in every detail right to the end of the project. This is true if for no other reason than we have put so much effort into the plan in the first place. There are several reasons why we should look at a rolling-wave approach to planning. Involvement of people who join the team later is just one. The important part of any plan is the need to develop key points when certain deliverables are needed. These deliverables and when they are needed are easy to identify. They are the ones that involve several different groups or stakeholders and are critical to the

It's the only way we can keep current with the team's organization.

project success. They are needed by the target dates set in the 3-D schedule. Within the constraints set by these key dates, we should plan the intermediate processes with the team members who will be involved. If we organize the team well, these participants will be on board to participate in the detail of how the work will be done and all of the associated trivia of resources needed, durations of each step, how the step is to be done, coordination, and more. The degrees of freedom decrease as the project evolves, but the opportunity to participate in planning at the micro-level should be maintained all through the system.

 Opportunities to participate at some level in planning our own work should be maintained throughout the project planning and implementation process.

This is probably the second-easiest element for effective teams to implement. It does, however, require that the project manager and the project management office (if there is one) try hard to stay away from the controlling end of the management style spectrum!

Ownership needs to be nurtured. Part of that process is inherent in the management style adopted for the project. Be flexible—there are many ways to skin a cat!

12.3 Propensity to Take Risk

When I started my academic career, I had a graduate student whose background was with a large integrated and multinational oil and gas company. He was very much the *company* man. He and I argued one day about the importance of following corporate policy. He was adamant that small breaks from corporate policy quickly led to anarchy and should be aggressively squashed. I begged to differ. Perhaps as a result, I gave him a special assignment. "Go," I said, "and find as many performance improvements, management breakthroughs, significant technical innovations, or other significant contributors to any organization's competitive edge that was a direct result of rigidly following policy." He found none in the university library, the corporate libraries and reports, the Internet, or anywhere else. The lesson: We need something more than policy to sustain our competitive edge. In fact, in some organizations we need to have a degree of anarchy if we are to be truly competitive.

 To be competitive today, we need at least a bit of the spirit of anarchy in our businesses!

What are we really getting at? We need the ability to take risk. We cannot afford to stand still. We need innovation, and we do not get it if we punish failure. Failure means that we took a risk; by implication we punish risk-taking. Safe behavior in today's business world is the same as what it has always been. You do not get fired for following policy, doing things the way they were always done, or otherwise keeping your head down. But that is not where competitive edges are honed. Remember, the first sign of insanity is to keep doing things the way that we have always done them but expecting a different result.

 Our competitive edge lies in continuous improvement. Improvement comes from trying something different.

We need to be able to take reasonable risks. To create an environment where this can occur, we need to be able to set behavior guidelines that everyone can buy into. Again, balance is important, as we do not want to battle unduly with corporate culture, especially if it is ultraconservative. This is a policy issue; if you cannot make the policy yourself, get approval to do so.

 Risk-taking is a policy issue. There should be a clear policy in place enabling us and our team to take appropriate risks.

Before we go any further, let's examine whether we have the real or implicit authority to create a risk-taking policy for your project. Following are some questions that will help sort out where we stand on this issue.

Do we work for a dictatorial organization, where one may be fired for any breach of policy or procedure with little tolerance for divergence? If yes, we probably have to get our organization's support for what we are doing if it is different from established business practice. However, there are few organizations seriously in the project business operating this way any longer; those that are left are probably dinosaurs. If you work for an organization like this, consider a career change or a different employer!

If there is some flexibility in the organization allowing us to develop a reasonable approach to risk-taking on our project, we need to consider the protocols next. If we act independently in developing a policy and presenting it to management for approval, will it be accepted or rejected? If it stands a chance of being accepted, we next consider the level of risk acceptable to the business and more particularly to our boss (and maybe to her boss, too). If our proposed policy will likely be rejected, we will need to negotiate. Remember that we want the boss to own the policy as well, so we need her involvement.

 A policy to accept risk at some level will require acceptance—and ideally ownership—by the organization's management.

Determining the level of acceptable risk-taking in a given organization is not easy, but it is the next step. Some organizations are notoriously risk averse. Some industries are particularly full of risk-averse people, and there are professions that seem to be dominated by risk aversion. Accountants, banks, and insurance companies come to mind. This is not a bad thing because, again, we need balance. Nobody in his right mind will risk an entire business on one deal, unless there are extenuating circumstances. Chief among those extenuating circumstances is the opportunity to bail out of a project or situation. Safe bailout requires a parachute. What does this tell us about our organization's propensity to take risk? First, we need to contain the risk within our project; then we look at the project in the context of the business as a whole. If it will have a small impact on the bottom line, then we have low risk, and we can probably be much bolder with our risk-taking policy than if the project were to have a big bottom-line impact. In the latter case, we may wish to consider an approach that allows us to contain the risk even further—perhaps set a maximum exposure limit in terms of delay or cost or another variable that can be readily assessed.

 The risk-taking policy we develop should be based on containing the overall risk to the sponsor organization. The smaller the risk, the more likely that management will accept it.

Now that was not too difficult, was it? At this point, we should have reached a number of conclusions that will help us formulate a policy. The next piece is to understand what that policy should look like. Here are a few tips and suggestions:

- Any project that will affect business performance of the organization by more than 5 percent should probably have a steering committee to oversee risks and review the project at key bailout points (off ramps, checkpoints, and so on).
- Any risk that will change cost or schedule by more than 5 percent should be reviewed with the project manager and the steering committee, if the project is big enough to justify such a committee.
- These more significant risks should be assessed and specific guidelines for their management should be determined before including the risk in the plan and in its subsequent execution.
- Any smaller risks should be reviewed with the project manager before proceeding. The project manager should be open to suggestions and willing to take appropriate risks.
- *If* a risk is taken, the results should be treated as a learning experience. If it was successful, we should know how to replicate the circumstances and take advantage of similar opportunities in the

future. If the risk results in failure, we need to learn from what went wrong to avoid making the same mistake twice.

- Either way, we should reward people for taking appropriate risks. If they succeed, we may have gained a competitive advantage, and that is worth something. If they failed, we have at least learned how to avoid the same failure in the future. This too is worth something, and I believe that it should be rewarded.

- Repeated failure, as a result of taking the same risk many times and getting the same results, should not be rewarded!

 A policy for risk-taking is a starting point. If we want the propensity to take risk to work positively for us, we need to make it more than policy. We need to nurture the habits that go with this way of doing business.

Without a propensity to take risk, stress levels are unnaturally high, and we miss out on the most creative ideas available to us. People will simply not take the risk of identifying and articulating opportunities. Or, if they took the risk, they won't risk admitting to it.

12.4　Creativity

The opportunity to be creative is a big selling feature in almost any business. It attracts the best people to your company and keeps them going. It is largely based on our propensity to take risk, but it goes beyond this.

If a propensity to take risks is a prerequisite for creativity, what are the other characteristics that need to be considered? What do starving artists working in freezing garrets have in common with nuclear scientists developing the atomic bomb or with engineers designing the first rocket or jet engine? We could throw Napoleon's chef, who created Pear Belle Helene, in with them. They all had adversity to challenge them. We can also consider great movies, discoveries of life-saving drugs, and amazing violin performances. The inspiration for these may have derived from a focus on clear objectives and internal motivation to challenge the unknown or to improve on the known. All are drivers, generating creativity. On our projects, we need to have determination to be the best (or at least better), and we need to recognize that there is always room for improvement.

Creativity needs a focus and a driver to allow it to develop. Look for natural drivers for creativity on your project. Develop an awareness of them within the team.

We simply need to encourage creativity in all of the team members. Administrators should look for ways to reduce overhead, streamline the process, and make project delivery even less bureaucratic. Technical people should be looking for clever solutions. They should be given enough time in their days to think about what they do and how it will affect others. You get the drift.

 Creativity needs encouragement, and it needs time—that we normally deny the team in our haste to deliver.

Finally, we cannot encourage people on the one hand and discourage them on the other. We need to anticipate and eliminate elements that may discourage creativity. There are numerous ways to deflate creativity; we see them all of the time in the workplace:

- We snigger at or dismiss too quickly the odd ideas that could lead to neat solutions. This kills the original train of thought, as well as discourages the originator from proposing other ideas in the future.
- We force ideas through too much bureaucracy (or democracy!) for them to survive.
- We do not listen well enough to catch opportunities.
- The source of the idea may be the biggest barrier to acceptance.
- Pride in our own solutions may eliminate better ones (i.e., the *not-invented-here* syndrome).

Most of the time we are oblivious to the things that we do to discourage creativity. We need to raise our awareness of these bad habits and avoid them.

 Encouraging creativity is part of the solution. Not discouraging it is another important part.

12.5 Fun

Fun is important. (We discussed this in Chapter 5.) Making fun happen is not difficult; it starts with open communication and creativity. These two elements help us discover what fun means to others and allow us to help others on the team to be successful.

 Although fun is not necessarily dependent on open communication and creativity, these two factors certainly help us have fun.

Plan to have fun. When was the last time you saw fun included as a deliverable (or even an activity) on a project schedule? Where is the money in your budget to cover fun? This is a strange concept to many people; the very thought of spending company or taxpayer money on fun is actually unacceptable in many circles. Yet, think about it for a bit. If $100 spent on having fun, recognizing people's contributions, and helping to get a team working together saves a team of ten people earning on average just $20 per hour, all we need to do is save half an hour of the team's time to recover the cost. The spin-off benefits are huge in comparison. If you're not convinced yet, make an effort to measure how much time we waste at the water cooler (or its equivalent) complaining about how we operate, the incompetence of senior management, the ignorance of the client, and how we cannot work with this department, those disciplines, or that individual. It doesn't take much to eliminate this behavior.

 In the end, it is people who deliver projects. People having fun are much more productive than those who are not— fun pays.

Also, fun does not have to cost much; we are really talking about motivation. When I've asked project teams to work on how they would have fun, many neat ideas have invariably emerged. Most of them have cost virtually nothing but showed reasonable recognition for effort, hard work, and appreciation by the whole team for an individual's effort. The common elements in almost every scheme included the following:

- low cost
- recognition for effort, creativity, or other contribution to the team or the project
- peer reward system (It was not the boss, but the team that made the awards.)
- flexibility in the reward system (You could use rewards in one of many different ways, depending on your preferences.)
- system unique to the team—also created by the team.

Let's look at a few examples.

One team decided to award millions of dollars. It used *funny money* from a board game. Rewards were shared at the weekly progress meeting. There was no set formula, but the team members would encourage the project manager to reward specific achievements and contributions. The rule was that you could not reward yourself, but you could recommend some other team member. Someone may point out how a person saved her effort by doing part of her assignment, freeing her to fix a problem. Someone else may identify how a group within the team worked so well together that the schedule was a day ahead of target. Another person may point out a clever solution to a problem. And so on.

As these were pointed out, the team would suggest a reward:

That must be worth at least $7,500.

No. It was worth more because it also saved me a bundle of effort. Make it at least $12,000.

Hang on, did Mary not help with that also?

The value was in the exchange of appreciation. It was not abused, and everyone tried extra hard to help each other, because just doing your own bit didn't generate the larger rewards. Maybe to some, size did matter. But to the majority, I believe that the recognition itself was most important, and it was followed by the enhanced teamwork that resulted. But fun did not stop there for the team; it worked out a reward exchange system. I cannot remember all of the details, but here are a few things that could be done:

- Five million dollars got you the president's parking spot near the door on a cold winter's day. All you had to do was get there before he did—apparently not too difficult a task.
- Two million dollars got you a moaning session with the vice president of your choice—and he would have to buy you a coffee and donut or muffin.

Don't Park Your Brain Outside

- You could exchange funny money for dinner for two, time off with pay, and a host of other things. You could pool the money and go for a team reward, such as a beer and pizza evening for the team and significant others.

In another organization, a similar idea was used more generally. The management distributed *high five* cards in recognition of special contributions. They could be collected and exchanged for various items.

Another team—this one working on a software development project—decided to use large plastic building blocks. Members bought two large buckets of the blocks; on each of two matching blocks, they wrote the name of each deliverable required for the project. As these deliverables were completed, the team, led by the person who received the deliverable for the next step in the process, would decide who contributed the most to its completion. That person was given the two pieces. One was used to build the project sculpture. This sculpture was housed in a part of the office that was much traveled by the team. The individual added her piece wherever she wanted; the second piece she kept. Above the sculpture was a counter that started with the total number of deliverables required to complete the project. As each piece was added, the counter was reduced by one; everyone could see how much was left to do. For the first time, the team and the customer could actually see the project reach completion.

Another team used a bell—this was the project manager's idea. Every time something of note happened—usually a key deliverable was produced, or a milestone was met—he'd walk around the five floors of the office building where the team was housed and clang the bell.

 Fun is all about sharing, recognition, and a touch of spontaneity and silliness. We have to let our hair down a bit and relax in each other's company.

12.6   Tribalism

Tribalism is all about belonging; it's a bit about exclusivity and a whole lot about being a successful team. The idea came from a discussion with an anthropologist. It seems we are good at belonging to tribes. The idea goes back a long way and has powerful roots in all of us. Families are tribes, as are companies and divisions within companies. So most of us belong to at least two tribes: the home tribe and the work one. If you stop and think about it, each tribe has its own language, culture, dress code, hierarchy, taboos, and traditions. We

The TIE Tribe

Testing SMART Management has possessed many great moments; one involved the first real forming of a tribe.

We were working in a *blame* culture organization. It seemed important to isolate the project team from the generally prevailing corporate culture in order to see open communication, trust, and other regenerative team signs. After discussion, we agreed that we would carefully plan the *fun* part of the project. I offered a few examples from other companies for similar projects. I mentioned the company where the team decided to award lots of money. I described the team in another company that used Lego blocks, awarding them to the team member who contributed the most to each project deliverable.

Armed (and dangerous) with these examples and more, the project manager decided to buy a project tie. He would award the tie each week to a team member who would wear it the following week. The chosen tie was covered in pink pigs.

I got a call the following week from the project manager. The fun thing was not working, and it was, of course, all my fault. I asked for details. The manager had awarded the tie at the last meeting, and the recipient refused to wear it. Nobody else seemed to think it a good idea, either. It turned out that the tie was being given to the person who, in the project manager's opinion, had contributed the *least* to the project in the preceding week. We agreed to meet.

By the time I got there, the team had already decided to award the tie to the person who had contributed the most (a novel concept!). The original tie had been rejected as it now had a bad aura. A new tie was not possible, because the project manager had blown the $50 budget allocated for *fun* on the pig tie. A team member had brought in an old tie, which the team could use. He produced the tie. It was from the 1960s: wide orange, brown, and olive horizontal stripes with ugly, furry, woven bits. General disapproval was avowed. Someone suggested cutting it up; someone else recommended coloring it black with an indelible marker. These suggestions led to the decision to write all of the project deliverables on the stripes—one per stripe—starting with the last one at the thin end. There were a few stripes left over, so the team promptly agreed to cut them off.

At this point, everyone on the team was involved. It was agreed that the tie would be awarded to the biggest overall contributor to the project each week. The stripes representing the delivered deliverables were also cut off, as they were produced and awarded to the team members contributing the most to these specific deliverables.

continued on next page

Don't Park Your Brain Outside

probably have our own special symbols, too: companies have logos, families have favorite relatives, a family joke, a coat of arms, pets, and so on. We also have our own traditions. All are tribal artifacts.

If tribalism is so powerful, we should harness the best of it to help build our project team. Now read *tribe*, not *team*. If we've incorporated all of the previously suggested ideas, we will have started on the path to building a tribe for the project. This is so powerful that it can almost be dangerous. On one project, we ended up with a problem. The team we built did not want to separate as we began to wind down resources after we'd peaked, just after the midpoint. People kept turning up for meetings long after their roles had well and truly been completed. They were still part of the tribe. This is best illustrated with an example; read about the TIE Tribe in the sidebar.

 Tribalism is part of our heritage. It is powerful. We can use it to help us be better than just teams.

12.7   Trust

If we succeed with the first six elements of high-performance teams, we will build trust, the glue that binds us into more effective teams.

In the past seven years of research at the University of Calgary into various aspects of effective project management, this is the one element that has emerged as common to all.

Faster project delivery requires trust in communication, in our subcontractors and suppliers to deliver, and in our team to meet targets. Lower cost requires better collaboration with others, especially our supply chain, and it only seems to happen if there is a sufficiently high level of trust. Improvements in the quality of products generally stem from collaborative effort. It, too, needs trust. Management of contracts is easier in a trusting environment.

What do we really know about trust? In Chapter 5, we looked at a construct for trust and identified three distinct types. Each one behaves differently, so let's consider them in turn.

Before we do so, however, we need to understand that how we define trust is very personal. We can probably agree on the concept but not the detail. Thus, I do not even try to define trust for you; instead, we look at three distinct elements that normally we do not separate.

12.7.1 The Hartman-Romahn Trust Color Model

What follows is a short and superficial description of the Hartman-Romahn Trust Color Model. The model is the basis of some new research into project management process improvement and was developed in collaboration with one of my research team members at the University of Calgary, Dr. Elke Romahn—hence, the name in the heading.

Trust for many is simply a black-and-white issue; for others, it comes in shades of gray. If we have three distinct types of trust, we can represent them as three primary colors. When they are together, and we are on the same wavelength, then we have a balance of the three types: white trust. Their total absence is black. In between, we have shades of gray. Unfortunately, trust breaks down if it is not in balance, so we do not have just gray. There is a whole spectrum with which to play, and each color has both advantages and challenges when working with them in a business environment. Once we have identified the three types of trust, we will look at how they behave and the *mechanics* of how trust is built.

Of the three, *competence trust* is the easiest to transfer and build. It is transferable and builds in steps. The transfer is made through our trust of others' opinions (references and referrals), reputations (not everyone can be wrong), and verifiable track records. We have assigned to competence trust the color blue (as in blue chip). We measure our trust in someone's capability to do what he is supposed to do. A mechanic, a dentist, a lawyer, an engineer, a carpenter, or any

At the end of the project, we turn this around.
There is an "F" on the other side.

other trade or profession will need to have some level of trust in order to function reasonably well. This type of trust can be rebuilt over time if it is breached.

Ethical trust is the ability to trust someone with our best interests and to behave predictably. It is much more difficult to earn. It is typically only partially transferable and is heavily dependent on our experiences. We will accept someone at a certain level of ethical trust, but they will need to prove themselves. If this trust is breached, the breach is usually permanent and nonrecoverable. We have assigned the color of yellow (or gold) to this type of trust.

Finally, we have *emotional trust*, based, of course, on how we feel. It includes everything from love at first sight to how we pick our politicians! It is about *chemistry*. We pick our friends with this type of trust in the foreground. It seems unpredictable and perhaps somewhat random; I would leave this in the capable hands of psychologists and social sciences experts. For the purpose of business, we need to acknowledge that it exists and in fact plays an important role in how we work. We have assigned the color of danger to this one: red.

To do business, in most cases we need a balance of competence and ethics—blue and yellow trust. This gives us green (the *go* color) trust. It is perhaps not coincidental that green also represents naiveté and innocence!

Trust does not happen because we decide to make it so. It requires a sender and a receiver; the trustor needs to be able to trust the trustee. Building trust is a bit like forming a contract. We need to offer our ability to be trusted and to have that trustworthiness assessed and accepted. If we look again at the descriptions of the three types of trust, we can see that they behave independently. Now let's look at the trust types together with the six other elements of effective teams, to see how each element can contribute to creating balanced trust for our team (see Table 12.7).

It is up to you—try the ideas in this chapter. If you have the same success I've consistently had, your projects will do well because your teams will do well.

 Teams do well when we balance business and technical issues with social ones.

12.8   SMART Teams and Team Building

The classical process for team formation is to form the team, storm through establishing group behaviors, establish the norms for team behavior—then perform. Integrating team building into planning processes and subsequent management of the project is a relatively new idea, but it offers some powerful ways of accelerating effective team formation. We eliminate the storming phase.

In developing the SMART approach to teams, we have focused on the following:

- Team building should be a natural part of project delivery, not a separate exercise.
- Teams need trust. We need to work to make it happen.
- There is a lot of unnecessary stress in project delivery. Team-work, done correctly, helps us eliminate or reduce it.
- Fun is important and will help us be more effective, so we need to plan this component into our projects. The added time and cost is recovered many times.

Trust Types > Team Building Element V	Competence Blue	Ethical Yellow	Emotional Red
Open Communication	Work on technical issues that are common ground between team members.	Some information is shared in confidence. Respect that confidence. Minimize scuttlebutt and rumors.	If you are uncomfortable with someone, try to understand his point of view.
Ownership	Respect people's expertise and contributions to how the project may be best delivered.	Declare weaknesses and needs. Be prepared to accept help if this is in the best interests of the team. Offer to help where it can contribute.	It is not enough to value expertise. We need to work well with the experts. This is easy if we like them. If we do not, try to understand why, and put emotion to one side in those dealings. Maybe consider using less expert but nicer people next time!
Propensity to Take Risk	Understand the risks that are being taken in the context of the skills and experience of the whole team, including contractors and suppliers.	Be open in discussing concerns, risks, and opportunities. Do not try to hide problems. Everyone should be set up for success—never for failure.	Treat everyone equally as far as is humanly possible. Do not pick on people you don't like.
Creativity	Allow team members to use their skills and experiences—even if these are not directly related to the work environment.	Respect others' contributions to the project. Acknowledge good ideas and who thought of them.	Do not let emotion color your judgment in sorting through innovative ideas.
Fun	Take time to recognize expertise and other individual and group contributions.	Fun should never be at someone else's expense. Have fun *with* people.	Work a lot harder at this if you have a dysfunctional team!
Tribalism	Define primary and support roles for each team member. Consider cross-functional training and other ways to help people understand each other's technical challenges.	A tribe protects itself from *outsiders*. Be careful who you put into that category. Be sure to invite all of the larger team to join the tribe. Treat all members as partners.	Tribes survive internal conflict by containing it. There is nothing wrong with emotional responses to people. We just need to maintain enough objectivity to be both good team players and managers.

Table 12.7   Trust Building in Teams

 SMART teams are tribes that trust each other and know how to have fun.

Chapter 13

GETTING BACK ON TARGET

I have to tell you: This chapter was inspired by the absence of a thirteenth floor in a building (several buildings, come to that!).

I need eighteen chapters for this book. I am behind schedule, so here I catch up. My choice in this case is not to write this chapter. You need to pick your own way to catch up: do things faster, cut scope, or allocate more resources. There are many options. Remember to check your priorities. In this case, I created this chapter so I could delete it to make this point!

Hope you are not superstitious!

End of chapter.

There—now we're back on schedule.

Chapter 14

PROJECT CONTROL AND METRICS

Often we put all sorts of controls and metrics into the management of projects. Many people fill in timesheets. Others will have a scheduler with a Gantt chart chase us with demands for estimates of percentage complete for an activity or, worse, an estimate of how long it will take us to get done. We may use performance measures against a budget, although this is often hard to do, because information comes too slowly from accounting. Thus, we have to guess what was done in addition to what accounting may be able to report. Sound familiar? Try answering these questions:

- What do *you* use to measure progress and control the progression of a project toward success?
- How would you do this if you were producing a creative live performance such as a play, a rock concert, or television show?
- In what ways did you answer the previous questions differently; why?

In our quest for success in effective and efficient management of projects, we came across one industry that routinely produces projects on time—so much so that we would be profoundly shocked it were ever late. Which industry would this be? Live entertainment. Imagine going to opening night of a big musical. You have straightened your bow tie or corsage, sipped your glass of champagne, and settled into your plush red seat in the dress circle. The lights dim, and an expectant hush descends on the audience. Through the dim light of the orchestra pit, you see some movement as someone approaches the conductor's podium. The curtain opens, and we see a bare stage and a bunch of people in street dress on the stage rehearsing. Someone on the stage looks around startled, then yells into the wings, "Shut that curtain; we aren't ready yet!" Sound stupid? Hard to conceive? Yet we do the equivalent on project after project in other industries. We wanted to know what really happened in live entertainment that does not happen in other areas. The answers came in part from observation and in part from the explanations of project managers in other industries, as they rationalized why they were different:

- We have a real product to deliver. So does live entertainment—and, like software, for example, it's not a tangible one.
- We do not have time for rehearsals. Why not, if that is what we need? Examples of an equivalent in other industries include commissioning, testing, and market validation. Interestingly, unlike live entertainment, where we have learned over the centuries that we need time to rehearse, we still plan for inadequate time in equivalent phases in other project types.
- There are no quality assurance or quality control requirements. What—no reviews or critics, no people lining up to buy tickets? Just like other industries, the internal controls are there for minimizing box office disasters.
- In live entertainment you can always take bits out, if you think that you will not get done on time. And so we do in other industries where we take out functionality, eliminate architectural details, or otherwise make changes or declare limitations.

What are the commonalties and differences between industries? What are the basic traditional project controls and metrics? When and how do they work? How can we improve our current planning and control of projects? These questions are answered as we work through the following topics in this chapter.

- classical project planning and control model
- focus on deliverables for all aspects of planning and control
- important metrics and the priority triangle
- estimating and scheduling
- risk analysis and iterations
- risk mitigation options and influence on expected outcomes
- changes by phase in project control issues
- managing the project culture through project phases
- creative problem solving
- managing scope, cost, schedule, quality, and safety: a toolkit
  - project charter
  - project dashboard
  - change order management
  - risk management.

14.1 Classical Project Planning and Control Model

If we can learn from live entertainment, we can also learn from other sources. Classical approaches to project management all have things in common. The planning process is of vital importance to all of them. We're unlikely to deliver a successful project if we do not think through how we are going to accomplish the objective. In working through the planning, we arrive at estimates of time and resources required for achieving our objectives.

The planning process offers us an opportunity to mentally work through the entire project. Unfortunately, we often do so assuming perfect or near-perfect circumstances. (More on this topic in a moment.) If we consider the planning process as a rehearsal, then the first benefit we derive from project planning is an appreciation of what it will take to deliver the project successfully. A second benefit is a plan, budget, and schedule. We use these to help manage the project, keep people informed of what is required of them, and where the project is in its development.

 It is important to adequately plan a project by thinking it through. In many cases, this is as close to a rehearsal for the real thing as we will ever get.

Planning at the outset of a project is essential if we are to manage effectively. We make the most significant project decisions at the beginning. The single largest decision is whether or not to proceed with the project. This decision will typically be based on a specific definition of what the project will deliver in terms of benefits, what those benefits will cost, and when they will be delivered. This gives us the standard metrics upon which classical project management is based:

- quality
- scope
- cost (budget)
- time (schedule).

Definition of the scope and quality of the project will dictate the cost and schedule. As we lock into decisions and definitions, they become harder to influence over time. When we just have an idea, that idea can change quite freely. Once we have reduced the idea to a set of deliverables, a matching budget, and a schedule, the idea itself is harder to change. Once the project plan is approved, the budget and schedule are more difficult to change. As we bring the project team on board, do

You are new here, aren't you?

work, retain consultants, contractors, and suppliers, and make progress on the project, so the level of difficulty in implementing change increases. Equally, once work is done, we have no further influence on it. The time has passed, and the resources have been expended.

It is important to get the plan as close to right the first time, so allow enough time to plan. In fact, we need to plan to plan. All too often we do not allow sufficient time for this all-important task. Our eagerness to get going will take over, and we start the project (then do it and finish it) with an inadequate plan and correspondingly inadequate results.

 The ability to influence the final cost and completion of a project decreases over time. Effort in planning at the front-end of a project is invariably worthwhile.

Don't Park Your Brain Outside

All I did was say, "Let's plan the project this time."

Once we have an initial plan in place, we need to continue developing and refining it to reflect ongoing changes, feedback on actual performance, and the changing project environment. It is extremely unlikely that all of the assumptions and guesses that went into the original project plan were correct at the start, so we will need to adjust for reality as we progress.

This means that the project plan needs to be a living document. It is important that we manage expectations around this idea from the outset. There seems to be an almost irrational expectation that projects behave differently than anything else in this world. While we know that circumstances will change, and even the simplest operations can go awry as a result, we deny this possibility on projects!

 Planning does not stop until after the project is done.

The plan itself has little value unless we work with it in the implementation of the project. Sounds silly to say this, because it is so obvious. But think about how many of the projects on which you've worked actually followed the plan. How many of the team members have seen the budgets (at least the bit that relates to what they are doing), the schedule, and the scope of work. How often do people at the sharp end of a project see the specifications for the final product? Surprisingly rarely, truth be known!

We need to measure what is being done against what was planned. On larger projects, and mandated on certain government and other projects, is a process known as earned value, a technique used to compare planned performance with what was actually done and what was expended to do it. In itself, it is a powerful tool traditionally used to help determine where you are in your plan. It is one way to measure progress against a plan.

As you will see later in SMART Project Management, we take the idea further. In SMART, we do not need to figure where we are in our plan; we already know. The worth of earned value lies in determining if we will still be on target in the future. Either way, we need a feedback loop to determine our progress with the project. Control loops are common in many engineering applications; the one we use every day is the thermostat. The wires connect the control device to the thing that is being controlled. Without the wires, the controller is useless. We need the equivalent in our projects. The wires carry information to and from the controller. Information conduits are a key part of effective project control.

 Control of a project requires a closed loop. Without feedback, control has no impact on the project. Feedback is information that needs to reach all of the right people so that we can correctly influence the future of the project.

Many of the numerous project plans that I've had the privilege of reviewing over the years had a different approach to them than the normal way we actually manage our work. Classically, we develop schedules based on activities. The problem with this is that we have great difficulty in identifying where we are. If, for example, I have an activity with a ten-week duration to "develop user documentation," I have the following problems:

- Exactly what does this mean?
- How do I know when the activity is finished? Who decides?
- How do I know, in week five, say, how complete the activity is?
- What are the chances that I can readily assess progress or required effort and time to complete?
- If someone says the activity is 50 percent complete, how do I verify this?

Information goes in the hopper, and the system produces all of the
reports we need to keep management happy.

If we now take a break from where I am going with this idea, and
look at how we intuitively manage work, we will see how to resolve
these problems. We manage our own work by looking at what we
need to get done. We can normally manage a whole week's work in
this way; we know on Monday what we have to deliver by Friday. On
a day-to-day basis, we know what needs to get done by the end of
the day if we are to be on target for the end of the week. For the day,
we may break into more detail—like what you need to get done by
lunchtime or what you need to do by the end of the day. In other
words, we manage by deliverables, and we break down each deliverable, as we go, into mini-deliverables. If we deliver them, we're on
target; if not, we're late. It is so simple that we probably don't even
think about what we're doing.

So, if this is how we manage, should we not plan that way as well?
It will make the plan easy to follow and implement.

 The way we plan a project and the way we control it are often different, which makes many plans hard to implement and sometimes even seem irrelevant.

Our project plans need to be deliverable based. The next important item to address is the level of detail that we need on a project.

Too much detail, and the plan becomes cumbersome and hard to follow. Yet with too little detail, we cannot assess where we are. Where is the happy medium? The answer lies in using different levels of detail, dependant on which part of the plan we are working.

Many plans that I see are presented at the same level of detail throughout. We describe what needs to be done in the first week of a three-year project in the same granularity as the last week. While the first week may be easy to predict, and the plan may be reasonably accurate, we can be sure only of one thing in the last week: the plan is wrong!

 It is important to plan at the right level of detail. Too much detail too soon, and the plan becomes too rigid and cumbersome to be useful to the project team.

14.2   Focus on Deliverables for Planning and Control

I've suggested that we should focus on deliverables as the basis for planning. This applies not only to the schedule but also to every other aspect.

Table 14.2 shows just some of the areas where a focus on deliverables can help in management of projects. If we are consistent and careful in doing everything based on deliverables, we can streamline the project management process. Coordination between tools and processes becomes simple and even automatic. As deliverables are the core of this approach, they can be used as a reference point for collection and collation of just about any information on the project.

 The only project element that constantly remains throughout a project and is linked to every key component of good project management is the project deliverable.

Don't Park Your Brain Outside

	Deliverables Approach	**Tools to Use**
Planning	Define the success of a project in terms of what needs to be delivered. Lay out on a timeline when each deliverable is needed for efficient project completion. Break each larger deliverable into smaller pieces as needed to describe the plan in more detail as work becomes current.	Deliverables breakdown structure (DBS), 3-D schedule, and RACI+ chart
Scope Definition	Only those deliverables identified as part of the project are included in the scope. Specifically exclude deliverables that you will not deliver but that someone may expect.	DBS
Schedules	All actions must produce something; if they don't, why have them? Tools marked with an asterisk (*) need to be deliverables, not activities, based.	3-D schedule, Gantt chart*, CPM schedule*, and RACI+ chart
Budget	Price out each deliverable. Break estimates and budgets into deliverables. Once you start collecting actual costs in this way, future estimating is easier and can be done without changing the basis of the estimate as more detail becomes available.	Estimates*, budget*, RACI+ chart, and DBS
Risk Management	Assess risks for each deliverable. Assign contingency (alternative plans, money, resources, and float) to deliverables.	Project dashboard (Carley chart), Monte Carlo risk analysis, and other tools (see Chapter 9)
Communications	Plan communications based on who needs to be involved in each deliverable or mini-deliverable.	RACI+ chart and checklists
Progress Assessment	Break deliverables into mini-deliverables as needed, and reassign budget, effort, and time. Are deliverables done?	Project dashboard (Carley chart)
Team Motivation	Assign responsibility for specific deliverables. Recognize achievement as deliverables are completed.	Progress meetings
Expectation Management	Expect only the deliverables that are included in the project plan. Manage expectations around each individual deliverable.	All of the above tools
Continuous Improvement	Learn as you go what is involved in producing a deliverable. Identify risks and shortcuts. Reuse this learning on the next similar deliverable on this or other projects.	Checklists, templates, and samples of similar projects

*Conventional project management tools adapted to deliverables based

Table 14.2   Use of Deliverables in All Aspects of Project Management

To avoid any confusion, we need to understand what a project deliverable is. In SMART project and program management, we specifically mean anything required for the successful completion of the project. I like to put a client orientation on this: all deliverables need to add value to the client—either directly or indirectly.

For example, on a software project, deliverables may be based on end-product items like reports, documentation, input screens, and specific functionality. Indirect components would include testing, code, sample data, approvals of proposed screen layouts before the coding is done, system architecture, and specific reviews by the client or others. Anything that contributes to the project by adding value, involving and getting ownership of key stakeholders, or eliminating rework, for example, may be a deliverable.

Each deliverable needs to have a physical component to it. An approval, for instance, needs a document—perhaps with a signature—confirming the approval and its circumstances.

 Project deliverables are those things that need to be produced in order to satisfy the client and other stakeholders in the successful delivery of a project.

Managing projects by deliverables leads to a more cohesive approach to both planning and implementation. More than this, it also makes both the planning and delivery of projects easier. The planning process now has a few steps leading to a project charter. The content of the charter will depend on the type of project, but it likely will have at least a deliverables breakdown structure (DBS), a 3-D schedule, and a risk register. Other project charter components will be included if it makes sense to do so. (Contents and tools are described in Chapter 8.) The project charter map in Figure 14.2 shows a number of elements that could appear in a project plan. Using deliverables allows us to crosscheck details from the different components of a plan. Once we have a plan for a project, it automatically becomes a template for other similar projects, expediting the planning process. If we develop our deliverables and mini-deliverables with care, we can reuse these deliverables on future projects, again speeding up and simplifying the planning process.

 Plans are much easier to prepare if they are deliverables based.

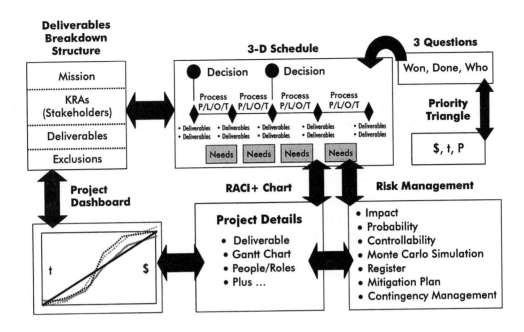

Figure 14.2 Project Charter Map

Once we have a plan referring to deliverables as the basis for schedule, budget, scope, and quality, it's easy to know what needs to be worked on in the project and when it needs to be delivered. There is no second-guessing or ambiguity.

We'll look at the mechanics of planning and managing projects using the SMART approach in the next few sections. We've already seen in Chapter 8 what goes into a SMART project charter and how to put it together. What comes next?

14.3   Important Metrics and the Priority Triangle

In preparing the project plan, it is worth understanding the key drivers for the project. Which is most important: quality and scope, cost, or schedule? I have deliberately lumped together scope and quality, as sometimes it is hard to differentiate between them. For example, adding functionality to software is considered by some a change in scope, and, by others, simply a shift in quality. Similarly, deleting granite cladding from a set of columns in a new building may fall under either heading. Different people may consider a cameo spot by a well-known star in a TV series to be a quality enhancement, and someone else may categorize it as a change in scope.

Now we have three variables to prioritize if we are to make tactical decisions aligned with the project priorities. Give a project manager any set of requirements couched in terms of all three of these variables, and she will probably be able to deliver on two. Put another way, let me restate and paraphrase the sign in a hardware shop in a small town in the mountains near Calgary:

You can have it fast, cheap, or good—pick any two!

In order to get a sense of a client's priorities, we may have some work to do. Most clients take the position that all three of these variables are equally important, which puts project managers in a very difficult position. It doesn't matter what decision we make, it will be wrong, because we will almost inevitably compromise one of the variables. I now use the priority triangle, as illustrated in Figure 14.3. This simple tool originated as a research instrument to test where people were focused at different stages of a project. (The results are interesting and useful enough to repeat here, so I will give you a summary in a moment.)

The priority triangle in Figure 14.3 is drawn as it is because we want to shorten schedule (t), maximize quality and scope or performance (P), and keep costs ($) down. The *no-go* zones are to keep people from putting an X where doing so creates ambiguity. We use the triangle to allow stakeholders—especially the client—to identify where they think the focus should be on these three variables. If they were to put the X in the center, they would be making all three variables equally important. The closer the X is to a corner, the more important that corner. The corners are not acceptable locations, as they leave the opposite two corners with the same level of priority. Similarly, the midpoints between corners should not be used. That leaves six white areas. The X in Figure 14.3 tells us that the person who put it there ranks performance as most important. Time has second priority, and cost is third on the list. If these are the project priorities, then we know that we should spend money where necessary to maintain performance (quality and scope) and, wherever possible, maintain schedule. If something will take a bit longer to get right, that is the better way of going rather than trying to rush and compromise on performance. This is a simplistic view, because we know that priorities will differ depending on our roles, where we are in the project, and on what we are focused at the time.

In the end, however, our planning and implementation of any project will be influenced by what we believe to be priorities. As we

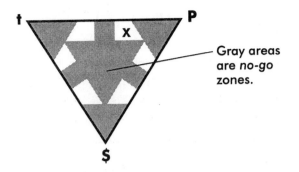

Figure 14.3 Project Priority Triangle

assemble the detail of the plan, we will make calls on whether to spend money on overtime, whether the risk associated with fast-tracking is worthwhile, whether part of the scope can be compromised in order to stay within budget, and a myriad of other decisions. If our thinking on what is important to the client is incorrect, we will not produce the best plan. As this type of thinking is not immediately apparent on the surface of the plan, the client may approve it, and we are on the path to project failure.

 Good planning and control reflects what is important to the success of the project.

I mentioned the little study I did to understand priorities on projects; Table 14.3 presents a simplified summary of its results. It is a fairly coarse summary, looking at some 140 projects in different industries. We interviewed representatives of the sponsor organization (client), a consultant to the project, and a major contractor or supplier of goods or materials.

In Table 14.3, the symbols (such as $ > t > P) tell us which of the three variables of performance (P), cost ($), and time (t) is more important. The first symbol is the most important. Subsequent symbols are of lesser importance if there is a > between the two, and they are of equal importance if there is an = between them. Although not a strictly scientific study, the review did show significant consistency over projects, regardless of the industry or project type, so we can reasonably conclude that a degree of predictability exists. If you look at Table 14.3, you should find that the pattern rings at least partly true for most of your projects.

Timing: Project Phase	Client Priority	Project Manager Priority	Consultant Priority	Contractor Priority
	Profit:	Usually Not Involved	Not Involved	Not Involved
Concept	$ > t > P Overall Value:	Usually Not Involved, But If So:	Not Involved	Not Involved
Project Approval	$ = t = P Urgency of Delivery, Performance of Product:	$ > t > P Need to Plan and Deliver Performance Product:	Performance and Time to Get It Right:	Usually Not Involved
Design	t > P > $ Overall Value	t = P > $ Design Is Complete and Late:	P > t > $ Try to Complete Design and Watch Costs:	Cheapest wins!:
Contractor Selection	$ = t = P Overall Value	P > t > $ Can we deliver for the price?	P > $ > t Compliance to Design:	$ > t > P Make a Profit:
Start of Implementation	$ = t = P Overall Value	P = t > $ Whose fault is it?	P > t > $ Don't blame me!	$ > t > P Will I get paid?
First Major Changes	$ = t = P Overall Value	$ = t = P Will it work?	P > $ > t Will the client be happy?	$ > t > P Let's get out of here as quickly as possible!
Close to Completion	$ = t = P Overall Value	P > t = P Will the operators complain?	$ = t = P Where is my project?	t > $ > P Will I get paid for all the work I did?
Completion	P = t = $ Performance of Product:	P > $ = t How do I make this project look good?	P = t = $ How do I make this project look good?	$ > t > P Am I still owed something?
Follow-up	P > t > $	P > $ > t	P > $ > t	$ > t > P

P = Performance $ = Cost   t = Time

Table 14.3 Priority Alignment on Projects

We can learn from this. First, the focus of stakeholders is different at any point in time; there is little overlap in priorities. This can lead to misunderstandings and conflict.

Our priorities also change over time. If we look at specifics, we also see a tendency for priorities to be different concurrently for the same stakeholder. For example, during the design phase, the designer may be more concerned about performance on a critical project component but more concerned about schedule on production of technical specifications, and cost is a priority in developing some of those specifications.

 What is important in the short-term changes over time and by stakeholder. It is rarely aligned with what is important to the project overall.

To keep things in perspective, we need to identify the relative priorities of the client for the overall project. This should remain fairly constant but can change. Because a change in priorities will influence how decisions need to be made, we should check from time to time. The project dashboard should have a gauge that keeps such information in our range of vision all the time; include the priority triangle on the project dashboard.

 The priority triangle helps us focus on overall project priorities, and lets us develop a strategy that is congruent with the expectations of the client.

As we've learned, the classical metrics on a project are quality and scope, cost and time. To this we can now add one more: priorities. Others that we've considered elsewhere in this book include stakeholder alignment, risk, team effectiveness (such as tribalism), and communication. These are relatively soft measures, but they give us warning of potential future problems. The priority triangle will help us keep an eye on alignment, as well as on shifts in project priority. If the priority shifts, the chances are good that we need to realign at least some of our stakeholders.

14.4 Estimating and Scheduling

This book does not attempt to describe how to best estimate or schedule your project. There are already many books and papers on

Weird—I've tried ninety-eight different scheduling packages,
and the project is still late.

the subject. I want to focus on a few of the considerations to make estimating and scheduling both easier and more reliable. Over the years, we have in many cases separated the functions of planning, estimating, and scheduling. The plan tells us what we are going to do and how. The schedule tells us who is going to do the work and when. In order to get from a plan to a schedule, we need to estimate what will be required. Specifically, we need to estimate effort by people and cost for everything else. Normally we reduce people effort to cost as well so that the overall project cost can be determined. The human-effort component of an estimate is much more volatile than the hard cost of materials and equipment or the fixed price for services, so it is useful to manage it separately from other costs.

If we consider the outlined sequence, we can see that estimating is the bridge between planning and scheduling. In preparing the estimate, the estimator needs to consider what the planner had in mind regarding how the project would be delivered. The estimate needs to reflect the plan; if it doesn't, the plan or estimate will be wrong—by definition! Once we have an estimate, the schedule should use the resources included in the estimate, not more and not less. The schedule should also reflect the plans on which the estimate was based. Scheduling is therefore largely a mechanical process that lays out a plan and estimated resource usage on a timeline. If a critical path method (CPM) is used in scheduling, then we also add logical constraints to the sequence of activities.

Let's consider a simple—trivial even—example. We're going out for dinner, then a movie. We need a babysitter. Our favorite sitter charges $10 per hour. We will be out for about four hours. Dinner will be at our favorite Italian restaurant. The scope of the meal is an appetizer, entrée, and dessert with coffee; the meal budget is $100. The other things we need to consider are:

■ The movie starts at 7:30 P.M.
■ The sitter needs to be driven home.
■ We need to get gas for the car; the budget is $20.

From this, we can see we have a plan and a start on the estimate. To complete the estimate, we need to add all of the components:

Sitter: 4 hours x $10	$40
Dinner	$100
Movie theater 2 x $8.50	$17
Gas	$20
Total	**$177**

With this information, we can put together our schedule. Fixed points are the start and end of the movie. We have to guess the time required to be served a meal and the duration of the movie in the absence of any firm information. Our schedule may look like the bar (or Gantt Chart) in Figure 14.4. Note that this plan is *not* deliverables based, because I want to show how things go wrong. If we did everything based on deliverables, we would just need to check that we have the same deliverables in the plan, estimate, and schedule and that they are aligned.

If we coordinate the information, we can spot the flaws (see Figure 14.4). First, we have a few missing deliverables: Sitter to House, Gas Purchased, Movie Tickets Purchased. All three take time, so we can see that the schedule is wrong. Do we pay the sitter for travel time? Should the consumed gas and any parking fees be included in the budget? We have not necessarily got expectations aligned around the scope or the budget.

From the simple example in Figure 14.4, we can readily see that planning, estimating, and scheduling are related activities.

The estimate needs just one more item added;
then, it will be complete.

 Estimating and scheduling are *not* stovepipe activities. They need to be integrated, and they are easier if everything is deliverables based.

Estimators need to make assumptions about what they are estimating and how the project is to be delivered. This is inevitable, because there will be gaps in the information needed to develop a precise estimate. These gaps include actual information about future events, assumptions about people's productivity, continuity of work, and more. If these assumptions are not discussed and, ideally, recorded for future reference, the next person may make different assumptions.

If planner, estimator, and scheduler are the same person, this problem largely disappears. This assumes that the one person is consistent and can remember the assumptions long enough! The problem remains, however, if the project manager is a different person and does not know the assumptions on which the plans were based. If—

Don't Park Your Brain Outside

as is often the case—different people develop these different parts of the project plan, they should align their assumptions, and discuss the differences. That way, you can capture the best ideas and develop a better (and coordinated) plan.

 The three skills of planning, estimating, and scheduling must work in tandem.

Remember that we talked about ownership of the plan in Chapter 12? Well, it needs to happen here. If the planners, estimators, and schedulers are not part of the project delivery team, we need to allow the project manager and the core delivery team (as a minimum) to review and buy in to the project plan. If they do not, it will not be their plan and working to it will, at best, happen as a token exercise. The best way of dealing with this is to involve the people who will do the work in the planning, estimating, and scheduling process.

 We need to be sensitive to the process that follows planning, estimating, and scheduling, namely, project delivery! Involve the people who do the work whenever possible.

We saw in our earlier trivial example (see Figure 14.4) that there were inconsistencies in the overall plan for our evening out. On real projects, where the process is perhaps not as well understood, or is harder to define and certainly more complex, we will have many opportunities to make mistakes—and it will be more difficult to find those errors. Thus, we need a process to help us plan, and then estimate and schedule the work. The process should make it easier to avoid problems and find errors, should we make any.

Using SMART tools, we know from Chapter 8 that there is a process that we can use to prepare a plan. If you review this process, you will see that we first plan what we need to do (scope) and how we are going to do it (methodology). Then we can estimate the required resources and how best to deploy them. Only when we have done this can we complete the mechanics of scheduling. Scheduling at a high level involves setting milestones, based on reasonable target durations, for getting from the previous one to the next one.

More detailed scheduling can be done using tools like CPM scheduling or Gantt charts. I recommend using Gantt charts within RACI+

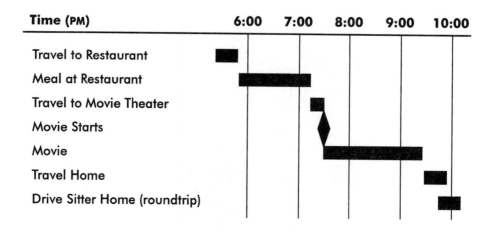

Figure 14.4 Gantt Chart

charts for short-range and CPM for mid-range scheduling. Whatever the chosen tools, we need to have an idea of what we are doing and what resources are required to do the work. For example, if we need two hundred hours to do something that must be completed in two weeks or less, then we can calculate how many resources are needed to achieve it. If we work a forty-hour week, we will need the equivalent of 2.5 full-time people to get the work done in the available time. I use the term *equivalent* deliberately; we need to know the assumption made by the estimator to arrive at the two hundred hours. If she assumed one person working, we need to factor in more time for coordination and for the fact that we will possibly have one person working only part time. This will affect productivity, and we may decide that we really require three full-time people for nine working days, which changes the estimate to 216 hours (3 people x 9 days x 8 hours each). Note how both the schedule and the estimate are different as a result of the interchange.

For the estimator to assess what's involved in getting something done, he will need an abundance of information about the project scope and planned methods for delivering that scope.

 First plan, then estimate, and only then schedule—and remember that it is an iterative process!

     Don't Park Your Brain Outside

This used to be our fiction-writers department, till we started doing projects.

14.5   Risk Analysis and Iterations

So far in this chapter, I have used single-point estimates for time and resources. We know that this is not the best way to work; in SMART Management, we use ranges. We take these ranges, and pick a target usually within the range that becomes the estimate of time, money, or effort toward which we will work. (Arriving at this target was discussed in Chapter 9.) We're going to look at a few of the practical things requiring attention to make introducing risk management into our plans a practical proposition.

When we develop range estimates, we can ask simple questions, and get a pretty good idea of what might influence that range. We then try to minimize the negative influences, and maximize the positive ones. When we do this, we are putting in place a risk management and mitigation plan. Often, such a plan will require new or different resources, changes in timing, and other modifications to the original plan. We need to remember to work these changes through, modify the plan, adjust the estimate, and make any changes to the schedule that may result.

When we have made the changes, we should assess the overall impact on the project. Have we added value or not? Are we spending time and money that is worth spending on eliminating or reducing a risk? If our solution is simply to add money or time to our contingency fund, does the additional burden on the project still leave it viable?

 Risk mitigation is always a tradeoff. Make sure that you are getting value from the mitigation approach you are using.

 When you have put together your risk management plan, check to ensure that the additional costs, resources, and time are included in the project charter and that the outcome ranges are, in fact, better than they were before.

As the project risks are identified, it is useful to add them to a risk register, which should become part of the project charter. It serves several purposes. First, it shows that the risks listed in the register were considered in the planning process. Second, it helps to communicate possible risks in delivery of the project. Finally, it shows the stakeholders what could go wrong and where, identifying the probability of occurrence and likely impact for each of these risks and what is being done about each one.

A common reaction to such a register is that the sponsor may cancel the project. If this is the case, then the project should be canceled. Most investors like to know in what they are investing; understanding the risks involved is an important part of the process. I've not yet found a client who—as a result of looking at a risk register—canceled a project that should have gone forward. I have seen projects canceled, but all of them should never have reached the stage of developing a risk register in the first place!

 Build a risk register. Include all identified risks—even those for which you plan not to do anything.

Any risk register will contain numerous risks; most are likely to occur over a limited time span. The project is therefore only exposed to specific risks at certain times. In other words, at any one time, only a limited number of risks will be *live*. Not only that, but also there will be risks only remotely likely to occur and others that will have little impact, should they occur. Awareness makes it easier for stakeholders to appreciate the likely impact of all the risks in the register.

 Know when a risk is live, and understand what it might do to your project. Ensure that relevant stakeholders understand these risks.

14.6   Changes by Project Phase: Control Issues

Change causes a lot of grief in projects. There are endless horror stories, with change at their roots, about runaway projects, scope creep, claims and lawsuits, and more. Change is often seen in a negative light, because it triggers additional cost and delays that are typically greater than originally anticipated.

Managing project changes has a lot to do with managing expectations. We need to ensure that clients and others understand that the impact of a change will increase over time. Changing the operating platform for a large software implementation will be a relatively small issue (as far as the software implementation is concerned) when the software is still being selected. However, the impact is huge by the time we are in beta test. Similarly, changing a valve from a manually operated one at the preliminary design stage of a process plant or factory is trivial and will not impact the project in any significant way. Doing so after the valve has been ordered has a much larger impact. By the time we are commissioning the facility, the impact could be even more significant if start-up is dependent on the change. All of this is obvious, you may say. But is it obvious to the client who asks for a price on a change, then defers the decision for six months without feedback that there was an expiry date on the original quotation?

 The same change will have a markedly different impact at different stages of a project.

Not only will the same change be more expensive and time wasting as time passes, but it will also be more difficult to implement. Most people do not like redoing something that they have done well once. This seems to be especially true if the change could have been avoided. The result is lower morale and productivity; lower quality is also likely—why bother if they are going to change it anyhow?

It is hugely important that we manage expectations around change throughout the team from client to whoever has to deliver! Any early warnings of change should be passed to those who may be affected, together with recommendations or instructions on how to respond. Such instructions could vary from "stop work" to "continue" with "slow down," or "do something else until we know for certain about the impending change" in between.

Any assessment of the change and its impact should take into consideration all of the factors that have been considered so far, plus a few others:

- impact on work sequence
- need for rework
- impact on morale of team
- how this change affects work methods and availability of resources
- other project deliverables that may be affected by the change.

The bottom line is that it is always best to avoid changes whenever possible. Some are unavoidable, but there are those that we can eliminate in two ways. Some changes can be implemented as effectively—and sometimes more effectively—after the main project is completed. Other changes can be avoided by forcing the issue earlier on, ideally during the planning phase.

To help with the latter, I add 2-D and 1-D schedule components to the 3-D schedule. The 2-D components are definition dates, indicating when each deliverable should be defined—if there is no impact on cost, budget, or schedule. This is not a new idea; it has been used in engineering circles (often at a cruder level) and has been called design freeze dates or similar. The problem is that design freezes tend to thaw in the heat of the moment! Some discipline is important.

The 1-D schedule addition is for decisions. In order to arrive at definitive definitions, we invariably need decisions from the client. The connection between decisions and their urgency and the deliverables that they affect is often lost in normal schedules. The 1-D schedule addition helps preserve the connection by identifying when key decisions need to be made by the client. These decisions often coincide with checkpoints or other decision or review points.

 The later a change occurs, the harder it is to accommodate it, and the costlier it will be in terms of resources expended, delays, and morale of the project team.

Wherever possible, build in early warning systems to help find potential changes, and then trigger the change as quickly as possible, or eliminate it entirely.

14.7 Project Culture by Project Phase

Earlier we saw that the entertainment industry seems to manage and refocus creativity as the project moves from one phase to the next. The objective was to focus attention on what can reasonably be managed and controlled at any point in time. Without appropriate care and attention, we may produce a team culture that is too static or that is not aligned with where it needs to be for project success. Specifically consider identifying with the schedule where the team's focus should be at each phase of the project. Examples could include:

- Planning: Wacky ideas are good!
- Design/project development: Creative but business-like ways of delivering our solutions—but solutions are not sacred (yet)!
- Implementation: Teamwork is the key; how can we help each other be successful?
- Completion: Solve the problems! We are the *can do* team.

Sorry if this looks corny, but sometimes corny is good—if it does what we want. By involving the team in the process and deciding ahead of time where you need to focus team energy, the shift will not look like the project management team does not know what it is doing, and we are in another *flavor-of-the-month* management environment.

Managing the project culture is an important part of the planning and control cycle.

The cultural shift needs to be from creativity at the outset to creative problem solving, then to getting the project done.

Creativity is closely linked with fun. Most of our team members in any knowledge-based project will be there partly because they have an opportunity to be creative. Do not deny them this vital part of their jobs; harness it by focusing creative juices on what we need to accomplish.

At no point do we want to kill creativity, but we do need to channel and focus it where it is most needed.

14.8   Managing Project Variables: A Toolkit

In most cases, we need to measure things in order to manage them. For most business situations, and certainly for projects, we like to measure results. The classical results that we measure are quality, cost, schedule, scope, and safety. Further, we have learned that we cannot wait until the end of the project to determine whether these are likely to be met, because at the end we can do nothing about them! So we try to assess relative performance against the plan. If that relative performance is as good as or better than planned, we will probably meet the targets for the project. If our performance is below what was expected, then we may predict an end result below that which was planned.

 The variables we normally measure on projects are safety, scope, quality, cost, and time.

The value of metrics lies in the accuracy of the plan and in the precision with which we can determine performance to date. Precision needs to be matched with speed if we are to make timely adjustments to the project plan. All three pieces must be present for good project performance assessment. In Chapter 8, we looked at how we to develop realistic plans; now let's look at how we can readily determine where we are in the plan at any point in time. Again, there is a solution. As mentioned earlier, the classical approach is to use a concept known as earned value, originally developed for military projects in the United States. There are both simple and complex ways of calculating earned value; I will stick to the simple one!

 Earned value helps us discover, with a degree of objectivity, where we are on the project plan.

For every deliverable in our project, we have a budget. This budget is in two parts: hard money and work hours. The work-hour portion may well be converted to money by applying a cost per hour. I like to keep them separate, as I normally apply earned value to the work-hour portion only at the detailed level. The hard money portion is much more stable and easier to manage. Work-hours productivity—which is what we measure—is volatile, because we are dealing with people, and we all have good days and bad ones. We are fast at some things and slow at others. This is where we need to focus our management effort most of the time.

 We get the best value out of earned value by applying it to the most volatile of our resources: people.

Now let's work through a simple example for which I will use work hours, but we can use hard money or total budget as the basis for our calculations simply by substituting the other variables. I will also give you the acronyms that are used in many circles, so you can see how classical project management cross-references what I present. Finally, I will point out where the SMART version differs from the classical one and why.

Consider a set of six deliverables (in classical project management, this may be activities). Figure 14.8.1 shows the Gantt chart for these deliverables and the budget and actual work hours up to now, which is week five. The figures above the bars show the budget work hours for each week.

In SMART Project Management, we do not use percentages to estimate completeness of a deliverable. Any deliverable spanning more than one week is broken down into pieces that need to be done by the end of each week in order to be sure that the item will be delivered on time. The budget is then distributed over each week to reflect the required effort (and/or cost) for that particular mini-deliverable. Following is the breakdown for the five deliverables in Figure 14.8.1:

1. Technical Specification:
   1.1 Contents and standard specs. Complete .... 80 hours
   1.2 Specifications complete and agreed with client ... 60 hours
2. Detailed Design
   2.1 Layout of product agreed with client .... 120 hours
   2.2 All drawings ready for coordination .... 160 hours
   2.3 Drawings coordinated and checked .... 160 hours
3. Production
   3.1 Tooling complete .... 100 hours
   3.2 All materials and resources assembled .... 200 hours
   3.3 All product components assembled .... 200 hours
   3.4 Product checked against specs .... 120 hours

4. Testing
    4.1 Validate requirements and test process ready   40 hours
    4.2 Product tested and errors fixed   80 hours
5. Commissioning   80 hours
6. Product Acceptance   20 hours

This somewhat contrived list for making a generic product shows what is expected as a mini-deliverable for each main deliverable at the end of each week. In essence, we now have a weekly checklist of what we need to do by the end of the last workday of the week, and we have the associated budget for work hours. We can easily calculate (based on, say, a forty-hour week) how many people should be involved.

Table 14.8.1 shows some of the basic information we need to calculate earned value. In order to determine where we are on the project plan, we calculate the value earned at the end of each week. In SMART Project Management, this is simply the budget for everything that we have actually delivered by the end of the week. If we use the earlier example, and refer to the numbers in the list we prepared of the mini-deliverables, we can see what we have earned each week by adding the budget for the deliverables completed each week.

We can now combine the information in Figure 14.8.1 and Table 14.8.1 into an earned value chart (see Figure 14.8.2). It is conventionally drawn in a cumulative format with time on the horizontal axis and budget (for work hours in this case) on the vertical axis.

Note in particular that the SMART version of earned value measures schedule variance as the difference (in time) between where you are (earn curve) and where you should have been on the plan. Classical earned value measures this difference on the *time-now* line in terms of budget. I have never been able to understand what being a few hundred dollars late really meant!

Before we leave this section, I have a small acknowledgment. Ken Hanley, a former student and now a colleague and instructor at the University of Calgary, as well as a consultant with KPMG, deserves credit. He first started calling the ACWP (actual cost of work performed), BCWS (budgeted cost of work scheduled), and BCWP (budgeted cost of work performed) curves by simple titles like "Earn" and "Burn"—much easier to understand and work with!

 The earned value idea is very useful to help understand where you are, especially on large and complex projects.

Deliverable	Schedule (weeks)									Budget Work Hours	Actual Work Hours
	1	2	3	4	5	6	7	8	9		
Technical Specification	60	75									135
	80	60								140	
Detailed Design		90	160	140	30						420
		120	160	160						440	
Production				40	160						200
				100	20	20	120			620	
Testing							40	80		120	120
Commissioning								80		80	80
Product Acceptance								20		20	20
Weekly Total	60	165	160	180	190						755
Work Hours	80	180	160	260	200	200	160	80	100	1,420	

Figure 14.8.1   Project Gantt Chart

For most SMART projects, we should already know where we are, because we will know each week if we have delivered the deliverables or mini-deliverables that were due. The real value of a tool like this is to help predict the future. As we need to focus on what needs to be done rather than what has been done, this is an important issue to address. Now let's look at how to adapt the earned value idea into a predictive tool.

You won't be getting a paycheck this time—
we are now doing payroll based on earned value.

The best project managers use tools that help predict what
will happen—not those that tell us what did happen—as
guides to future action and decisions.

Proactive earned value simply takes what we have in the earned value curve and the data that are used to create it and combines it with a RACI+ chart (see Figure 14.8.3 for an example of putting this information on the same page).

The example in Figure 14.8.3 shows a generic RACI+ chart. Let's look at what's on it and how it can help us understand our plan better; then we'll look at a RACI+ chart for our little example.

The RACI+ chart in Figure 14.8.3 has a header that identifies the project, the manager, and the deliverable detailed. The deliverable has a reference number that, if this is part of a SMART plan, tells us exactly where it fits. The number tells us that this deliverable is part of Key Result 2. Under this key result, it is part of Deliverable 4, which has been further broken down into smaller components, of which this is the fifth item (5). The description tells us it is "Major Element." The person

Don't Park Your Brain Outside

Week	Deliverables Delivered	Budget for Deliverables	Cumulative Total Earned Value
1	1.1 Contents of Specifications	80	80
2	1.2 Complete Specifications	60	140
3	2.1 Agreed Product Layout	120	260
4	2.2 All Drawings Ready for Coordination	160	420
	3.1 Tooling Complete	100	520
5	2.3 Drawings Coordinated and Checked	160	680

Table 14.8.1   Weekly Earned Value (Deliverables Based)

responsible for this piece of the project is Amelia Drover. This is part of what must be a very large project with the name, Fred 2-5. Now if we have a lot of these RACI+ charts, are working on several projects, and we drop our folder with them, we can at least sort them! Other useful—and perhaps essential—information would be the latest revision number and when it was last updated, which would help us ensure that we have the latest version.

Now for the detail (see also Section 8.8; some of this material is a repeat of what we covered there):

- Each of the action items should result in a tangible product.
- The Gantt chart should be scaled to show about six to eight weeks ahead. Much more than that, and we are possibly wasting our time trying to accurately predict what might happen at this level of detail.
- As each week passes, eliminate the old week, and add a new week of detail.
- The initials for each member of Amelia Drover's team appear next. Under each person's initials is a letter or a dash.
  - The dash tells us that that person has no role in the corresponding action item.
  - We include the dash to be sure that we have considered the role of that person carefully, and that this is not just an omission.
  - An "R" (and there should be only one per action item) tells us who is responsible for its delivery. An "R" implies an "A," as well.
  - An "A" tells us that this person has to do something. "A" means action; it implies a "C."

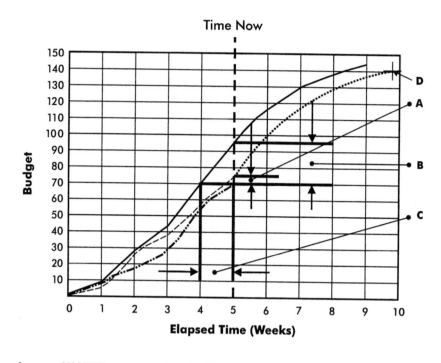

Figure 14.8.2 — Earned Value Chart

Item	SMART Term	Classical Term	Acronym
———	Plan Curve	Budgeted Cost of Work Scheduled	BCWS
– – – –	Burn Curve	Actual Cost of Work Performed	ACWP
–··–··–	Earn Curve	Budgeted Cost of Work Performed	BCWP
············	Forecast Curve	No Specific Term	—
D	Expected Outcome	Estimate at Completion	EAC
A	Budget Variance	Cost Variance	—
B	—	Schedule Variance	—
C	Schedule Variance	—	—

Figure 14.8.2 Earned Value Chart

- ◆ A "C" is for coordination, and we need to coordinate with that person. A "C" implies an "I."
- ◆ An "I" means that person needs to be kept informed.
- ◆ With this, we have two things: a communications road map and a clear understanding of expectations.
- ■ The budget work hours are next. They represent the distribution of expected effort taken from the estimate and applied to each action item, much as we did in Figure 14.8.1.

Now let us look at just one line, which will tell us that the information on this chart is rubbish (in terms of a reasonable plan)! The action labeled "Activity" has two people allocated for action, plus Angela who clearly has other responsibilities. The two people whom

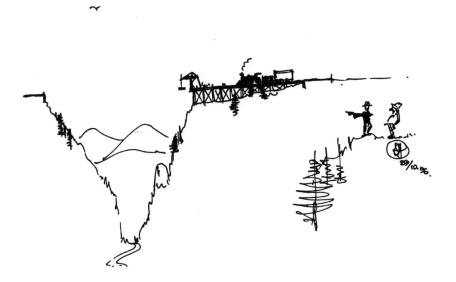

You're right, the bridge is half finished!

we've identified (CM and GH) also have other things going on in week two, so they will not be full time on this action item. If the scale is in weeks, then we need to burn an estimated 120 hours, using two part-time team members over these two weeks, representing an average of thirty hours per person. In week two, CM is responsible for "Another Activity" and has to do something on "Yet Another." GH, meanwhile, is working on "Build Something" in week two. As the only person allocated for action on this, GH has to find 345 work hours in weeks two and three. Clearly the plan is impossible, and we see this because the relevant information is on the same sheet. We've just analyzed the proactive use of earned value. By looking at the work that needs to be done (based on the estimate and validated by the people who are supposed to do it), we can test to see if the resources are available to get to where we are supposed to be in the future. In the example, we can see that these resources are not enough for the task in the available time. Now we can decide to real-locate tasks or change the schedule, or some other combination, to make it work.

Deliverable: _2.4.5 Major Element_   Manager: _Amelia Drover_   Project: _Fred 2-5_

ACTION	DATES	A D	C M	G H	C F	F W	M L	J S	W W	B E	Budget w/Hrs.	Actual w/Hrs.	Budget Cost	Actual Cost
Activity		R	A	A	C	I	I	–	I	C	120		400	
Another Activity		–	R	C	I	A	A	I	A	–	50		50	
Build Something		R	–	A	C	I	I	–	C	–	345		1,500	
Another Item		–	R	C	I	A	A	I	A	–	127		–	
Yet Another		R	A	A	C	I	I	–	I	C	90		9,000	
Design a Bit		R	–	A	C	I	I	–	C	–	55		1,700	
Design More		–	A	R	I	C	C	A	I	I	455		875	
Sneeze		R	C	A	A	I	C	I	–	–	200		7,785	
Gesundheit		–	R	I	I	C	–	–	–	–	65		–	
Another Thing		A	C	R	–	C	I	C	–	–	20		100,000	
Wait for Item		–	I	C	A	A	R	I	A	I	655		–	
More Stuff		R	A	–	I	C	I	A	A	A	80		–	
Finish		A	I	C	I	I	A	A	A	R	12		100	

Figure 14.8.3   RACI+ Chart

Back to our small example; Figure 14.8.4 shows what the RACI+ chart would look like.

In order to put together the chart in Figure 14.8.4, the team would have been identified, and its members would have developed the chart together. Note that it covers the whole of this small project. For many projects, just one RACI+ chart will be adequate for control. The granularity of detail required will be a judgment call by the project manager and her team.

Is there anything wrong with this plan? I'll leave it to you to check.

 Proactive earned value used with a RACI+ chart can help avoid problems by identifying them before they occur and getting team solutions to any schedule, budget, or other problems that may occur.

There are other tools to help us manage a project and measure where we are. All of them are rooted in the project charter. In the next few sections, we will look at some specific tools that are of the greatest value to managers on most projects.

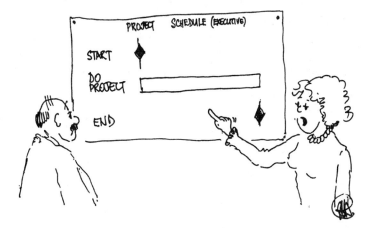

This is about all the detail that the Board can handle.

14.8.1 Project Charter

The project charter was described in detail in Chapter 8 as the document that should tell the sponsor how the project budget will be expended and when and what the inherent risks are in project delivery.

Any project sponsor will expect results from his investment. A good project manager will lay out the project plan and manage expectations carefully. Part of this process is the professional disclosure of progress, changes, options, and other things that may change the outcome of the project. For that we need a starting point: the project charter. We next need a simple, effective, and powerful way of showing what is going on.

 The project charter is the team's license to spend money. Such a license is issued with conditions; a key condition is that the project delivers results.

14.8.2 SMART Project Dashboard (or Carley Chart)

The chart we will examine evolved from implementation of SMART Project Management and the set up of a SMART Project Management office at a large Canadian oil and gas company, Pan Canadian Petroleum Limited (see Figure 14.8.2.1). David Carley is one of the two people from the company who played a very significant part in the success of this

Project: Simple Example   Project Manager: Mike O'Neil   Date: January 2000   Rev: A

Action Item	Schedule (weeks) 1 2 3 4 5 6 7 8	Resources M S K F B S L	Work Hours Budget	Actual	Cost Budget	Actual
1. Technical Specifications	▬	R A C I I – –	140	—	—	—
2. Detailed Design	▬	R A A C I – –	440	—	400	—
3. Production	▬	I C I R A A A	620	—	8,000	—
4. Testing	▬	C I R C I A –	120	—	500	—
5. Commissioning		R A C I A – –	80	—	100	—
6. Product Acceptance		R I I C I I I	20	—	200	—

Notes:

Figure 14.8.4   Example Simple RACI+ Chart

implementation; he also developed the chart, which explains its name. The basic version of this chart is shown in Figure 14.8.2.1.

The project dashboard concept evolved from a need to keep project reporting simple, foolproof, and as free as possible of bureaucracy and the need to rely on accounting or other systems. The dashboard contains the following information:

- schedule (based on milestones and deliverables)
- budget and rate of expenditure
- status of budget and schedule
- predicted future outcomes
- range of likely outcomes
- decision points (off ramps and checkpoints)
- risks and when they are live
- other information, such as:
  - ◆ expected project business performance against original target
  - ◆ priority triangle.

By putting critical information on one chart, we can present a single picture that summarizes the status of a project. The information on the dashboard is generated as a result of developing a complete project charter. The steps are as follows.

Reproduce the 3-D schedule, plotting elapsed time on the horizontal axis and the calendar dates on the vertical axis, which gives you a baseline appearing as a straight line at forty-five degrees. The 3-D schedule will be based on elapsed times that reflect the target durations for periods between milestones at which deliverables are due.

Don't Park Your Brain Outside

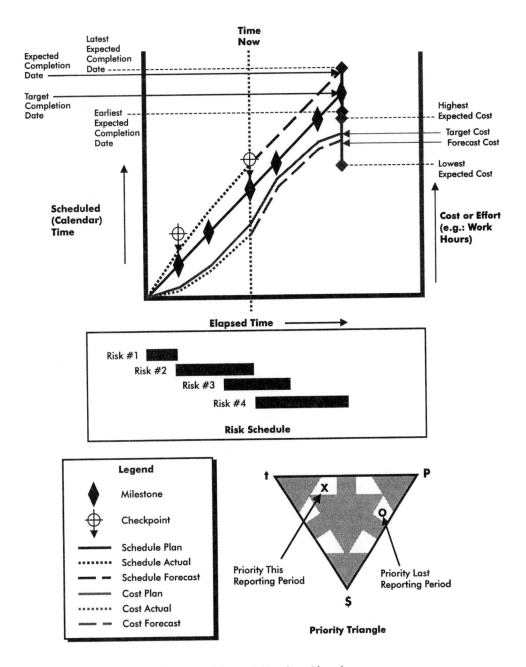

Figure 14.8.2.1 Project Dashboard (Carley Chart)

At the end of the 3-D schedule, plot the range of acceptable outcomes derived from a Monte Carlo risk simulation.

Add checkpoints and decision points. Checkpoints are where the team reports status to the client or the project advisory panel or its equivalent. Decision points are like checkpoints; they are passed if all is as planned, and the objectives and priorities of the project and the business are unchanged. If there is a change, or if the plans have not been made, the decision needs to be made to continue as planned, modify the plan or the project, or even defer or cancel it.

Plot the cash flow or expected work hours (or both), using the same horizontal axis as for the schedule, but a different vertical scale.

Add the range of acceptable outcomes for these at the end of the plot.

Plot where the major risks are live under the main chart, using the same horizontal scale. The thickness of the line will represent the likely impact on the project. In the example shown in Figure 14.8.2.1, each risk carries a reference number (e.g., R1 and R3), which refer to the risk mitigation plan that has been included in the overall project plan.

Add other information that may be useful.

When all of the deliverables for a milestone have been produced, we plot the actual date on the vertical axis against the planned elapsed time on the horizontal axis. If this point is above the plan line, we're late. If it is below, we're early. Similarly, we plot the actual work effort or the money expended at that point. Again, if the point is above the planned line, we're over budget, and if it is below, we're under budget.

To forecast where we are likely to end, there are basically two options. The simplest is to draw lines parallel to the plan but starting at the last actual performance point plotted. This basically says we do not expect the rest of the project to change, despite what has happened so far (see Figure 14.8.2.1). Alternatively, plot a new estimated time and cost line. If this line is different from the original plan, it alerts everyone that there has been a change. The client should be trained to look for this, and ask about the changes and how realistic they may be.

The project dashboard serves to keep the team informed of where they are at the time and where they are likely to end.

If we change a plan to show that we will finish on time despite being late now, the plot of the forecast dates for milestones will not be parallel to the original schedule. This leads to a natural question about how it might be achieved. If there is no additional expenditure, for example (the original budget curve and the current projection are parallel), then any intelligent reviewer of the dashboard will ask some hard questions about the reality of the current plan or the original one. How can we now do things faster than in the planning stages? Why does acceleration not cost more?

Don't Park Your Brain Outside

Basically, if you put the information on one display, it is easier to maintain a holistic view of the project while still paying attention to the detail.

 With this dashboard, it is harder to evade the truth!

Even the collection of data in order to report on the dashboard is simple. Deliverables are delivered, or they are not. We know this from progress meetings. Expenditures, we track through the project's approval process and validate through tracking of committed costs. If we are measuring effort (work hours), we simply do a head count for the project. If we keep timesheets, they provide a degree of validation. Accounting information is notoriously late and can be misleading if the coding is incorrect. The *quick and dirty* head count gives us timely information and is usually good enough for project performance monitoring purposes.

 One of the key elements of the project dashboard is that it keeps the critical information visible with minimal effort and no reliance on complex systems and tools.

14.8.3 Learning from Projects

I regularly hear about the importance of doing a *postmortem* on a project to learn from what went well and where there was room for improvement. I also hear how rarely and erratically such reviews are done. Typically, the team is disbanded, and its members are blown to the winds before we get around to the post-project analysis. If members are still around, the prime reason is likely to be because they are busy on a new project and so won't have time for a look back at an old one!

Instead of a look back at the end of a project, it is more useful to continuously look back at the current project—while memories and detail are still fresh. This can readily be done at weekly progress meetings. The focus must be on what we can learn, which should be based on deliverables because we want to depersonalize them. There should be no blame. We need to recognize opportunities for improvement as well as innovation and opportunities to repeat successes. This fits well with a carefully thought out recognition plan, and it is part of having fun.

The trouble with a postmortem on a project is that the project is already dead!

 The key to effective corporate learning on projects is to make the learning process both a normal part of the project delivery methodology and something that can be of immediate value to the team that learned the lessons, as well as to others.

14.8.4 **Managing Scope and other Changes**

We discussed changes and managing them in Section 14.6; now we'll look at the mechanics of managing a change. Changes are quite often a matter of opinion, so the first step in management of project changes is to define the project so clearly that a change can be recognized in the first place. There are two ways of doing this. One is to fix the scope, and the other is to fix cost and schedule. If we can fix the scope (and quality), we do so through the DBS; anything that is properly identified in the DBS is a part of the project. We carefully exclude what is not in the project by defining and listing specific exclusions.

This approach may not work on some projects or some parts of projects. The reason is simple: we cannot yet define the scope or quality of the end product or deliverable.

The second method comes in two steps. The first is to generally describe the intent of that part of the project we cannot properly define, and state that we cannot yet clearly define it; this helps manage expectations. The second step is to make the best assumption of the probable cost or schedule impact on the project. This will manifest itself in the form of a large PLO (perfect, likely, outrageous) range in our time, effort, and cost estimates.

We quite easily detect a change in the first type of project or deliverable within a project: what we are now doing no longer meets the original description. In the second case, we need a bit more care. Incompletely defined deliverables must be stewarded more cautiously. We allow the deliverables to be defined over time, always watching the updated estimates (yes, we do have to update these as new information allows) to see where they fit in the original range. If they stay within the original range, and the likely converges on our target schedule and cost, then we don't have a change. Anything else constitutes a change to the project and needs to be processed.

Don't Park Your Brain Outside

The first step in effective management of changes is to know that something is different.

Once we have identified a change, the next step is to determine whether there is any choice with accepting it or not. If there is a choice, we need to present it to the right authority to approve, reject, or modify. If there is no choice, we need to present the impact to the sponsor with due speed and care. The sponsor can then decide whether to accept the change or alter the project to accommodate it, by compromising or modifying another part of the project or even canceling the whole thing. It is usually good practice to offer recommendations for action in the event of any change when presenting to the decision-maker.

We need to consider business, technical, and social issues, a balance that was discussed in Section 14.6, when assessing the impact of a change and the possible implications on the project.

 Successful management of changes requires a balanced approach that considers technical, business, and social issues. Not everyone will have the same focus, so managing expectations and alignment are also important.

Change is invariably with us on projects; we should be prepared to manage it. The easiest way to accommodate change is to build flexibility into the project plan. The converse of flexibility is rigidity, and the most common form of rigidity in a project plan is planning at too great a level of detail too far out into the future.

Flexibility in a project plan usually pays off.

14.8.5 Getting a Project Done

Next to starting a project, this has to be the hardest thing to do. At the end of a project, we have run out of steam. We may be facing unemployment or uncertainty about our future. We may be in a position where our team is breaking up faster than we can afford, because the best folks are moving onto the next opportunity rather than risking it going by while they finish the current project. These and other issues create challenges for the project manager and the team.

After starting a project, getting it finished is the hardest thing to do.

Many of the best project managers treat the end of a project as a new project, infusing a fresh spirit of enthusiasm into it. They refocus the team by replanning and, if necessary, redefining completion. If there are contractors involved, it sometimes pays to renegotiate the terms of their contracts. Often there are favors to pull in or useful deals to be made that provide an incentive to get done.

 Treat project completion as a mini-project within a project. The last part of a project needs a *fresh start* with new enthusiasm and possibly different or modified objectives.

14.9   SMART Project Planning and Control

What have we been doing in this chapter? The main point is that a clear focus on what we need to deliver does several things for us:

- Helps define success.
- Keeps us focused on what needs to get done.
- Makes both planning and measurement easier.
- Ensures a common language for the most important issues on a project.
- Ensures that planning, delivery, measurement, and change management are all done on the same basis, using the same tools.

 The first thing that makes this approach SMART is its focus on deliverables.

SMART planning is based on how we intuitively manage. We are accustomed to managing by deliverables; it is the approach of choice for most of us. We understand it; it is so natural that many of us do it without even realizing that this is how we manage our material lives and businesses on a day-to-day basis.

Don't Park Your Brain Outside

SMART project planning and control requires that we plan the way we manage and control.

We've put together a set of simple and scaleable tools that give us all the key information we need to effectively manage our projects. They are not stovepipe tools, meaning that they do not deal with just one aspect at a time such as schedule, budget, or scope. They provide a way of integrating and cross checking information.

 Planning and control should be simple and easy. We do not need most of the complexity—even on large projects.

With this understanding of SMART planning and control, we can now look at the remaining issue for good project management. We need a good and nonbureaucratic administration, as it gives us our audit trail and provides the records needed for good business practices.

Chapter 15

ADMINISTRATION

Trick question: What is the difference between administration and bureaucracy?

Answer: If you aren't careful, nothing! When the administration of a project gets in the way of doing the work, the perception is generally that we have been overtaken by unnecessary bureaucracy.

Have you ever worked on a project where people:

■ asked for apparently useless information
■ required reports that seem to disappear into big black holes
■ demanded that forms be completed for every little thing
■ imposed seemingly endless *project reviews*
■ set up time-wasting meetings
■ insisted on lots of *coordination* that seems to have no purpose?

If so, you are not alone! The question we need to address is: Do these things just get in the way of progress, or do they have some real value? Which things do we really need to do? What is the value in them?

We have many stakeholders on our projects, including specialists with different perspectives from ours. They may be lawyers, accountants, or marketing specialists or experts in manufacturing or quality control. Specialists provide value; they may require information and material that is not necessarily obvious to us. Part of effective project administration is to establish the processes and procedures that we really need for each project.

This chapter will cover what processes and procedures we need and how to set them up to ensure success on our own projects. We will look at issues related to effective and good project administration and management. We should gain a better sense of how all of the different pieces of SMART Project Management fit together.

Just so I manage everyone's expectations here: this chapter is *not* about *administrivia* such as how to set up a filing system, procedures for processing an expense report, how to complete timesheets, and what size room you need for meetings!

15.1   Normal Issues in Project Administration

In an ideal world—for people like me at least—we would not have to do any of this administrative stuff! From a practical point of view, however, it is inevitable that we need to do some; the question is, "How much?" The answer lies in addressing the question of value to the project and the business. We need to provide the infrastructure—to support communication, record-keeping, and risk management—that allows us to get on with needed work while protecting the business for which we work. Records need to cover the right material and be retrievable. Good stewardship of money requires adequate accounting and management of expenditure, and we need to understand the normal business risks that we are taking, so we can mitigate them as effectively as possible.

 Project administration is an integral part of managing any project. Think of it as good housekeeping.

I once had the privilege of working with a very wise accountant who was CFO in a company I was running. When he joined the firm, the first thing he did was stop producing *all* accounting reports that were required weekly or monthly from various people across the organization. When I complained that my managers would not be able to do their work properly without the information, he said I was probably quite right. He had produced the reports, simply not issued them, because he wanted to see who asked for them. The reports that were not claimed were the ones that were not being used. If they were not claimed for three reporting periods in a row, we stopped producing them. In some cases, we asked how the manager was able to manage without the information. We uncovered both mismanagement and exceptional management skills. For example, one of my project managers tracked committed costs because he knew that the accounting system could only deliver expended costs, and the information came in many weeks too late. He noted whether bills were paid by checking both internally with accounts payable and with subcontractors and suppliers. The latter check showed concern for suppliers' cash flow and endeared him to them; they would bend over backwards for him. At the end of the day, we eliminated almost two-thirds of the previously produced reports and got better management practices as well!

On most projects, accounting information is valuable at the end of the project and for an audit. It has little value for managing money, cost, and expenditure. We do the managing when we make decisions and award work.

 A minimalist approach to administration is a good idea, as long as you know what minimum really is!

Project administration, over and above corporate administration, helps keep team members informed of what is going on, and vice versa. In the process, we want to capture the transmitted information in a concise and retrievable form. For this we have procedures that are unique—although they may be similar—to every organization.

 Project administration is about managing information and record-keeping.

The need for communication is driven by the need to keep team members aligned, avoid duplication of work or oversights, and keep everyone engaged. If we want to feel part of a team, we need to be *in the loop* for information. Typically, most of us prefer to know more about what's going on than we really need to know. A bit of human interest also spices up the exchange of information!

In the Toronto construction industry, there is a saying that if you've not heard a good rumor by noon, you should start one! On a geographically distributed telecommunications project with operations in Canada, France, Germany, and the United States, we started an electronic scuttlebutt on the projects' virtual water cooler, where you could wander (on the intranet) to gather information on the project. Just to make life a bit more interesting, and to get people to visit the site, there was a rumor board where outrageous rumors about people could be posted. The only rule was that the information must be untrue! The idea was to post a rumor about anyone whom the team felt was not paying attention. Once the individual heard the rumor, she seemed more inclined to visit the project web page. Note here the balance between the use of technology, the business need to get people to communicate, and the social component to encourage the behaviors that promote the communication.

 People make projects happen. Administration should support this in every way possible while still meeting business objectives.

Project administration needs to be set up to address the needs and expectations of the project stakeholders. One example of this is the need to allocate costs to specific cost codes. There can be many reasons for the way we structure our cost codes; read the sidebar, A Capital Idea?, for one story.

Harnessing the expertise of the whole team and using it to identify the risks and opportunities on the project are important. Then we look at how we can eliminate procedures that add less value than the cost of administering them. Countering this is the need for reasonable precautions against human error and other human weaknesses.

 Business objectives require a foundation of support, checks, and balances commensurate with the risks being taken and the expectations of shareholders and other key stakeholders. This includes the taxman!

15.1.1 Documentation

Whether for general reference, historical value, audit, self-protection, contractual reasons, or any other reason, we need to be sure that each decision and the expected impact on the budget, schedule, quality, and scope of the project is documented. This should be a formal record if the impact is viewed as significant at the time. If not considered significant, the minimum would be to make a note in your diary that the decision was made, and the expected impact was not significant.

Surprisingly often, decisions are made, and the impact on the project plan is not fully assessed and documented. Quite often this is because it's not easy to determine the expected impact at the time. If this is the case, the least we should do is document that we cannot determine the impact. We may wish to add a guess as to when such a determination may be possible. The point is that we should not

A Capital Idea?

A large manufacturing company expanded its facility at a cost of about $250 million. The cost codes used were those suggested by the construction manager, as they aligned with the way that the project control budget had been put together. The owner's accounting department was never consulted on this trivial matter.

However, when the project was complete, one of the accountants asked about assignment of capital expenditure to different categories. Was the work part of the structure of the building (one rate for expensing the capital), or was it part of the process (a faster rate)? The tax rules had been ignored by the designers and the contractors, as well as by the in-house engineering team. The result was a bit more efficient in terms of capital expenditure (by about $2 million) but had cost the company almost $10 million in lost tax breaks (or in additional taxes, depending on your view).

Just one example was a small additional cost of one support for a conveyor system. (At the time, the system was supported on the building structure.) This transferred the entire conveyor system from *process* to *structure* with a tax implication worth many times the cost of the additional independent support.

allow a decision to be made in complete ignorance. If the decision must be made before the real impact can be assessed, this constitutes a risk that should be documented.

 All major decisions or ones that materially affect the expected outcome of the project should be documented, together with the rationale that led to the decision at the time. Document all changes to the plan.

As project managers, we are responsible for the investment of time and money into change. We should therefore be careful, and treat this process in the same way that we would expect of others if they were entrusted to spend our money. What does this mean? It's easy to work out, if we look at any significant expense we may face in our private lives. (We are using the Idaho Test again!) Consider, for example, a significant repair to a car or house. Here is what we are likely to expect, and (surprise!) also what the clients on our projects expect:

- If there is a change, or something that was not expected, we want to know what the impact will be on completion time and on how much we have to spend. If it is significant enough, we may have to adjust other plans for other projects, find alternative ways of financing, and may even need time to adjust to the shock of the change!
- If there is an option for how to proceed, we want to know what those options are, and we want to be able to make an informed decision. We certainly do *not* want someone else making that type of decision on our behalf.
- We probably expect the original budget to be fairly accurate. If we are quoted what looks like a firm price, we do not expect to pay more. If we are given an approximate price, we make our decision based on other criteria, such as an assessment of competence or based on past experience with the person or organization with whom or which we are dealing.
- Generally, we appreciate being told what is going on. The sooner we are aware of a problem, the sooner we can respond to the situation—and we probably have more options at that point too.
- We do not really want to know what the contractor or mechanic's problems are; we want our job done.

Basically, we need to keep our client in close touch with the project. Yet, just as we probably do not want all of the fine details about what is going on with our kitchen renovation, so we probably don't want to tell our project clients everything. It is quite easy to get a feel for what a client wants by walking in his shoes a short distance.

 Remember that we are spending someone else's money. It is reasonable for the spender to expect an accounting, especially when the expenditures were not in accordance with an approved plan.

Over the years, I've found that keeping a record of any significant deviation from the project plan and the expected outcome, together with the reason for the change, has paid off. There are several reasons:
- My memory is not the best. I cannot remember what I was doing on 17 June 1998 without going back to my diary. Can you?
- If I have a record of what happened, and the record is both contemporary and tamperproof, it is good evidence of my understanding at the time. If I acted reasonably and professionally at

the time and know what I did, I'll be able to justify the decision or defend a position. (Yes, we do need to be bulletproof!)

- The records should tell who was informed and of what, when.
- The records should document any other relevant information, such as who was consulted in the decision process and what information was available that is unclear from other records.

If information is documented in meeting minutes, correspondence, or reports, for example, there is usually little point in reproducing it in a diary. Yet, there is a point in doing so if you disagree with the formal record. In such a case, you need not only to keep the record, but you also need to let the appropriate people know that you disagree. Then convince them of your point of view or stand corrected.

 If people need to know what is going on, it is worth documenting the event. Documentation need not be formal: use appropriate levels of record-keeping.

It is not always easy to know what to record. Most of us do not like to be bogged down with documentation. Therefore, use whatever knowledge is around to help steer your assessment of what is worth recording. Your own experience and the stories of team members are both excellent sources of wisdom.

 Knowing what records to keep is partly based on experience. Use the experience of the team.

 The other part of knowing what records to keep is to apply a test: will anyone query this action or decision later? If yes, keep records!

15.1.2 Record-Keeping

For most of us, record-keeping is tedious. Many of the essential records are maintained simply by following good business practices. We account for expenditures through receipts, invoices, payment records, and so on. We keep minutes of meetings. We file copies of purchase orders and contracts, change orders and other instructions to contractors. We keep copies of correspondence. There's no magic to any of this, so we need not pound it to pulp.

A significant amount of record-keeping is a natural outcome of following good business practices.

Where we need to put a bit of effort is in capturing the stuff that does not get caught through normal processes. The three most useful techniques for this are outlined; in order of value (in my opinion), these are professional diaries, communication confirmation, and personal notes.

A professional diary has three distinct features: 1) the right hardware, 2) the right style, and 3) appropriate content.

Hardware is the book you use. It needs to be tamperproof and robust. I use acid-free paper for a hardbound book with blank, lined and numbered pages. (I get mine from Lee Valley Tools.) At the end of each day, I draw a line across the bottom of the last record and enter the next day's date. There are no large blank sections and never more than one blank line. The layout should be neat. I try to always enter information on the day that the event occurred. Most important, however, is the content itself.

Content is useful in two ways. First, it is a reminder of what happened and what you understood at the time. Second, it is evidence of what you perceived, decided, and so on. As evidence, it becomes something that will be shared with others; in a lawsuit, it becomes public domain. The content should be written with its possible future use in mind. Be objective; stick to facts. If you include opinion, be professional and identify the opinion as such (i.e., state that it is not a fact).

 Professional diaries not only help in keeping a record of what is important to you but can save an inordinate amount of subsequent argument. The key to their power lies in consistent, tamperproof, honest, and objective reporting.

In my contracting days, I got into the habit of confirming telephone and field instructions in writing. This habit grew out of following client directions (or what I understood to be such) and then not getting reimbursed for the additional expense involved. If either party misunderstood the instruction and consequences, the written version quickly brought out the difference in perception. All too often, it seems that we have selective memories. It pays to record decisions and instructions and ensure that the other party has a chance to respond to your understanding.

My mechanics involved keeping a pad of four-part, carbonless copy forms to identify who was involved in the communication, what type it was, the time and location, and a summary of what was discussed. The original went to the person with whom I'd communicated, the next copy went into the project files, the originator kept the third copy, and the fourth one went to anyone else who needed it. Photocopies can be used for any additional requirements.

 Records of verbal communications serve to document what was discussed and agreed while confirming understanding of intent.

I have often been reminded—sometimes many years later—of how much someone appreciated a handwritten thank-you note. It is personal and shows a degree of care that a commercially printed or typed note does not. Personal notes of any kind can be powerful and very effective ways of communicating both good and bad news. Consider using them, but avoid overusing them.

 Personal notes are, well, personal! They deliver a message of thanks, concern, or anything else with a power that other conventional communications do not have. If you need a record, note what you said in your diary, or keep a photocopy.

We mentioned meeting minutes a moment ago. Let's back up. Who reads minutes? If they are read, who reads them carefully? Do we pick up on items that were not as well recorded as they should have been? How about those statements that are downright wrong? Do we bother to get them corrected? It is really important to read minutes of meetings that we attended. If they are wrong and are not corrected, they—not us—are corrected later!

 It is important to read and respond to minutes of meetings. If you have an action item, act. If you disagree with the way something was recorded, say so—preferably in writing.

 The *best* way to manage meeting minutes is to write them yourself!

15.1.3 Business, Legal and Other Obligations (Safety, Taxes, Regulatory Compliance)

Safety is normally associated with physical safety. Yet, a safe work environment should be one that is safe in every sense of the word. It should be safe for us to do anything that will help the project or the business be a success, provided it does not compromise the physical safety and well-being of others. What we do must also be legal; typically, if it is not legal, it will compromise the safety or well-being of others. *We should never compromise on safety.*

If we cannot safely achieve a particular objective as planned, we should change the plan. If we take shortcuts around safe practices, it's to save time or money. If the result is damage to a person, we really need to ask: "Was it worth it?" I have yet to find a situation outside war where the damage can in any way be justified. Even then ...

 Safety—in the broadest sense—should never be compromised.

A quick story: I was once asked to prepare a database including all of the regulations for a particular industry by an association serving that industry. The request was canceled a few days later. Why? First, the number of regulations were increasing so fast that whatever we produced would be out of date in a matter of weeks. Second, the cost of compliance could be kept down by not knowing all of the regulations. The chances were good that the regulating agencies would not know either!

Many of our regulations are being overtaken by technology—or by irrational thinking. Let me give you an example. In one jurisdiction, the use of plastic pipes for water is not permitted in ceiling spaces above publicly accessible rooms, because plastic is a combustible material. Thus, sprinkler-system pipe must be made of metal. In the same jurisdiction, it is acceptable to run as much electrical cable, telephone wire, security system, and control wire as you want in the same space. How is this wire coated for insulation? With plastic. Which of the two is likely to be a hazard? The wire—if the pipe melted, it would release the water it contained and, chances are, help put out the fire. This is especially true if the routing of the fire system was such that other areas requiring sprinkler water would not be deprived of water by that pipe's failure (the only reason you might want to have metal pipes).

In another example, a hotel was being built near an airport. The fifteen-floor hotel was under construction, with permits in place, when someone noticed that it was too high for the area. The maximum height (because of proximity to the runway) was five floors. They had to complete construction of a hotel that would never be able to return the revenue that was expected, because it was far too small.

 Regulations continue to be added to an already burgeoning collection in almost every developed country. Large and complex projects will be more significantly impacted than smaller ones. It pays to monitor compliance or obtain specific exemption from regulations.

15.2   Controls You Need

Don't be tempted by project controls for their own sake. Many of the controls we see imposed on projects are there because they have always been done that way. Some are justifiable, from a business or project perspective. Often we do things that add no value and may even get in the way of effective project management. Project controls were discussed earlier; here we look at links between different types of project metrics and controls, so we can see which ones will serve us best.

 Check to see if you are being a control freak! Use only those controls you need to manage your project effectively and in compliance with good business practices and corporate policy. Challenge policy.

15.2.1   Schedule (Milestones, Deliverables, Links, People, Culture and Focus)

The easiest way of knowing if we are on schedule is to know exactly what has to be done each week by the end of that week. If it's done, we're on schedule. We can work in finer detail, such as daily or even hourly requirements. Aircraft maintenance often has an hourly schedule. Running a TV show or a large sports event may have deliverables separated by minutes. Maintenance on a nuclear plant in a radioactive area may be down to seconds. Working with deliverables at the appropriate level of detail helps monitor schedule progress.

At a coarser level, we should know when we've reached a milestone in the delivery of a project. Again, achieving a milestone is readily associated with completion of one or more deliverables, so seeing if we are there is easy.

Knowing where you are on the schedule is useless if you do not plan to do anything about not being where you expected to be.

We can link schedule performance to several things. It affects the rate of spending money, so it will affect both the budget and the cash flow for the project. If either of these do not line up with the plan, then there's a good chance that our schedule is off too, and vice versa. We can also link schedule performance to softer issues such as morale and enthusiasm of the team. This is readily affected by delays. The worst time for a delay is right after everyone has worked extra hard to meet a deadline. It damages morale, makes a mockery of the deadline, and makes it very difficult to build enthusiasm for the next schedule challenge! We can generally get a feel for schedule and performance by being sensitive to the team's enthusiasm for a particular aspect of the project.

Cultural attitudes toward schedule vary as well. Managers, companies, parts of a country, and entire countries may have a different sense of urgency than we do. The sense of urgency will be reflected in how much care is expended in managing time, reporting on it, and even reacting to delays or other schedule changes. The right focus at the right time on schedule is one of the most effective ways of addressing management of schedule. Record delays and their causes. Note additional efforts to catch up, and reward them. Celebrate achieving milestones. But, most important, manage the attitude toward schedule. Shift creativity and enthusiasm away from innovation toward delivery and timely completion.

On a large construction project in Calgary, the project manager decided to emulate what happens in live entertainment. He created a *first night* imperative by announcing a party on *completion day* for all of the people involved in the construction of this large facility. It was announced about six weeks prior to the event. Everyone involved could bring his family and friends to show off the completed project. The result was a shift in attitude, because of a chance to show our families what we did at work. Not only was the project complete, it was also spotless. It was a tangible achievement that team members could show their families. The party cost a few thousand dollars, no doubt, but it probably cost less than the overtime and dragged-out work that normal completion would have cost.

Any acceleration or delay of the schedule will affect many other things too. Keep an eye on the *big picture*.

15.2.2 Cost (Development, Design, Implementation, History, Estimating)

We need to remind ourselves that estimates are best guesses. Ideally, they are informed guesses. The very best estimates are developed based on experience, past performance, and the estimator's ability to visualize how to best use this knowledge in the context of the new project. A lot of effort is being put into capturing the expertise of estimators through expert systems, databases, use of neural nets, and fuzzy logic, and progress is certainly being made in this arena. But the real trick is not in replicating the past but in creating a new and better future.

 Cost estimates are derived from past experience applied to future situations. At best, they are guesses! And they do not necessarily take into account the impact of better solutions.

We normally try to estimate the final cost of a project at different stages in its life. Each time we hope that we will have better information and therefore a better estimate. Again, basing estimates on deliverables helps us determine where the impact of this greater detail in information is affecting the expected cost outcome.

 Our ability to influence cost decreases over time. *Control* shifts from a definitive style to an audit style.

 Do not have too many cost codes. At some point, you start to collect useless information!

 As with all other control, cost is easiest to manage when we plan, deliver, and measure based on deliverables.

It needs to be a real crisis before anyone will actually look at it.

15.2.3 Quality

Quality can be split into two parts: product and process. Think about a great meal delivered with atrocious service—not a good experience. Equally, wonderful service with a terrible meal is a disappointment. We do not change the rules when we become a client on a project, so we need both.

I bought a car that I had looked forward to owning for the longest time, made in England but by a company that is no longer owned in England. The car worked well, apart from a few niggling things that had never been fixed; I could live with it. But I then discovered that the specifications were misrepresented, the product was delivered with a known flaw (a potential fire hazard), and the price had several hidden extras. The service since then has involved joy rides (of about 100 km), theft from the car while with the dealer, and other odd things. For example, the car has two sunroofs: the front one got stuck in warm weather, and the rear one leaked. When I got them repaired, I was told that were two new units; now the front one leaks, and the rear one gets stuck in warm weather. Is this coincidence? Maybe, but after numerous other coincidences and inexplicable events, surprises, and so on, I'm dubious. At one point, I even contacted the manufacturer in England, which suggested that I sue the Canadian company and the dealer!

The quality *process* is important for two reasons. First, we need to keep the client happy. Second, we need to manage the client's expectations. If the process is thought through and validated as one that can reasonably deliver the expected quality, we are not taking any undue risk.

 It is too late to manage quality after we have delivered the product. All we can do is apologize if it is not good enough!

We still see specifications that tell the supplier how to produce the product. Because we know what we want does not mean that we know how to build it! Leave the details to the experts. The best specifications are ones that define the end result, as they leave room for the supplier to respond cost effectively or even offer a better solution.

 Leave production to the experts. Focus on functionality and expectations.

Too many specifications reflect what we did on the last project, or what our consultants did on their last project. This is driven partly by schedule pressures to get something started before we really have time to understand the problem. It is also driven by cost, especially when we ask our designers to be efficient, which often translates into reusing old designs or design elements.

 Understand why technical specifications are the way they are. If the requirements cannot be justified based on safety, value, or some other basis, you probably need to change the specifications.

15.2.4   Safety (Issues and Drivers)

Here it is again, just in case you missed it earlier!

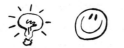 **Safety is important for all sorts of reasons. Never compromise it.**

Bob McTague, president of Optima Engineers and Constructors in Calgary, and one of the wisest people I have had the joy of working with, offers this advice: Safety is about doing things right the first time.

When you think about it, we are after quality, safety, avoidance of rework, and a host of other things. But accomplishing these ends requires planning and careful thought. We can benefit from involvement of the people who will do the work; they know the pitfalls better than anyone.

 Safety is achieved by *doing it right first time*. The benefits flow to everyone.

Safe work environments do not happen by themselves. They require a conscious effort to maintain awareness and sensitivity to the issue. Regular training and inclusion of any safety issues in assigning and discussing work are helpful. The relevance of a safe workplace can be promoted through posters and other media; some people use awards to further promote safety.

 Safety is largely an issue of awareness, which can be maintained through education and continuous reminders. The effort and cost of a good safety program are much lower than the cost of a serious accident.

As a responsible project manager, you should record any significant event involving safety issues, whether they are positive or negative.

 Keep good records of what you do in this area. Record safety training, awareness, infractions, and responses.

15.2.5 Scope

We used a deliverables breakdown structure (DBS) to plan our project. When we have incomplete definition of a deliverable, we should make a stab at defining it, even if we know our guess is probably wrong. Make a note that the definition is provisional. This is important because we can at least estimate and schedule, based on the best guess. When something changes later or is properly defined, we can see the difference between our original assumption and the final item. By showing in some way (I draw clouds around incompletely defined or assumed elements of the DBS) that we expect a change in the future, we are also managing the client's expectations about the precision of our estimates and schedules at the time.

Scope is hardest to manage when you cannot define it! So define it—even if that definition is wrong; at least you have a reference point.

Monitoring the scope of work on a project is more important for those projects that have a tradition for uncertainty, such as software development or R&D projects. It is also important in any environment where rapid technological change or business uncertainty is present.

Monitor scope with great care on uncertain projects or when you are working in a volatile business or technical environment.

15.3   Effective Progress Meetings

I like to run progress meetings on Monday mornings so we can see where we need to be by Friday. There are two other reasons that the first day after the weekend is good. We can run around toward the end of the previous week to make sure that our deliverables are going to be done on time. The other reason is that we have the weekend in which to fix any problems with delivery.

Especially near the beginning of the project, we do not want to get team members into a habit of being late. This is almost a tradition on many projects. We normally start with a fairly ambitious schedule, yet we rarely take the learning curve of a new team into account. The result is that we are late on something by the first week. Usually we accept this, as we have lots of time to catch up, but we have all of next week's deliverables to produce, plus the ones we missed this week. Before we know it, we are running late with something every week. The schedule is now meaningless to most of the team; we have trained it to be late.

We want to train team members to be on time; we must ensure that our progress meetings allow us to achieve this objective. Part of the solution is to have an appropriate schedule from the beginning. The other part is that we do not want any surprises at our progress meetings.

Progress meetings should not have surprises.

We especially want no surprises at the project kickoff meeting. Think of the kickoff meeting as the first progress meeting, to set the pace of the project work. Keep the meeting to an hour or less. If people see that meetings are going to be efficient and useful, they are likely to turn up and be prepared for future ones. I used to keep a collection box for my meetings, as everyone who was late or unprepared had to contribute a dollar. Once in a while, when there was enough money in the box, I would buy a book on time management and award it to the biggest contributor. I cannot remember ever having to buy a second book on a project.

 Part of having efficient progress meetings is to have a fixed agenda.

Following is an example of a progress meeting agenda:

1. What has been delivered this week?	5–10 minutes
2. What have we missed?	5–10 minutes
3. What is the impact on future work?	10–20 minutes
4. What do we have to deliver next week?	2–5 minutes
5. What problems do we foresee next week?	5–10 minutes
6. How do we fix those problems?	10–20 minutes
7. What else that will affect project success needs work?	5–10 minutes
8. Hidden-agenda items	Optional
9. Celebrate success	However long it takes!

Add up the times; the total is more than an hour. Be prepared, and we get a whole lot less. If everything is on target, you get rid of the first three items. If you are prepared, we know the answer to item 4. (Take a few seconds to make sure that everyone has this week's checklist of deliverables in front of them.) Thirty seconds into the meeting, we are starting on item 5 of the agenda. That's a great way to start the week!

 Have a predictable agenda. Stick to it.

The focus of the progress meeting is on future progress. With the SMART approach, we can easily see where we are in terms of what needed to be delivered and what was indeed delivered. If we plan and replan reasonably well, we will have delivered everything to be on target. Making sure that we are still on target next week becomes the focus of our meeting. Then we have time to celebrate success by recognizing the contribution of individuals and groups within the team.

 Be forward looking. Recognize performance. Celebrate success.

Progress (and other) meetings are only useful if you get something out of them. Ensure that everyone gets useful information, such as informing the team about the project as a whole.

Staying motivated and committed to the project in hand is important. Use progress meetings to assess levels of motivation and commitment, and work on maintaining or improving them. Deal with problems. Celebrate successes. Successes include what we have learned from mistakes. Recognition of contributions should be peer based, uncontrived, and unbiased.

 **Take the time to celebrate.**

15.4 Cash Flow

Getting paid is important—duh! If we work with contractors and suppliers, we need to be sure that they are paid promptly. They need constant cash flow out of the business to cover payroll, rent, overheads, and payments to their suppliers. Without at least as much money coming in, they cannot meet these obligations and will eventually go out of business. This does not help us if they play key roles in the delivery of our project.

Many accounts payable departments work on the basis that delaying payment is good practice. Arguably, and certainly superficially, it is. The argument is simple. I hang on to money that is owed to someone else, and I can use it to get a return through investments, such as T-bills or some other vehicle, depending on how much of this type of money I expect to have over the foreseeable future. So where's the flaw? The flaw is in two primary areas: the cost of money to the vendor and the quality of service you get from someone to whom you owe money.

The cost of the goods or services from your supplier includes the cost of it doing business, part of which is the cost of financing. Some suppliers make this cost (and perhaps a bit of a penalty for late payment) visible in their pricing structure by offering a *discount* for prompt payment. The discount represents the additional cost of the supplier providing financing for the purchaser.

In a nutshell, any business needs money in-bound that exceeds money out-bound in order to stay in business. Slow down the money coming in, and working capital increases. If the cash cannot be obtained to cover this additional demand, the company goes under.

 Cash flow is to business what blood circulation is to the body. Stop it, and you kill the corporation.

Again, if we are purchasing goods or services, we need to be sensitive to the supplier's cash flow. If the supplier cannot stay in business because it is cash starved, our project will suffer. If it cannot purchase materials as quickly as we need them, or if it has to downsize staff to manage a reduced cash flow, our project suffers. Prompt payment to suppliers of any type will do two things for us, in addition to keeping them in business. First, it will potentially reduce the cost of the product; it's worth trying to negotiate a discount for guaranteed early payment. Second, it improves relationships. If the supplier can only serve a limited number of clients, which ones will it pick? Clients who pay promptly will get preferred treatment over those who delay, in most cases.

 We need to be sensitive to our suppliers' cash flow, as well as our own.

Our customers also need to manage their cash in order to pay us. If we have a large contract involving large monthly payments, for example, the client needs to ensure that the money is available. If it's not, our payments will be delayed. In these sorts of situations, a project cash flow projection is an essential tool for the client to manage its treasury.

Most companies finance projects out of one or more of four sources: 1) cash flow, 2) operating capital, 3) debt, and 4) equity. The time scale for release of each source of money is different. Cash flow (taxes, revenue) has a degree of risk, as it's usually subject to sales, market conditions, and other factors. Often this source is hedged through use of a line of credit or a draw on operating capital.

Companies don't normally keep large amounts of cash just sitting in the bank; money is put to work. It is invested in anything from T-bills and guaranteed income certificates to new business ventures. It takes time to liquidate such investments or for them to mature. Draws on such money generally need to be planned.

Loans are a second form of financing. Project-specific loans are normally tied to progress, especially if they have been negotiated on a nonrecourse basis. Lines of credit are a bit more flexible but also have practical limitations, as they are often based on a percentage of the current accounts receivable for the organization. Loans take time to obtain. Lines of credit are usually established for filling gaps in the organization's cash flow, so they are faster to access.

Another way to finance projects is raising the money through a public or private offering of company stock. This takes time, requires regulatory approval for public offerings, and either way needs to be sold to the potential investors.

Whatever approach taken by the client, the budget and a reasonable contingency will be needed as the basis on which the money is allocated and committed to the project. If the project costs run away, the allocated funds will no longer cover the cost, and the client has to scramble to find the difference. The harder it is to find this additional money, the slower will be payments and agreement to changes and extras.

 Our cash flow is affected by our customers' cash flow. It is in our best interests to be sensitive to this.

15.5   Business Issues

Just a quick reminder: All projects have their roots in a decision to do something. We rarely do things for no reason. To manage our projects, we need to understand the reason.

From the point of view of project administration, this is important because we will make decisions on how we will manage not just the production of whatever we are doing but also the process itself. The business context will dictate certain things. The type and detail of the records being kept, detail and structure of accounting procedures, frequency of approvals and project reviews, amount of public relations effort required, records to be maintained, and more will be affected.

All projects happen in a business context. We should be aware of the context and how our project influences and is influenced by it.

15.5.1 Marketing

On virtually every project, we buy or sell goods or services at some point. Sales and purchases require two things to be in place: we need to know about the item we are buying, and a relationship needs to exist between the buyer and the vendor.

We do not buy things that we do not know exist. Although this is self-evident, we probably don't think too hard about what it means. Our project will involve products and services produced by others who may well be within our own organization. We will use only what we know, so we need to know what is available if we want the best for our project. We need to be receptive toward new technologies, better ways of doing things, the competition's activities, and the trends for new products and services. We need market intelligence, which takes time and effort.

In addition, we need relationships with suppliers of the goods and services, so we can work better with them and they with us. If we have a good relationship with a vendor, then that vendor will keep us informed of what is new. This translates into less effort for us. If we have previously worked with someone, we can usually rely on the resulting relationship as a foundation on which to build the next project.

Most projects involve selling something to someone. Sales are based on product, price, and relationships. We need to constantly work relationships with our client and our supply chain so they are there when we need them.

 Marketing is no longer a one-way street. Relationships require effort on both sides—albeit not equal effort!

15.5.2 Customer Satisfaction

Much has been written about customer satisfaction, but I want to reduce it to a simple concept, one we've seen before: Our customer will be happy if his expectations are met. Often our customer has more than one representative. Just as often, these representatives do not share the exact same ideas about what constitutes project success. Therefore, we need to stay in touch with and manage expectations.

Don't Park Your Brain Outside

Customers are satisfied if their expectations are met or exceeded.

Project administration involves our client in many ways. We typically communicate at meetings, formally in correspondence, and informally on the job and in social settings. With every contact, we have an opportunity to test client expectations and manage them. Project managers self-select themselves into this career because we are optimists. Optimists paint optimistic pictures of what the future holds. If that's not enough, we've typically been preceded by sales types who have been known to oversell a project. We need to be sensitive to managing expectations of the client back to reality.

While doing a bit of work recently for some homebuilders, the conversation wandered to client satisfaction. Typically, this group of builders had the same experience. The sales people were evaluated as helpful and positive. The building foreman was evaluated as either slightly positive or slightly negative. The poor warranty work foreman was always evaluated as poor or worse. Sales made the promises, and these promises met or exceeded the buyer's dreams. The builder did not deliver on these dreams, so failed to meet them. The good ones worked at managing the customer's expectations and got slightly better evaluations. The poor people who did the repairs and warranty work were always in the wrong; their very presence meant that the customer was disappointed with the product.

 To meet or exceed customer expectations, we need to know what they are, and we need to manage them if they are unreasonably high.

15.5.3 Insurance
On some projects, we need to become involved in the acquisition of insurance coverage, which can cover anything from accidents, fire, and theft to the life of a key person or professional liability. Whenever we have identified an insurance solution for managing or mitigating a specific risk, we need to be certain that the insurance we want can be obtained at a cost that is reasonable for the project. Then we need to be sure that the insurance will work for us. Finally we need to check that we are not unnecessarily duplicating other insurance coverage. (See also Chapter 9.)

Buying insurance means we are farming out risk to others. We need to know what it will cost, and whether we have really got rid of the risk that we think we have insured against.

15.5.4 Bonding

Bonds in this context are assurances by a third party of a second party's performance. There are three commonly used types of bonds: 1) bid bond, 2) performance bond, and 3) labor and materials payment bond. (See also Chapter 9.) A bid bond provides for a situation in which a bidder on a project is the lowest and then withdraws its bid. The bonding company (also known as a surety) then pays the owner the difference between its client's bid (the lowest one) and the next highest bid.

A performance bond provides for coverage to the owner in the event that a contractor fails to complete the work under the terms of the contract. The surety will then cover the cost of completing the work. There may be limitations on the coverage, and the process of obtaining the assistance of the surety can be very tedious and long.

In some jurisdictions and under certain circumstances, if a vendor fails to pay, a project owner is liable for some or all of the payments its contractors owe to subcontractors, suppliers, and labor. If these circumstances exist, a payment bond will help to mitigate the risk, as the surety will cover the cost.

Often, the real value found in a bond is the very fact that the supplier can obtain one. If it can, this is because it's unlikely to ever need it. This is often the basis on which a surety will sell the bond to the vendor in the first place.

On a purely practical point, it pays to remember who the client is for the surety. The client is the vendor or contractor, not the project owner. Often sureties demand additional assurances of their clients. For example, they may ask for personal commitments from senior management or owners of the vendor company to cover the deductible. These deductibles will often be high enough to bankrupt the individuals concerned. As it is bad business to put your client out of business, and better to collect premiums than to pay out, be prepared for long delays and possible legal battles before you get your money from a bond.

If you use bid, performance, or payment bonds, understand the practical issues surrounding their use.

15.5.5 Investors' and Lenders' Concerns

Investors have a right to know how their money is being spent and what the involved risks are. Lenders must have a reasonable expectation of recovering the money they lend, together with a return on the loan. Lenders are usually brokers, lending other people's money. They have responsibilities to the owners of the money to return it, plus interest.

 Lenders and investors do not necessarily understand your business. Expect to take time to explain in *layman's terms* what you do. Treat the money folks as part of your team because they are, whether you like it or not!

15.6   Staying in Touch

Earlier in this book, we looked at organizations and who is on our team. I suggested that anyone who affects or is affected by the project is a stakeholder. Each stakeholder is a potential team member. Stay in touch with people, and you can work with them more easily. Regulators like to know what is coming at them. They can often provide very useful input to your project, saving effort and delays. Contractors have brains! We can take advantage of this little-known phenomenon. The worker bees know more about making honey than you or I do. We can benefit from bringing the project workforce into the planning process and keeping its members informed of our expectations and plans as they evolve.

There are passive and active ways of maintaining contact with our stakeholders. Following are a few ideas to consider:

- web pages
- newsletters
- progress reports
- progress meetings
- informal communication
- parties and celebrations of milestones.

Hey Bill, how badly do we want this project anyhow?

Everyone in the target organization model is part of your team. Stay in touch with your team; it's the only way that its members will be able to help you deliver the project.

Clients need to see value. Sometimes it is hard for them to see it. Take the time to explain. Clients who have confidence in you ask for less information. Confidence stems from your relationship and ability to perform. Part of it is based on how openly you communicate.

The team delivers the project. To do so effectively and with minimum churn and rework—and with the best possible results—team members must be kept informed. They need both essential information to do the job plus peripheral information to provide the context in which the team can work more effectively.

Do not give suppliers and contractors solutions to solve. Help them understand what you are trying to achieve, and allow them to contribute better solutions.

Other stakeholders include the general public, regulatory agencies, competitors, and more. We will recognize them as important if we ask ourselves the right questions about our project:

■ Who can influence the outcome?

- Who will determine whether the project is a success?
- Where does the power lie?
- Who makes the real decisions, sets policy, and directs strategic objectives?

Anyone identified with any of these questions is a potential stakeholder with whom to work and get involved in the business of delivering the project. The more questions lead us to the same stakeholder for an answer, the more influential that stakeholder is likely to be.

Chapter 16

BIG VERSUS SMALL PROJECTS—ADAPTING SMART TO YOUR WORK ENVIRONMENT

In the previous chapter, we looked at administration and suggested that too much administration or the wrong administration was tantamount to bureaucracy—a mortal sin in my mind! The other element that can lead to sinning in this fashion is doing too much project management for a particular project. None of us likes being managed to death.

In this chapter, the differences between managing large and small projects and other varieties are discussed to provide the reader with some guidelines on how to select the tools and processes that will yield the best return on project management time and effort.

Before we get into detail on how to adapt tools for projects of different sizes, let us look at managing programs that are a collection of projects—usually with some common objective or synergy but not necessarily so. If we look at programs, then the next step is to look at whole businesses that increasingly are a collection of programs loosely held together with corporate administration and infrastructure.

This is a short chapter. As every project is unique, all I can do is provide guidelines. Use your judgment in selecting and *scaling* the tools, processes, and competencies you need to make your project a success.

16.1   The Fern and Spider Analogy

SMART Management tools were originally developed for managing change. Change has three components in varying degrees present in just about any situation: social, business, and technical. Business process improvement (BPI), change management, and many other terms are used to describe parts of the process of managing technological change. A holistic approach does not permit us to use just one tool kit. Therefore, blend what's in this book with other tools and processes to create a full suite of skills needed to achieve success.

That said, another constant differentiation is between project management and program management. Also, they are perceived to be separate from corporate management. As with the blurring of lines between technologies and industries, we need to blur the lines between management mindsets and approaches. There are merits in all; what we need to do is take the best for the work we have in hand. This is where the fern and spider model comes into the picture.

The concept behind the fern and spider analogy is that the stem of the fern represents the main business of the organization, supported by a series of branches representing its programs and larger projects. They in turn support the leaves that represent the projects or major deliverables on the larger projects.

Each leaf, as a deliverable item, can be treated as a mini-project. At the other end of the spectrum, the entire fern can be treated as a very large project. SMART is used to define corporate strategy and develop business plans. The basic idea is the same as for a regular project. We define success in three years' time (or whatever the planning horizon is). This is the project; it should tie into the corporate vision.

Now why a spider? That's you—busy making connections between elements of the business and the project in which you are involved. You need a real network—a web, if you like—of contacts and communication channels. Spiders are sensitive to vibrations in the web and can make the connections between cause and effect.

 Bear this analogy in mind as we work through the four main dimensions of projects.

16.2   Assessing Your Project

When we consider the relative difficulty of managing projects, there are four main elements that affect the process: 1) size, 2) clarity of definition

Figure 16.1 Fern and Spider Model for Organizations, Programs, and Projects

(uncertainty), 3) complexity, and 4) attitude (desirability, appeal). These are largely relative terms and may be subjective. Management of a particular project requires a specific set of tools, processes, and competencies to support the team. The selection of these tools is easier when we have a basis for evaluating the project and knowing, as a result of the evaluation, which parts of the project or program management process to emphasize.

16.2.1 Size: Big versus Small

Size is a relative term. The impact that the project has on the bottom line determines size. Primarily, we will be concerned with our own profitability and success, but we should also consider the needs of other team players.

A large project will have a significant impact on the success of our organization. It may also be a large project if it will significantly impact our careers. The same project can be large and small at the same time. For example, a project to design a new wiper blade for a new model car may be a large project for the small company commissioned to do so, but it will be a small one for the large auto manufacturer.

The larger the project, the more attention we need to give planning, record-keeping, and project controls. Within planning, special attention to risk management and management of stakeholder expectations will be needed.

16.2.2 Clarity of Definition: Wild versus Tame

Wild projects are those that we cannot define at the outset. They include research and development projects and may also include new technology implementation, live entertainment projects, software projects, corporate reorganizations, marketing projects, and so on.

As the project gets wilder, we need to put more effort into managing the scope and stakeholder expectations. More checkpoints will be required. We will need more objective reviews of the project at these checkpoints, so an independent team to perform the review may be an advantage.

Risk analysis and the use of range estimates are of particular importance. In defining the project scope, clarity will be needed. Management of changes will be harder too, as we use a false baseline to determine what has changed.

16.2.3 Complexity: Simple versus Complex

Complexity in this situation refers to the number of different types of expertise that will be involved in the project. In a simple project, only one discipline in one department in one organization is involved; probably the ultimate simple project is done by one person! Complexity increases as we add layers to our target organization model.

Some of the factors affecting complexity include different:

- professions involved (even mechanical engineers and electrical engineers speak different languages)
- departments in the organization (for example, marketing and accounting—again a language problem, to say nothing about different priorities)
- companies
- locations
- countries, languages, time zones, cultures, and so on.

As complexity increases, we need to put more effort into communication, expectation management, and building the project's own unique culture. Attention to team effectiveness is important, and the time needed to build the team will increase significantly as we add each new level of complexity.

16.2.4 Attitude: Beautiful versus Ugly

This variable is probably the most subjective. What is attractive to one person will not necessarily be to another and vice versa. This variable

356

is about motivation, excitement, interest, profile, opportunity, and all those other things that make a particular project interesting—or not. The opposites of these attributes also exist and make some project work painfully unpleasant. Examples of what I consider unpleasant projects include organization downsizing (layoffs), litigation (especially if I were to be involved directly), and clean up of a disaster or atrocity. They are all pretty horrible. Less awful are those projects we know are doomed to failure, where the client is particularly unpleasant or litigious, or perhaps when we are forced to work in uncomfortable or dangerous circumstances.

I am sure you've grasped the concept! Basically, the uglier the project, the more we need to focus on motivation of the team, safety, individual concerns, and the image of the project. (Public relations can play a big part in project success.)

16.3   Other Factors

We have just looked at the four primary factors that help us identify where to focus. There are other more specific issues that often appear, and the following sections discuss a few of the more common ones.

16.3.1 Location

We will discuss type and distribution of location(s) for the project in this section. Pleasant locations attract people, even if it means time away from the family. Perhaps for some, even time away from the family can be an attraction!

Unpleasant, boring, isolated, polluted, unhealthy areas (not necessarily all at the same time) are likely to require persuasion for people to travel there permanently or for the duration of the project. If this is so, the cost of incentives, costs, and delays associated with recruiting and staff turnover all need to be included in the project plan.

The other dimension to this is the geographical distribution of the team. My theory is that misunderstandings increase with the square of the distance between sites multiplied by the number of sites involved.

The opportunity for communications breakdowns increases significantly as the number of people involved increases. The same is true of locations involved. Figure 16.3.1 illustrates that there is just one channel of communication between two locations and three between three locations. By the time we get to five locations, we are at eight channels.

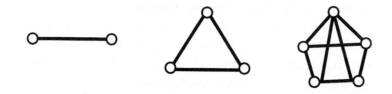

Figure 16.3.1 Growing Number of Channels as Locations Increase

16.3.2 Environment (Business, Social, Political, and Natural)

Unstable conditions will require more care in management. These factors will primarily influence the need to identify and mitigate risks, and, once this is done, it's important to manage expectations around the resulting uncertainty. Changes, in all likelihood, will occur frequently, so these circumstances are quite similar to those for an uncertain or hard-to-define project.

16.3.3 Time Frame and Duration

The longer a project will take, the more uncertain the outcome will be. Also, maintenance of team enthusiasm is much harder. Consider breaking long-duration projects into discrete pieces that deliver something useful at least every three months. Be sure to celebrate successes as you go.

A six-month project will behave differently at different times of the year. An outside construction project will clearly do better in the summer than in the winter. A software project may do better in the winter, when people have less to do outdoors. Again, local conditions and team make-up will have an influence.

16.3.4 Technology

Complexity and novelty of technology will affect the outcome of a project. It will also affect whom we pick for our team and how we select them. The more exotic and novel the technology, the more attention we need to place on recruiting, rewarding, and keeping the individual specialists that we need to implement the technology. Novelty of technology also acts as a motivator in itself, representing the reason that some people choose to work on a project. With leading-edge technology, we also tend to get an imbalance of people on the project with a larger focus on technocracy rather than team and social skills, or possibly even business skills. Attention to managing this imbalance then becomes important.

Don't Park Your Brain Outside

16.3.5 Other Risks and Uncertainties

Clearly, the topics covered in this chapter are not exhaustive. They are intended to cover some of the more significant factors that need to be considered when we pick and modify the tools, processes, and competencies of SMART Project Management.

16.4 Selecting and Modifying Tools

If you look at the SMART approach to project and program management, you will see that it's really a framework rather than a methodology. This is deliberate. Each time I've helped an organization implement the SMART approach, it's turned out differently; this is as it should be. We need to adapt what we do to the task, the people, and the culture of the organization. The message is that we need to be creative in using the approach. What is important—and what makes this all SMART—is that we pay attention to the following principles:

- We understand the business that is the driver of the project. We know what we are trying to achieve and why. This is the difference between building a bridge and improving access across a river at a particular point.
- We maintain a balance among business, technical, and social issues at all times, and we never compromise safety, in the broadest sense of the word.
- We build high-performance teams that include fun, creativity, and tribalism in their make-up.
- We do everything based on deliverables, including defining success, planning, managing, organizing, producing, and recording.
- We actively manage risk, uncertainty, and stakeholder expectations.

Section D

SELF-EVALUATION AND PROBLEM SOLVING

This facility cost us $749 million.
Now the cable is too short, and we have the wrong plug.

Chapter 17

ABSOLUTE PERFORMANCE— A MATURITY MODEL FOR PROJECTS

The material presented in the first part of this chapter has been previously published in *Project Management* 4 (1), 1998. The original article was co-authored with Greg Skulmoski, one of the doctoral candidates who works with me at the University of Calgary. It is reprinted here with the kind permission of the editor-in-chief, Dr. Karlos Artto.

17.1   Maturity in Project Management

The issue of what makes some project managers and organizations better than others at delivering projects is a question that has been studied for many years. Studies have examined critical success factors, key result areas, and project manager's skills and personalities. More traditional research has continued to investigate important areas such as scheduling tools, risk management, bidding strategies, and other tools that support the project management process. Studies of human issues in temporary organizations, teamwork and teambuilding, motivation, and perceptions of success also continue. All have contributed in their own way, and each is linked to the others.

In this model we map the many facets in project management in a way that will help us work with and understand its growing body of knowledge. The presented framework is modeled on the work of the Software Engineering Institute (SEI) and other concepts and studies published primarily through the Project Management Institute (PMI). It is referred to as the project management competence model, as it is intended to reflect the competencies required for an effective project manager. It is a working framework that will continue to evolve over time.

17.2   Background Information

Project management traditionally has dealt with the work that takes an idea from project funding to delivery; Lundin (1998) conceptualized this as the "inverted black box"—what happens before we get into traditional project management, and what happens after commissioning plays a pivotal role in the definition and measurement of success of a project. We need to start with the original idea, its business context, and how it was funded. We should also determine what happens to the project once it is completed. With too many projects, the *customer* is rarely consulted. This is easily seen in the literature, couched in terms of end-user frustrations with software, operators' dissatisfaction with the facilities they must operate, and so on. The competence model is one way to map project management knowledge and not only provide the links to serve a number of purposes, but also create an opportunity to study and understand the growth of excellent project managers. It helps to understand the mechanism that underlies this growth. As such, it also helps us understand the layout of knowledge needed for developing excellence beyond classical and modern project management. It should influence how we develop our training curricula. Finally, it may help define a cohesive approach to certification.

The debate on how to certify project managers continues, with different views on this from different national professional associations. PMI in North America has a knowledge-based model for its project management professional (PMP®) designation. Experience and project management competencies provide the basis of models favored in some European countries. The link between maturity models and certification within the profession of project management is a natural one. In this chapter, we will look at it and other links, with growth of the body of knowledge moving beyond the traditional bounds of project management and the changing work environment. That done, we will look at a framework for a more universally applicable model to assess and develop project management effectiveness and competence.

17.3 General Competence Models

The models for competence and maturity in project management that have appeared since 1997 began the process of building this concept. The published models are briefly described in this section, starting with the one that got this idea going: the SEI capability maturity model (CMM).

17.3.1 SEI Capability Maturity Model

It includes five levels; the *initial* level is based upon no stable environment existing in the organization for development of software. Often commitments are made and not met. It's difficult to achieve a methodical process that results in any consistency in project delivery. The objective is simply to produce software.

At the *repeatable* level, the goals have shifted to delivering projects in a controlled fashion, usually taking the form of schedules that drive the project. At this level, the organization will also control cost and functionality and will have developed policies and procedures around the process it needs to achieve these objectives.

The third level is the *defined* level. There's a coherent and consistent approach to project delivery with organizationwide training to ensure that the participants in the process have the required skills to fill their project roles. The organization's standard practices are now modified on each project to suit the specific needs and demands of the situation. At this level, the focus is not on managing the project but on managing the product.

At the fourth or *managed* level, the focus shifts to managing the process to ensure that customer needs are properly met and balanced with cost and other standard measures. Quantitative quality measures are set, and there is an organizationwide quality and productivity measurement process. The objective is to achieve improved consistency and predictability of outcomes.

At the fifth level, we have achieved the *optimized* process. What sets this level apart is that the organization is now continuing to improve on what it has done to grow from level one to four, and it is doing so in a structured way.

Although the SEI CMM has been widely accepted and adopted, it's been the target of some criticism. The three primary criticisms are that 1) it increases corporate bureaucracy and rigidity, 2) it causes organizations to focus on CMM issues at the expense of others that are important to its business, and, finally, 3) organizations will tend to avoid risky projects in order to get better CMM ratings. All have been proven wrong by studies investigating these phenomena.

The next three models reflect a strong basis in PMI's *A Guide to the Project Management Body of Knowledge* (*PMBOK® Guide*). As such, they may all be open to criticism because they are limited to more traditional approaches to project management, meaning that they look specifically at the project execution phase.

17.3.2 Project Management Maturity Model

Fincher and Levin proposed their project management maturity model on the basis of goals that an organization may use to assess its maturity level (1997). By focusing on the weak areas identified in a comparison to the suggested goals, it is possible to identify where improvements may be made to improve project management performance. All nine of the *PMBOK® Guide* areas of knowledge are included at each level in this model. It is a fairly close adaptation of the SEI CMM, so it too has five levels, and their definitions reflect the same types of goals as the CMM. An analysis of these levels by Skulmoski suggests that there are inconsistencies between the different levels in the model (1998). There is no evidence that it has been empirically tested. Mastery of the *PMBOK® Guide* effectively constitutes level 4, so it does not challenge the status quo in any significant way.

17.3.3 Capability Maturity Model/Project Management Maturity Model

Goldsmith developed this *PMBOK® Guide*-based model (1997). It is specific to software projects, and Goldsmith's focus was on accelerating development time. The process includes steps such as learning about project management and then becoming certified by PMI as a PMP. This model simply brings together the structure of SEI's CMM and the *PMBOK® Guide*; it adds nothing new beyond this.

17.3.4 Project Management Process Maturity Model

This is the last and the most comprehensive of the *PMBOK® Guide*-based models, developed by Ibbs and Kwak and reported in a PMI publication (1997). It is based on a study intended to identify the organizational and financial benefits of project management. The authors looked at thirty-eight organizations and assessed their maturity, using a simple and prescriptive model. The model was developed to help project managers assess maturity and return on investment that might accrue from this process; it is also loosely based on SEI's CMM. It starts with an ad hoc approach to project management at level one and grows to continuous improvement at level five. At level two, some informal procedures and plans are in place. At level three, organizations have partially developed procedures and practices, and trend data is collected and shared between teams; systematic and structured project management occurs at this level. At level four, integration across the entire organization occurs; also, at this level, project management is documented and well understood.

The authors of this model point out that previous studies and models trying to identify the benefits to project management have been unsubstantiated and anecdotal.

The next two models (one published, the other under development) are not based directly on the *PMBOK® Guide*.

17.3.5   The Project Management Maturity Model

This model was developed and trademarked by Remy (1997). It, like the others, is loosely based on the one by SEI; it has five levels. The creator of this model does not advocate trying to get the entire organization to the top level. Instead, he suggests that the organization achieve a balance that best suits its business objectives. This model differs significantly in that it is based on the domain of modern project management as defined by Kerzner (1996). It is similar to Ibbs and Kwak's model in that an organization can have several different levels of maturity and still be effective.

One of the prime differences in this model is that it recognizes that "effective project management is the evolving interaction of process, systems, and culture. Addressing one aspect without considering the others produces little more than expensive frustration" (Remy 1997). This model is, however, not backed by any empirical research. It is anecdotal and from a consulting company that makes a living in this business.

17.4   SMART Project Management-Based Maturity Model

This early concept of a maturity model is also loosely based on the SEI model. It is the result of five years of empirical study in the application of derived best performance studies (described later). It challenges many of the standard practices in project management by pushing the envelope of accepted expertise and processes. As we have seen, the SMART model is based on the following elements:

- Projects are *strategically managed* and integrated with corporate objectives.
- Teams and objectives are properly *aligned*, and this alignment is tested and validated.

- The project is performed in a *regenerative* culture that encourages and supports high-performance teams.
- The project is defined, planned, and managed in the context of a continuously changing (*transitional*) environment with corresponding shifts in demands on the project and its assigned resources.

These models, when applied to projects in organizations, consistently yielded significantly better project performance in terms of customer satisfaction and cost and time required. However, it proved to be unsustainable when implemented in an environment that was at level one, two, or even three on most of the maturity models previously defined. In order to understand why this might be, further study was undertaken, based generally on the principles of identifying best practices.

17.5 Successful Projects and Successful Project Managers

In order to understand competence, we need to define it specifically. We're familiar with the notion of competence in the context of professional skills; we have our own benchmarks that we use when selecting a dentist, doctor, lawyer, or even a motor mechanic. Some of the ingredients that we consider include the following:

- Is the personal chemistry right?
- Is the candidate professional qualified and certified by his professional association (peers)?
- Does the professional have a good reputation?
- Does he have the tools to do the job efficiently and well?
- What is his track record?
- Does he listen to—and understand—what I need?
- How well does he explain the risks and manage my expectations, especially if they are unreasonable?
- How easy is it to work with this person?

This is not an exhaustive list, nor is it in the right order, as the priorities will be largely dependent on the situation.

What we can immediately see from such a list is that there is more to our perception of competence in other established professions than just technical and business capabilities. Further, when we look at the attributes or skills of project managers who stand out from the crowd as truly competent, we will find at least one common element: they are able to balance the many different issues and drivers behind a project, and manage the stakeholders toward the common goal of a successful project.

This brings us to the issue of defining project success. For the purposes of this book, the definition is encapsulated in the following short but complex statement: "A successful project is one where the stakeholders are satisfied with the outcome." Now, let's look at the outcome, who the stakeholders might be, and what "satisfied" may mean.

Outcome is the end product of the project; this needs to be defined at the outset and redefined as the project evolves. The definition will not necessarily be detailed or correct at the start of the project; it will include the traditional cost, schedule, scope, and quality definitions. It should also include definition of the process to be used, the business or other drivers, the risks and uncertainties at each stage of the project, and probably more in order to give the stakeholders a benchmark against which to assess their opinions of success.

The stakeholders that count are the ones that vote on the success of the project. They can include the project team members and all those who are affected by or can influence the outcome of the project. Their satisfaction will be based on how closely the project process and outcomes meet their expectations. Managing stakeholder expectations is an important aspect of effective project management.

Given this definition—general as it is—of project success, then effective project management is whatever it takes to achieve such an outcome efficiently and with minimal disruption and damage to the social, natural, political, corporate, or other environments within which the project is executed. Whether or not we subscribe to the traditional definitions of project management—which spawned Lundin's implied challenge in his "inverted black box" idea (1998)—or the more encompassing definitions, we need to consider what happens before we have a project and what goes on after the *project* phase is over. It helps us understand the environment in which the project occurs.

In this broader context, a framework for better understanding of project management and its many facets starts to emerge. A significant amount of information synthesis has led to the development of a model for project management maturity that is based on setting level four at *world-class* performance. The other readily definable levels are level one, the entry level, and level five, the level at which structured and logical continuous improvement on performance at level four occurs. However, to put some meat on the bones of this skeletal definition of a maturity model, we need to consider the elements that constitute performance at the entry and world-class levels and clearly define these terms. That done, the next step in developing a rational maturity model is to determine the building blocks required to go from level one to level four. The final step is to find the right sequence for assembly of these blocks to allow individuals and organizations to develop their project management skills in a sustainable way.

17.6   Elements of Maturity

As a starting point, levels of the proposed framework may be defined as in the following sections.

Level One

At this level, we see the typical first-time project manager with little or no formal training but with a mandate to deliver a project. From an organizational point of view, this level would be defined as having no formal career path for project managers. The title of project manager may be assigned without any recognition in terms of promotion, training, pay increase, or added authority to do the work.

Level Two

This level requires that three elements are in place. The first is a formal training program with an appropriate certification, diploma, or other qualification associated with successful completion. This is needed to allow the individual project manager to obtain two important requirements: basic knowledge in accepted project management practices, and credibility in the organization and with the team. The project manager's credibility will also depend on a number of other— often more important—elements such as technical competence, experience, and reputation for success in some form. The second required element is acceptance at the organizational level of formal project management. Specifically this means that the organization expects projects to be managed, rather than merely allowing them to happen. Symptoms include formal recognition of the title *project manager*, perhaps with differing levels from assistant to senior or executive. The underlying organizational commitment is important—not lip service to a process and job titles. The third element of this level is that the organization permits its project managers to do what they must do in order to manage their projects effectively.

For the organization, this level requires that a formal and effective training program in project management be in place. It typically also requires that project management standards be in place, as well as a career path for project managers within the organization.

Level Three

The third level of project management maturity is one at which the definition of project management in the organization has been broadened to include all of the steps in the project life cycle. It begins when the idea first originates and continues through to final closeout of the project or its product at the end of its useful life. This is a much larger mandate. It does *not* mean that the same person is managing every step of the process. At this level, we expect project managers to consider the technical elements (classical project management), as well as the business context in which the project takes place (modern project management). Finally, we would expect the project manager to consider social and societal issues (integrated project management).

The organization needs to reflect these additional factors as well. First, the project selection process should consider how well aligned each project is with corporate strategy. It should also consider where the project fits in a risked portfolio of projects from which the organization must choose in order to achieve its objectives. Currently, most organizations using risked selection will include in the evaluation a risk factor for technical and commercial success of the project. They will not consider the risk in project delivery, however, and it can have a profound impact on the outcome of the project. This helps explain the significant difference between the expected return on investment when the project is approved and the actual return on completion that is commonly reported.

At level three, the project is developed as part of the corporate strategy. It's also routinely and predictably delivered at or below a stretch budget and schedule with little or no rework and with a satisfied customer.

Level Four

This is the level at which high performance is achieved. When we looked for differentiation between good and world-class project managers, one characteristic stood out in particular: the ability to make and maintain all connections between disparate elements of the project and its successful management. For example, how will approval of this project impact others in the organization and vice versa? What does selection of one contracting strategy over another have on schedule, team effectiveness, and the effort required to maintain effective communications, cost, administrative processes, and so on. No decision is made in isolation. The project manager finds solutions to the disease, not the symptom.

At the organizational level, teams cooperate between projects. Priorities are set to suit corporate goals—rather than those of the project with the strongest manager or sponsor. It is not just acceptable practice but good practice to cancel your own project—if that is the right thing to do. Unfortunately, it is currently a career-limiting move in many organizations.

Essentially, at this level, the project manager, with the conscious support of the organization, is working beyond corporate guidelines, procedures, and processes, adapting or changing them to suit the needs of the situation. The result of this final set of skills and competencies is that projects at this level are scheduled and budgeted aggressively to perform at up to 30 percent faster and more cost effectively than projects at level two. Projects at level four consistently come in on time and within expected cost, scope, safety, and quality expectations.

Level Five

This level, like that in the SEI CMM, is one at which controlled and organized process improvement is achieved.

It is not enough to define these elements; several other things need to be done. First, we need to develop ways to perform at level four. By the definition of the earlier model, this has been done with integrated project management, but has not been done yet in a sustainable way. Three pilot projects in organizations are currently under way to test the concept of this maturity model. Results will take several years to develop; faster approaches must be found.

Next, we need to detail what knowledge, experience, competencies, and other skills or attributes are required at each level for both the individual and the organization. The different levels can coexist within an organization. Career paths for project managers, organization standards, and other infrastructure elements need to be defined for each organization, so the framework for growth in this increasingly important area of management is in place.

Project management maturity will help us understand the real drivers for project management effectiveness, together with the myriad of peripheral factors that contribute to such success.

The SMART framework helps develop a platform for future growth of project management. If used, this platform will help us understand the elements required for developing truly competitive project delivery. Elements will include technical, business, and social issues such as the following:

- Technical Issues
  - more effective resource-based scheduling techniques
  - better tools for scope and change management
  - ways of measuring team alignment
  - simplified tools for earned value, risk analysis, and more to make them more accessible and user-friendly
  - tools to plan for and manage communication.
- Business Issues
  - multiproject management to include interproject communication and priority setting
  - planning that helps align projects with—and support—corporate strategy
  - risk plans for projects that are consistent with the risk-taking and investment policy of the sponsor organization.
- Social and Societal Issues
  - ensuring legal and regulatory compliance
  - understanding the long-term impact of the project on the community and the team
  - developing good working environments for the *whole* project team and stakeholders
  - ensuring a sustainable social infrastructure to support the project during implementation and in the operating phase
  - understanding and mitigating social, environmental, and economic damage to third parties.

There is still much to be learned about effective project management. The wider we cast the net, the sooner we will find the most critical factors to positively influence the outcomes of future projects.

17.7 Afterthoughts

No maturity model will ever be correct or complete. This is because project management will continue to evolve and, as a result, affect the model.

17.8 Project Management Maturity Model Self-Assessment

Step 1

Turn to Chapter 18, and read through the error messages. Then record how many of these (or very similiar ones)—under each of the categories—you hear on your project(s).

Number	Category		Score
18.1	Planning and Compliance to the Plan	_____	9
18.2	Uncertainty and Alignment	_____	8
18.3	The Right Project	_____	9
18.4	Stakeholders, Interference	_____	6
18.5	Changes	_____	5
18.6	Scheduling and Estimating and Control	_____	13
18.7	Strategic Issues, Corporate Interference	_____	7
18.8	Happy Customers	_____	7
18.9	Team Issues	_____	8
18.10	Trust and Contracts	_____	4
18.11	Planning and Communication	_____	7
18.12	Complicated Project Controls	_____	9
18.13	Priorities	_____	5
18.14	Uncertainty and Risk	_____	18
18.15	Suppliers and Contractual Arrangements	_____	10
18.16	Concurrent Work and Design, Cross-Functional Teams	_____	8
18.17	Responsibility Gap and Communication	_____	7
18.18	Project Organizations	_____	10
18.19	Managing Expectations	_____	8
18.20	Effective Project Controls	_____	15
18.21	Trust	_____	7
18.22	Oops!	_____	4
	Total		184

Step 2

See where you are:

- You are at level four if you score less than 2 under *all* of the categories combined.
- You are at level three if you have a score of less than 2 in any of the categories and zero in categories 1, 2, 3, 8, 9, 11, 12, 13, 14, 19, and 20.
- You are at level two if you have less than 3 in each category.
- You are probably at level one with any project or organization that has higher than a 3 score under any category.

Chapter 18

WHAT NORMALLY GOES WRONG ON PROJECTS?

This chapter lists the most common results seen as failures on projects, provides suggestions, and refers to the book sections that will help the reader address specific issues and resolve them.

Similar to the list of error messages at the back of many software manuals, we have common project errors and problems with tips on how to fix them and where to look in this book or elsewhere for help. The error messages have been grouped to make it easier to find the one that approximates yours. They likely will all sound depressingly familiar. Do not let that bother you. Look at the grouping and the message, then check the detail to see if you are heading in the right direction.

Your own experience will help. My experience has been that solutions to problems are not always obvious; this is reflected in the answers I suggest in this chapter.

If, after checking the error messages, you find that you have a new one—"Help, I cannot find my error message!"—please do not panic. There are so many things that can go wrong, we could not possibly list them all; I've tried my best. If you find a solution to your unlisted error message, send the information to me. Then I can include it in the next edition of this book (if there is one). At the very least, I would love to learn from your experience! (My contact information is at the end of the Acknowledgments at the beginning of the book.)

Before we start the list, following is a key to how it works:

18.x   Example Group of Error Messages

- ❏ First error message in this group.
- ❏ Second example.
- ❏ Here it the third one.
- ❏ Final example in this set.
  - ◆ A brief comment on what may be behind these comments.
    - ❖ Chapter and section references to possible relevant parts of the book.

18.1   Planning and Compliance to the Plan

- ❏ It's difficult to know when a project has started.
- ❏ Sometimes we feel this project is a waste of time.
- ❏ Some people do not know when the project is finished.
- ❏ We seem disorganized with this project.
- ❏ Some of our projects get done well, but people still complain about them.
- ❏ Our project is a moving target.
- ❏ There seem to be different rules for my project, compared to others in the organization.
- ❏ It's hard to get the resources or commitment we need.
- ❏ The rules change as our project moves forward.
  - ◆ The plan is incomplete, and there is no agreed project charter. If these were in place, you would know where you are, because you are working toward specific deliverables for next week's progress meeting.
  - ◆ There is no commitment to the project plan.
  - ◆ Scope is unclear or ambiguous.
  - ◆ Planning lacks client focus.
    - ❖ Sections 1.7, 2.2, 2.3; Chapter 3; Sections 4.1 and 6.7.2; Chapters 8 and 14.

18.2   Uncertainty and Alignment

- ❏ When some people get involved in a project, they want to change it.
- ❏ Defining the project seems to be an ongoing exercise.
- ❏ Our project lacks direction.
- ❏ The rules keep changing.
- ❏ How do we know that we are working on a useful project?
- ❏ Management will not give me the time to plan this project properly.
- ❏ My team is having trouble getting organized.

- ❑ Everything is great, but I have a nagging feeling that the project will not stay that way.
  - ◆ Appropriate priorities need to be set.
  - ◆ Alignment of stakeholders is missing or incomplete.
  - ◆ Roles are poorly defined.
    - ❖ Chapters 4 and 5; Section 8.6; Chapters 10 and 12.

18.3 The Right Project

- ❑ Are we wasting money or time in developing this project idea?
- ❑ Do we have enough information to request approval for this project?
- ❑ How can I be sure that senior management will not kill this project halfway through?
- ❑ What is this project doing for my career?
- ❑ What if this project goes wrong?
- ❑ Is working on this project a career-limiting move?
- ❑ Have we put together the right project?
- ❑ Should we invest in this project?
- ❑ What are the chances of this project being accepted by management?
- ❑ Is there a better project in which to invest our effort?
- ❑ How can we make this a better project, in which the organization can invest?
  - ◆ Value of the project to business is unclear.
  - ◆ We do not know why the project is being done.
  - ◆ Uncertain who the sponsor (senior manager) is for the project.
  - ◆ Project should have been canceled or significantly modified.
  - ◆ Plan is totally unrealistic.
    - ❖ Sections 1.7, 2.2, 2.3; Chapter 3; Sections 4.1, 5.4, 5.5, 6.3, 8.1, 8.2, 8.3, 9.1, 9.7, 9.8, 14.2.

18.4 Stakeholders, Interference

- ❑ Who will decide whether this is a successful project?
- ❑ Why do some people insist on poking their noses into this project?
- ❑ They should have said what they wanted when we started—not now.
- ❑ It's another change; this time it will cost them.
- ❑ We never seem to know what the customer really wants.

❑ Management seems to get off track with its expectations of what the project will produce.
  ◆ Uncertainty about objectives and resultant misalignment of team.
  ◆ Rapid change in the client's world.
  ◆ Communication breakdowns.
    ❖ Sections 2.3, 2.5, 3.4, 6.7, 8.4, 8.6, 11.6.4, 14.2, 14.3, 14.4, 15.2, 15.3.

18.5 Changes

❑ What was approved for this project is unclear.
❑ Half our projects get canceled—after we put a lot of effort into them.
❑ The rules for this project keep changing.
❑ How do we know that management will be interested in this project six months from now?
❑ It's hard to get support from the different departments involved in this project.
  ◆ Business drivers unclear.
  ◆ Project mission not defined or incorrect.
  ◆ Plan developed without input from one or more key stakeholders.
  ◆ Project environment very volatile.
    ❖ Sections 2.2, 2.3, 3.3, 3.4; Chapter 4; Sections 5.4, 5.5, 5.10, 6.3, 6.4, 6.7.3, 7.2, 7.3, 8.4, 8.5, 8.6, 8.7, 8.11; Chapters 10 and 14.

18.6 Scheduling, Estimating, and Control

❑ Every estimate we do seems to be inaccurate.
❑ When we schedule something, it seems to come in late more often than not.
❑ There are surprises on every project.
❑ With the uncertainty on this project, we seem to have trouble bringing senior management on board.
❑ If there is a problem with the project or the team, I get blamed.
❑ The objectives of the project are almost impossible to achieve.
❑ The customer always seems to want what cannot be done.
❑ Most of our projects seem to start badly, then they go downhill from there.
❑ Once we miss a deadline, none of the others seem to be met either.
❑ It's hard to know which is more important: quality, cost, or schedule.

❏ We never have enough time to plan the project properly.

❏ Planning seems to be a waste of time, and the plan is out of date almost as soon as we start on the project.

❏ There's no point in planning; nobody follows the plan.

♦ Risks not well understood.

♦ Risks not properly identified.

♦ No risk mitigation plan.

♦ Estimating based on single points.

♦ Estimates not done with input from team members responsible for delivery.

♦ No buy-in to plan by team.

♦ Unrealistic or overoptimistic planning and estimating.

❖ Chapter 2; Sections 4.3, 5.2, 5.5, 6.3, 8.3, 8.4, 8.5, 8.6, 8.10, 8.11; Chapter 9; Sections 10.7, 14.2, 15.2, 15.3.

18.7   Strategic Issues, Corporate Interference

❏ At some point in the project, we seem to lose corporate support.

❏ The organization seems to jump from one priority to another.

❏ It's hard to know which project has value and which does not.

❏ We seem to spend a lot of time doing the wrong thing.

❏ Getting other departments involved just slows us down.

❏ People from the other departments don't understand what's important in this project.

❏ There's no sense of urgency in some of the people with whom we need to deal on this project.

♦ Primary cause is likely lack of strategic direction of organization or project or both.

♦ Communication breakdown.

♦ Lack of alignment.

♦ Stakeholder buy-in not as good as it could be.

♦ Priorities unclear for organization or project or both.

❖ Chapters 2, 3, and 4; Sections 8.1 and 8.10; Chapters 10 and 12.

18.8   Happy Customers

❏ Often when we get to the end of a project, our customer has more for us to do before we get paid, or the project is considered complete.

❏ When we're finished, someone changes the rules, then says that we've failed.

❏ People who have nothing to do with the project try to interfere.

- ❑ It's always a surprise that kills the project or bends it out of shape.
- ❑ We have the wrong amount of contingency.
- ❑ Management cuts back on our budget but still expects us to deliver.
- ❑ We work impossible schedules.
  - ◆ Expectations are not being managed or met.
  - ◆ Lack of alignment with customer needs.
  - ◆ Priorities unclear.
  - ◆ No clarity with definitions of success and completion, or who gets to vote on them.
  - ◆ Communications flawed or too infrequent.
    - ❖ Sections 2.3, 2.4, 3.1, 3.2, 3.4; Chapters 4 and 5; Sections 8.1, 8.4, 8.6, 8.7, 8.11, 9.8, 10.11; Chapter 12; Sections 14.3, 14.4, 14.6, 14.8.

18.9 Team Issues

- ❑ The team is dysfunctional.
- ❑ We cannot get the right mix of skills needed for the project.
- ❑ Our team was assigned to this project; half either lack the experience or knowledge or simply are not interested in what must be done.
- ❑ I'm on this project, and it seems to be a career-limiting move!
- ❑ In this organization, it's everyone for herself.
- ❑ How do I know that this assignment is a good one?
- ❑ What are they really trying to do?
- ❑ I'm not sure why, but I feel that there's something wrong here.
  - ◆ Team disaster!
  - ◆ Missing communications and trust.
    - ❖ Chapters 5 and 12 (read twice if necessary!).

18.10 Trust and Contracts

- ❑ You can't trust any (or some) of the contractors or suppliers.
- ❑ I've been cheated before; it won't happen again!
- ❑ If anything goes wrong, I'll be blamed.
- ❑ There are probably lots more like these!
  - ◆ Contractors not part of the team.
  - ◆ Wrong contracting strategy.
  - ◆ Poor communications.
  - ◆ Need to better understand trust, and work on achieving it.
    - ❖ Chapters 4, 5, 11, 12.

18.11 Planning and Communication

- ❑ We plan projects but then go ahead and ignore the plan.
- ❑ Our plans for projects are not detailed enough to be of any use.

- Our plans are so detailed that they're bound to be wrong—and usually are, when it comes to trying to follow them.
- Only half the team seems to know that we even have a project plan.
- I do not know why we bother planning—it's a complete waste of time. We all know what we have to do.
- I do not understand the plan for this project.
- The plans are all too complicated.
- Nobody ever looks at the plan—it's just for the project manager.
  - Lack of alignment.
  - No real team.
  - Planning not understood.
  - No team involvement in the planning process.
  - Too much or irrelevant detail in the plan.
  - Poor communication.
  - No ownership of the project or its plan by the team.
    - Sections 4.3, 4.4, 5.1, 5.2, 5.4, 5.9, 5.10, 6.7; Chapter 8; Sections 9.7 and 9.8; Chapter 10.

18.12 Complicated Project Controls

- Look at all the different charge, cost, timesheet, and other codes we have on this project—it's ridiculous!
- I'm confused by the WBS, the RBS, and the OBS and how they are supposed to map together (or I do not even know that these are work breakdown structures, responsibility breakdown structure, or organization breakdown structures)!
- Why do we have to rework our budgets into control estimates?
- The schedules don't make sense from my discipline's point of view.
- We have too much data in this project, but it's still not enough to manage it properly.
- We always end up in a panic at the end of the project, trying to get everything done or reducing the scope, so we can say it's done!
- Half the time, something critical to the project is late, and we have to clean up the mess.
- Everyone else uses up the float time, and we have the mad panic to get stuff finished on schedule.
  - The planning and control of the project are not deliverables based.
  - We are planning or collecting performance information at too fine a level of detail.
  - We plan one way and manage another way.
    - Chapters 8 and 14.

18.13　Priorities

- ❑ We always seem to be in a panic about one thing or another on our projects.
- ❑ It sure would be nice for the team to have correct and meaningful deadlines toward which to work.
- ❑ Our projects suffer from *rush and stop*—it's very bad for morale!
- ❑ Decisions are hard to get on time; they hold up every project we have!
  - ◆ Priorities and expectations are not managed.
  - ◆ The plan is unclear.
  - ◆ Detailed planning is not on a far horizon.
  - ◆ There is no connection between the plan and what we do.
    - ❖ Chapters 8 and 14.

18.14　Uncertainty and Risk

- ❑ The client keeps changing the specifications for parts of the project; we waste a lot of time, as a result, and it makes planning a complete waste of time.
- ❑ Management demands estimates on items for which we can hardly even guess.
- ❑ Producing estimates around here is like sharpening the axe for your own execution!
- ❑ My boss keeps saying, "I won't hold you to the estimate." I don't think he knows what those words mean!
- ❑ Our projects are so leading edge that it is impossible to estimate what they will cost or how long they will take.
- ❑ We have a double standard on our projects: our client's estimates are allowed to be wrong, and ours are not.
- ❑ There are so many variables that it is impossible to estimate accurately.
- ❑ We prepare estimates, but they are always discounted or reduced by the client, so we have to artificially inflate them from the beginning.
- ❑ I always hide contingency, so nobody can take it away!
- ❑ Range estimating is OK in theory, but clients and management always expect a single-figure estimate.
- ❑ How can I get the client or management to understand that there are risks on this project?
- ❑ You made me produce range estimates; now how do I get them to work in a real project schedule and control estimate?

- How do I get my client engaged in the real risk and uncertainty in this project?
- Hidden contingencies are hard to manage—how can we get them in the open without having them taken away?
- When something goes wrong on our projects, there's always someone who says we should have known!
- How do we avoid panic when something unexpected happens on our project?
- There are some events that could happen and, if they do, they will kill this project. How do we avoid them?
- How do we pick the right contractor or supplier?
  - ◆ Corporate policy and style seem to be anti-risk and deny uncertainty.
  - ◆ No risk identification or management on the project.
    - ❖ Chapter 9.

18.15 Suppliers and Contractual Arrangements

- What type of contract should we use?
- How do we know that we are getting the best value for our money?
- It's hard to know what pieces of the project should be bundled together in a contract.
- We seem to struggle with what should be outsourced and what we should be doing in-house.
- We have to continuously chase our contractors and suppliers to get them to deliver on time.
- Too many of our contracts seem to be plagued with change orders and claims for additional payment.
- Once we have awarded a contract, the contractor seems to lose interest in our project.
- There's never enough time to write careful and detailed specifications for our suppliers and contractors.
- We keep getting asked to change our specifications to suit the supplier's needs, rather than those of our project.
- Alternatives are included by bidders in their proposals—how do we know that they are equivalent to what we specified?
  - ◆ Wrong contracting strategy.
  - ◆ Contracting and purchasing out of control of project team.
  - ◆ Corporate policy on how outside services are acquired is fixed and cannot respond to project needs.
    - ❖ Chapter 11.

18.16 Concurrent Work and Design, Cross-Functional Teams

- ❏ How can we take advantage of the rest of the team's knowledge when there is not enough time for all of our normal project activities?
- ❏ We keep recycling information, specifications, and other project deliverables because someone is not happy with the product.
- ❏ Our team is made up of such diverse functions that it is difficult to get everyone to work together.
- ❏ The corporate culture will not allow us to do things the way this book says we should.
- ❏ We struggle to get people from competing departments to work on this project.
- ❏ There are so many hidden agendas that we keep losing direction for our project.
- ❏ Who has to conform to which organization's culture when we have more than one organization involved in a project?
- ❏ I do not get the right information for my job half the time.
- ❏ We end up reworking things because we had the wrong instructions in the beginning.
  - ◆ Communication breakdown.
  - ◆ Ineffective teamwork.
  - ◆ No team planning.
  - ◆ Lack of ownership of the project plan.
  - ◆ Unrealistic schedule.
  - ◆ Contract strategy not in line with project needs.
    - ❖ Chapters 8, 10, 11, 12.

18.17 The Responsibility Gap and Communication

- ❏ Some people never seem to know what's happening.
- ❏ There's a lot of useless information floating around—how do we know what's important?
- ❏ There's often confusion about who is responsible for what on our projects.
- ❏ We do not always know with whom we have to coordinate.
- ❏ Sometimes communication seriously breaks down, despite the best efforts of the team.
- ❏ We're sometimes not told about things that affect our work.

❑ It's difficult to keep everyone informed about every detail on the project.
  ◆ Communication breakdown.
  ◆ Incorrectly structured team.
  ◆ Inadequate planning tools and poor communication of intent.
  ◆ Other priorities seemingly more important to team members.
  ◆ Lack of motivation.
    ❖ Sections 1.7, 2.1, 2.4, 2.5, 3.4, 4.3; Chapter 5; Sections 6.6 and 7.7; Chapters 10 and 12.

18.18   Project Organizations

❑ Things don't get done sometimes, because the person who was assigned to do it didn't know it was needed or even that she was supposed to do it.
❑ Organization charts on our projects are meaningless because:
  — they are always out of date
  — they do not reflect what's really happening
  — the project is too small
  — the project is too large
  — everything changes too quickly.
❑ We work in a matrix organization, and it doesn't seem to help our project.
❑ We get pulled from one project to another, never knowing which is more important.
  ◆ Wrong organizational model—probably too rigid.
  ◆ Lack of tribalism.
  ◆ Unmanaged priorities.
  ◆ Missing program management.
  ◆ Project management office needed.
    ❖ Chapters 10 and 12.

18.19   Managing Expectations

❑ We'll know if we're on time and within budget when we're done.
❑ The client is not happy with the project, but now it's too late to do anything about it.
❑ The client always expects more than we contracted to deliver.
❑ What we thought needed to be done is different from what others expected.
❑ We have creeping change on our projects.

- The project keeps growing.
- Every time we think we are finished, there seems to be something else needed.
- We cannot get paid for changes or extras.
- We seem to have to pay more every time we sneeze on this project!
    - Expectations not managed.
    - Communications breakdown.
        - Sections 4.1, 5.1, 5.10, 6.7; Chapter 7; Sections 8.3, 8.5, 9.1, 9.8, 10.8; Chapter 12; Sections 14.8, 14.9, 15.2, 15.3, 15.6.

18.20 Effective Project Controls

- Sometimes it's unclear who is supposed to do what on the project.
- How do we know what is a real extra to our project or contract and what is not?
- Our budget overruns regularly.
- We are often late on projects.
- It's hard to define our projects.
- Where do we get reliable data?
- Whoever prepared this estimate was an optimist.
- The estimate bears no direct relationship to what we're doing.
- We need to rework the estimate to allow us to control against it.
- We have a pretty schedule, but the activities are different from the detail that we need to manage our work.
- How do we know when an activity is finished?
- It's hard to tell where we are with activities in progress.
- When things change, the schedule is not updated in time to be useful.
- We only seem to use scheduling to impress the client and explain why we're late!
- We've spent years developing corporate standards for our specifications, yet most of our suppliers and contractors ask for approval of something a bit different.
    - Project not in control, or plan was way out of line with reality.
        - Chapters 8, 14, 15.

18.21 Trust

- It's only after we award the contract that the supplier suggests cost-saving ideas.
- I suspect that the supplier's incentive for offering alternatives to what we asked is that he wants to make more money—so we're probably not going to get full value if we accept the proposal.

- Others claim to do things at lower cost or faster than we do—is this just an accounting issue?
- The field/manufacturing people always make a mountain out of a molehill when it comes to building what we need.
- Life would be simpler if people could follow simple instructions, especially when we go to so much trouble to get them clearly defined.
- Why do designers not learn how things are built?
  - Ineffective team.
  - Lack of trust and tribalism.
  - Inadequate cross-functional communication.
    - Chapter 4 (especially Sections 4.2.2, 4.2.3, 4.2.5, and 4.3); Sections 5.4, 5.6, 5.9, 5.10, 10.2; Chapter 12; Section 14.2.

18.22 Oops!

- If we'd read this contract properly, we would never have signed it.
- How do I know I'm getting the best value for money?
- What type of contract do I need to use?
- What happens if something goes wrong?
  - Contracting strategy not thought through holistically.
  - Contractor not part of team.
    - Chapter 11 (and maybe Chapter 12 too?).

BIBLIOGRAPHY

General

Ackoff, Russel L. 1999. *Ackoff's Best: His Classic Writings on Management*. John Wiley & Sons.

Badiru, A. S. Pulat. 1994. *Comprehensive Project Management*. Prentice Hall.

Barrier, D., and B. Paulson. 1992. *Professional Construction Management*, 3d ed. McGraw-Hill.

Cleland, D. I. 1997. *Field Guide to Project Management*. Van Nostrand Reinhold.

DeWeaver, M. F., and L. C. Gillespie. 1997. *Real-World Project Management*. Quality Resources.

Farkas, C., and P. De Backer. 1996. *Maximum Leadership*. Henry Holt & Co.

Goldsmith, Larry. 1997. Approaches Towards Effective Project Management, Project Management Maturity Model. *Proceedings of the 28th Annual Project Management Institute 1997 Seminars & Symposium*. Upper Darby, PA: Project Management Institute, 49–54.

Graham, R. 1989. *Project Management, as If People Mattered*. Primavera Press.

Gupta, R., and N. Stone. 1996. *Managerial Excellence*. McGraw-Hill, Inc.

Hartman, Francis. 1997. Trends and Improvements: Looking Beyond Modern Project Management. *Proceedings of the 28th Annual Project Management Institute 1997 Seminars & Symposium*. Upper Darby, PA: Project Management Institute.

Herbsleb, James, David Zubrow, Dennis Goldenson, Will Hayes, and Mark Paulk. 1997. Software Quality and the Capability Model. *Communications of the ACM* 40 (6): 31.

Hesselbein, F., M. Goldsmith, and R. Beckhard, eds. 1996. *The Leader of the Future*. Jossey-Bass Inc., Publishers.

Ibbs, William, and Young-Hoon Kwak. 1997. *The Benefits of Project Management: Financial and Organizational Rewards to Corporations*. Project Management Institute Educational Foundation.

Ireland, L. W. 1992. *Quality Management for Projects & Programs*. Project Management Institute.

Juran, J. M. 1994. *Managerial Breakthrough*. McGraw-Hill, Inc.

Kerzner, Harold. 1996. The Growth and Maturity of Modern Project Management. *Proceedings of the 27th Annual Project Management Institute 1996 Seminars & Symposium*. Upper Darby, PA: Project Management Institute.

———. 1997. *Project Management: A Systems Approach to Planning, Scheduling and Controlling*, 6th ed. Van Nostrand Reinhold.

Kimmons, R. L., and J. H. Loweree. 1989. *Project Management: A Reference for Professionals*. Marcel Dekker, Inc.

Kliem, R. L., K. L. Robertson, and I. S. Ludin. 1997. *Project Management Methodology*. Marcel Dekker, Inc.

Labovitz, George, and Victor Rosansky. 1997. *The Power of Alignment*. New York: John Wiley and Sons.

Leavitt, J. S., and P. C. Nunn. 1994. *Total Quality Through Project Management*. McGraw-Hill, Inc.

Lewis, J. P. 1993. *Project Manager's Desk Reference*. Irwin Professional Publishing.

Lientz, B. P., and K. P. Ross. 1995. *Project Management for the 21st Century*. Academic Press.

Meredith, J. R., and S. J. Mantel, Jr. 1994. *Project Management: A Managerial Approach*, 3d ed. New York: John Wiley & Sons.

O'Connell, F. 1996. *How to Run Successful Projects*, 2d ed. Prentice Hall Prof. Tech Reference (PTR) Group.

Pfeffer, J. 1996. *Competitive Advantage through People*. McGraw-Hill, Inc.

Pinto, Jeffrey K. 1994. *Successful Information Systems Implementation: The Human Side*. Upper Darby, PA: Project Management Institute.

PMI Standards Committee. 1996. *A Guide to the Project Management Body of Knowledge*. Upper Darby, PA: Project Management Institute.

Remy, Ron. 1997. Adding Focus to Improvement Efforts with PM³. *PM Network* (July).

Rosenau, M. D. 1992. *Successful Project Management*, 2d ed. Van Nostrand Reinhold.

Toney, Frank, and Ray Powers. 1997. *Best Practices of Project Management Groups in Large Functional Organizations*. Upper Darby, PA: Project Management Insitute.

Verma, V. K. 1996. *Human Resource Skills for the Project Manager*, vol. 2. Upper Darby, PA: Project Management Institute.

Whitten, N. 1995. *Becoming an Indispensable Employee in a Disposable World*. Prentice Hall: 1995.

Chapter 1   Introduction to SMART Management

Cohen, D. J., and J. Kuehn. 1997. Value Added Project Management: Doing the Project Right Is Not Enough. *Proceedings of the 28th Annual Project Management Institute 1997 Seminars & Symposium*. Upper Darby, PA: Project Management Institute, 915–20.

Dorf, R. C., ed. 1998. *The Handbook of Technology Management*. Boca Raton, FL: CRC Inc. Publications.

Fangel, M. Comment: 1993. The Broadening of Project Management. *International Journal of Project Management* 11 (2): 72.

Frame, D. J. 1994. *The New Project Management*. Jossey-Bass Inc., Publishers.

Hartman, F. 1995a. A Case Study of the Application of Self-Managing Project Team Principles. *Proceedings of the 26th Annual Project Management Institute 1995 Seminars & Symposium*. Upper Darby, PA: Project Management Institute, 290–98.

———. 1995b. *The Definition of a Mature and Complete Megascience Project Proposal*. Paris France: OECD.

———. 1995c. Self-Managing Projects: Addressing the Realities of Today's Projects. *Proceedings of the Frontiers in Project Management Conference and Exhibition*.

———. 1996. Innovation in Project Management: Using Industry as the Testing Laboratory. *Proceedings of the IRNOP Conference on Aspects of Society and Business Organized by Project*, 49–59.

———. 1997. SMART Project Management. *Proceedings Construction and Engineering Leadership Conference*, 104–15.

Hartman, F., A. Ilincuta, and E. Vindevoghel. 1997. Who Will Change the Diapers? *Proceedings of the 28th Annual Project Management Institute 1997 Seminars & Symposium.* Upper Darby, PA: Project Management Institute, 947–51.

Kiernan, M. 1995. *Get Innovative or Dead.* Vancouver, Toronto: Douglas & McIntyre.

Lundin, R., and C. Midler, eds. 1998. *Projects as Arenas for Renewal and Learning Processes.* Kluwer Academic Publishers, European Union.

Thamhain, H. 1995. Designing Modern Project Management Systems for a Radically Changing World. *Project Management Journal* 25 (4): 6–7.

Turner, R. 1994. Project Management: Future Developments for the Short and Medium Term. Editorial. *International Journal of Project Management* 12 (1): 3–4.

Chapter 2   Understanding Success and Failure

Gilbreath, R. D. 1996. *Winning at Project Management: What Works, What Fails and Why.* New York: John Wiley & Sons, Inc.

Hartman, F., and R. Ashrafi. 1996. Failed Successes and Successful Failures. *Proceedings of the 27th Annual Project Management Institute 1996 Seminars & Symposium.* Upper Darby, PA: Project Management Institute, 907–11.

Kanabar, V. 1997. *Project Risk Management: A Step-by-Step Guide to Reducing Project Risk.* Copley Publishing Group.

Morris, P. 1994. *The Management of Projects.* Thomas Telford.

Pinto, J., and D. Slevin. 1988. Critical Success Factors Across the Project Life Cycle. *Project Management Journal* 19 (3): 67–75.

Verma, V. K. 1995. *Organizing Projects for Success: The Human Aspects of Project Management,* vol. 1. Upper Darby, PA: Project Management Institute.

Chapter 3   Strategically Managed Projects

Ashrafi, R., and F. Hartman. 1996. Setting Priorities and Identifying Critical Success Factors at the Early Stages of a Project. *Proceedings 1996 Annual Conference of the Canadian Society for Civil Engineering,* 392–401.

Bartmess, A., and K. Cerny. 1996. Building Competitive Advantage through a Global Network of Capabilities. *IEEE Engineering Management Review* (Summer): 29–42.

Cleland, D. I. 1994. *Project Management: Strategic Design and Implementation.* McGraw-Hill, Inc.

———. 1997. The Strategic Pathway of Project Management. *Proceedings of the 28th Annual Project Management Institute 1997 Seminars & Symposium.* Upper Darby, PA: Project Management Institute, 519–23.

Dinsmore, P. C. 1993. *The AMA Handbook of Project Management.* Amacom Books, A Division of AMA.

Frame, D. J. 1995. *Managing Projects in Organizations,* 2d ed. Jossey-Bass Inc., Publishers.

Hartman, F. 1995. *The Definition of a Mature and Complete Megascience Project Proposal.* Paris, France: OECD Megascience Forum.

Miller, B. 1997. Linking Corporate Strategy to the Selection of IT Projects. *Proceedings of the 28th Annual Project Management Institute 1997 Seminars & Symposium.* Upper Darby, PA: Project Management Institute, 803–07.

Pinto, J. K., and O. P. Kharabanda. 1995. *Successful Project Managers: Leading Your Team to Success.* New York: John Wiley & Sons Inc.

Pinto, J. K., ed. 1998. *Project Management Handbook.* San Francisco: Jossey-Bass Publishers.

Smith, L. A., H. Smith, and A. Niederhoffer. 1997. Project Management 2000: The New Behaviours. *Proceedings of the 28th Annual Project Management Institute 1997 Seminars & Symposium.* Upper Darby, PA: Project Management Institute, 442–46.

Turner, R., K. V. Grude, and L. Thurloway, eds. 1996. *The Project Manager as Change Agent*. London: McGraw Hill.

Zaas, B. M., and M. M. Geaney. 1997. A New Era of Program Management Steering Systems Integration Solutions With Next Generation Management. *Proceedings of the 28th Annual Project Management Institute 1997 Seminars & Symposium*. Upper Darby, PA: Project Management Institute, 667–75.

Chapter 4 Alignment

Griffith, A., and E. Gibson. 1995. Project Communication and Alignment During the Pre-Project Planning. *Proceedings of the 26th Annual Project Management Institute 1995 Seminars & Symposium*. Upper Darby, PA: Project Management Institute, 76–83.

Griffith, A. F., and E. Gibson. 1997. Alignment of Cross-Functional Teams During Pre-Project Planning. *Proceedings of the 28th Annual Project Management Institute 1997 Seminars & Symposium*. Upper Darby, PA: Project Management Institute, 194–99.

Henderson, J. C., and J. Sifonis. 1992. *Strategic Alignment: A Model for Organizational Transformation through Information Technology, in Transforming Organizations*, edited by T.A. Kochman and M. Useem. Oxford UP.

Chapter 5 Regenerative Work Environment

Cahoon, A., and J. Rowney. 1996. Discussion on Work in Progress, University of Calgary.

Capowski, G. 1996. Managing Diversity. *Management Review* (June): 85–86.

Fitz-enz, J. 1997. *The 8 Practices of Exceptional Companies*. Amacom, A Division of AMA.

Price, S. M., and R. Mangin. 1997. Project Horizons: A Perspective for Project Management in the Twenty-First Century. *Proceedings of the 28th Annual Project Management Institute 1997 Seminars & Symposium*. Upper Darby, PA: Project Management Institute, 545–50.

Stewart, T. A. 1997. The Corporate Jungle Spawns a New Species: The Project Manager. *Fortune* (July 10): 179–80.

Van Oech, Roger. 1990. *A Whack on the Side of the Head*. Warner Books.

Whiting, K. 1997. Project Management in the Next Century: Engage! *Proceedings of the 28th Annual Project Management Institute 1997 Seminars & Symposium*. Upper Darby, PA: Project Management Institute, 535–40.

Chapter 6 Transition: Managing Change and Uncertainty

Carr, D. K., and H. J. Johansson. 1995. *Best Practices in Reengineering*. McGraw-Hill, Inc.

Hartman, F. 1996. Management of Uncertainty and Portfolio Management. Invited Speaker, Management of Technology Interest Group, Calgary (November).

Kezsbom, D. S. 1997. Making Change a "Constant": Becoming a "Change Master." *Proceedings of the 28th Annual Project Management Institute 1997 Seminars & Symposium*. Upper Darby, PA: Project Management Institute, 1046–049.

Kinni, T. B. 1996. *America's Best*. New York: John Wiley & Sons, Inc.

Laufer, A., and J. Kusek. 1997. Project Surprises—Expecting the Unexpected. *Proceedings of the 28th Annual Project Management Institute 1997 Seminars & Symposium*. Upper Darby, PA: Project Management Institute, 641–45.

Leban, W. V. 1997. Competition Drives Change in Organizational Structure—Functional to Project Matrix. *Proceedings of the 28th Annual Project Management Institute 1997 Seminars & Symposium*. Upper Darby, PA: Project Management Institute, 921–26.

Naisbitt, J., and P. Aburdene. 1990. *Megatrends 2000—Ten New Directions for the 1990's*. New York: Avon Books.

Shtub, A., J. F. Bard, and S. Globerson. 1994. *Project Management: Engineering, Technology and Implementation*. Prentice Hall Prof. Tech Reference (PTR) Group.

Taylor, J., and W. Wacker. 1997. *The 500 Year Delta—What Happens After What Comes Next*. New York: Harper Business Books.

Wagner, S. A., and M. Mercer. 1997. Implementing Project Management: Success into the Next Century Utilizing Change Management Strategies. *Proceedings of the 28th Annual Project Management Institute 1997 Seminars & Symposium*. Upper Darby, PA: Project Management Institute, 706–11.

Wesley, D., and K. Whitefeather. 1996. Making a Positive Difference When Your Organization Is Changing. Available from Internet site at http://www.changecraft.com/Ccbk-3.htm.

Chapter 7   SMART: Putting the Pieces Together

Hartman, F. 1998. Successfully Delivering Chaotic Technology Projects. International Conference on Management of Technology (Feb. 16–20), Orlando, FL.

Thamhain, H. 1995. Best Practices for Controlling Technology-Based Projects According to Plan. *Proceedings of the 26th Annual Project Management Institute 1995 Seminars & Symposium*. Upper Darby, PA: Project Management Institute, 550–59.

Shenhar, A. 1996. Project Management Theory: The Road to Better Practice. *Proceedings of the 27th Annual Project Management Institute 1996 Seminars & Symposium*, 704–09.

Chapter 8   Planning Processes—The Project Charter

Burke, R. 1994. *Project Management: Planning and Control*, 2d ed. New York: John Wiley & Sons, Inc.

Kelley, R. M. 1988. *Planning Techniques (Basic and Advanced)*. Kelley Communication Development.

Kerzner, H., and P. J. Rea. 1997. *Strategic Planning: A Practical Guide for Managers*. Van Nostrand Reinhold.

Knutson, J., and I. Bitz. 1991. *Project Management: How to Plan and Manage a Successful Project*. Amacom Books, A Division of AMA.

Lewis, J. P. 1995. *Project Planning, Scheduling & Control*. Irwin Professional Publishing.

Nelson, B., B. Gill, and S. Spring. 1997. Building on the Stage/Gate: An Enterprise-Wide Architecture for New Product Development. *Proceedings of the 28th Annual Project Management Institute 1997 Seminars & Symposium*. Upper Darby, PA: Project Management Institute, 893–98.

Skimin, W. E. 1997. A Process-Based Model for Project Planning and Management. *Proceedings of the 28th Annual Project Management Institute 1997 Seminars & Symposium*. Upper Darby, PA: Project Management Institute, 994–99.

Chapter 9   Risk Assessment and Management

Chapman, C., and S. Ward. 1997. *Project Risk Management*. New York: John Wiley & Sons.

Grey, S. 1995. *Practical Risk Assessment for Project Management*. New York: John Wiley & Sons.

Hartman, F. 1996. Risk in Project Management. *Proceedings of the Third Annual Project Leadership Conference*, 1–12.

———. 1997. Proactive Risk Management—Myth or Reality? Invited Speaker, IPMA International Symposium on Project Management, Helsinki, Finland (Sept).

Kahkonen, K. 1997. A Framework for Applying Various Project Risk Management Methods and Tools. *Proceedings of the 28th Annual Project Management Institute 1997 Seminars & Symposium*. Upper Darby, PA: Project Management Institute, 988–93.

Kliem, R. J., and I. S. Ludin. 1997. *Reducing Project Risk*. Gower (Ashgate Pub. Co.).

Kolluru, R. S. Bartell, R. Pitblado, and S. Stricoff. 1996. *Risk Assessment and Management Handbook*. McGraw-Hill.

Levine, H. 1995. Risk Management for Dummies: Managing Schedule, Cost and Technical Risk and Uncertainty. *PM Network* (Oct.): 30–32.

———. 1996. Risk Management for Dummies, Part 2, Three Computer-Based Approaches to Schedule Risk Analysis. *PM Network* (April): 11–13.

Norris, C., J. Perry, and P. Simon. 1992. Project Risk Analysis and Management. The Association of Project Managers, UK.

Raftery, J. 1994. *Risk Analysis in Project Management*. London: E & FN Spon.

Wideman, M. R. 1991. *Project & Program Risk Management*. Upper Darby, PA: Project Management Institute.

Chapter 10 Organizations for Projects

Aaron, J. M. 1995. *Managing the Change Process*. Milestone Planning and Research Inc.

Davidson, M. 1996. *The Transformation of Management*. Butterworth-Heinemann.

Head, C. W. 1997. *Beyond Corporate Transformation*. Productivity Press, Inc.

Hesselbein, F., M. Goldsmith, and R. Beckhard, eds. 1997. *The Organization of the Future*. Jossey-Bass Inc. Publishers.

Lindsay, W. M., and J. A. Petrick. 1996. *Total Quality and Organization Development*. CRC Press LLC.

Schneidmuller, J. J. 1997. The Making of a Professional Project Management Organization. *Proceedings of the 28th Annual Project Management Institute 1997 Seminars & Symposium*. Upper Darby, PA: Project Management Institute, 676–81.

Thompson, D. S. 1997. Corporate Pathfinders: The Future of Project Management. *Proceedings of the 28th Annual Project Management Institute 1997 Seminars & Symposium*. Upper Darby, PA: Project Management Institute, 437–41.

Chapter 11 Contracts and Contracting Options

Dozzi, S. P., F. Hartman, N. Tidsbury, and R. Ashrafi. 1996. More Stable Owner-Contractor Relationships. *ASCE Journal of Construction Engineering and Management* 122 (1): 30–35.

Hartman, F. 1994. Reducing or Eliminating Construction Claims by Changing the Contracting Process. *Project Management Journal* 25 (3): 25–31.

Hartman, F., and P. Snelgrove. 1996. Risk Allocation in Lump Sum Contracts: Concept of a Latent Dispute. *ASCE Journal of Construction Engineering and Management* (Sept.): 291–96.

Hartman, F., P. Snelgove, and R. Ashrafi. 1997. Appropriate Risk Allocation in Lump Sum Contracts: Who Should Take What Risks? *ASCE Journal of Construction and Engineering Management* (Dec.).

Jergeas, G., and F. Hartman. 1994. Contractors Construction Claims Avoidance. *AACE Journal of Construction Engineering and Management* 120 (3): 533–60.

Jergeas, G., R. Beekhuizen, and V. L. Herzog. 1997. The Nature and Sources of Disputes in Information Technology Projects. *Proceedings of the 28th Annual Project Management Institute 1997 Seminars & Symposium*. Upper Darby, PA: Project Management Institute, 691–97.

Pedwell, K., F. Hartman, and G. Jergeas. 1996. Project Capital Cost Risks and Contracting Strategies. *Proceedings of the 40th Meeting of the AACE International,* D&RM.3.1–D&R.M.3.5.

Chapter 12   Teamwork

Bennis, W., and P. W. Biederman. 1997. *Organizing Genius.* Addison-Wesley Publishing Co.

Buchholz, S. 1987. *Creating the High Performance Team.* New York: John Wiley & Sons.

Culp, G., and A. Smith. 1992. *Managing People (including Yourself) for Project Success.* Van Nostrand Reinhold.

Darnall, R. W. 1996. *The World's Greatest Project: One Project Team on the Path to Quality.* Upper Darby, PA: Project Management Institute.

Lewis, J. P. 1997. *Team-Based Project Management.* Amacom Books, A division of AMA.

Lipnack, J., and J. Stamps. 1997. *Virtual Teams.* New York: John Wiley & Sons.

Parker, G. M. 1996. *The Handbook of Best Practices for Teams.* HRD Press.

Shonk, J. H. 1996. *Team-Based Organizations.* Irwin Professional Publishing.

Uhlfelder, H. F., ed. 1996. *Team Management.* Pfeiffer and Company.

Verma, V. K. 1997. *Managing the Project Team: The Human Aspect of Project Management,* vol. 3. Upper Darby, PA: Project Management Institute.

Weiss, D. H. 1991. *How to Build High-Performance Teams.* American Management Association.

Wellins, R. S., et al. 1993. *Empowered Teams.* Jossey-Bass Inc.

Zenger, J. 1993. *Leading Teams.* Irwin Professional Publishing.

Chapter 14   Project Control and Metrics

Granot, M. 1997. A Practical Approach to Project Control. *Proceedings of the 28th Annual Project Management Institute 1997 Seminar & Symposium.* Upper Darby, PA: Project Management Institute, 1012–015.

Hartman, F., and G. Jergeas. 1996. Simplifying Project Success Metrics. *AACE Transactions,* PM7.1–PM7.4.

Hegde, S., I. Pal, and K. Rao. 1997. Integrating a Metrics Framework into an Integrated Circuits Development Process. *Proceedings of the 28th Annual Project Management Institute 1997 Seminars & Symposium.* Upper Darby, PA: Project Management Institute, 856–61.

Chapter 15   Administration

Adams, J. R. 1997. *Principles of Project Management.* Upper Darby, PA: Project Management Institute.

Crainer, S., and R. Tate. 1996. *Key Management Ideas.* Pitman Publishing.

Fisk, E. R. 1997. *Construction Project Administration,* 5th ed. Prentice Hall.

Wideman, M. R. 1986. *A Framework for Project & Program Management Integration.* Upper Darby, PA: Project Management Institute.

Chapter 16   Big versus Small Projects—Adapting SMART to Your Work Environment

Ferrell, W. G., and D. Galsworth. 1997. *TQM-based Project Planning.* Chapman & Hall.

Beatty, R. 1997. The Roadrunner Project: Toward World-Class Practices in the Next Century. *Proceedings of the 28th Annual Project Management Institute 1997 Seminars & Symposium.* Upper Darby, PA: Project Management Institute, 879–83.

Graham, R. J., and R. Englund. 1996. Leading the Change to Project Management. *Proceedings of the 27th Annual Project Management Institute 1996 Seminars & Symposium*. Upper Darby, PA: Project Management Institute, 886–90.

Chapter 17   Absolute Performance—A Maturity Model for Projects

Fincher, A., and G. Levin. 1997. Project Management Maturity Model. *Proceedings of the 28th Annual Project Management Institute 1997 Seminars & Symposium*. Upper Darby, PA: Project Management Institute, 1028–035.

Goldsmith, L. 1997. Approaches Towards Effective Project Management. *Proceedings of the 28th Annual Project Management Institute 1997 Seminars & Symposium*. Upper Darby, PA: Project Management Institute, 797–802.

Hartman, F. 1997. Trends and Improvements: Looking Beyond Modern Project Management. *Proceedings of the 28th Annual Project Management Institute Seminars & Symposium*. Upper Darby, PA: Project Management Institute, 398–402.

———. 1998. *Project Management* 4 (1).

Ibbs, C. W., and Y. H. Kwak. 1997. Financial and Organizational Impacts of Project Management. *Proceedings of the 28th Annual Project Management Institute Seminars & Symposium*. Upper Darby, PA: Project Management Institute, 496–500.

Kerzner, H. 1996. The Growth and Maturity of Modern Project Management. *Proceedings of the 27th Annual Project Management Institue Seminars & Symposium*. Upper Darby, PA: Project Management Institute, 697–703.

Lundin, Rolf A., and Anders Soderholm. 1998. Managing the Black Boxes of the Project Environment. In *Project Management Handbook*, edited by J. Pinto. San Francisco: Jossey-Bass Publishers, 41–54.

McCauley, M., and B. Seidman. 1996. Measuring the Revolution: Quantitative Metrics of Project Management Maturity. *Proceedings of the 27th Annual Project Management Institute Seminars & Symposium*. Upper Darby, PA: Project Management Institute, 1000–005.

Remy, Ron. 1997. Adding Focus to Improvement Efforts with PM^3. *PM Network* (July).

Skulmoski, G. 1998. Doctoral Studies Work in Progress, University of Calgary.

INDEX

success   7, 20
   framework for   *See* framework, for success
   probability of   27–28, 47, 50, 106, 136–37,
      140, 156–57, 170, 188, 245
   range of outcomes for   27, 60, 105–08, 115,
      141, 156, 160, 162, 176, 178
   See also contracting, success; failure(s), suc-
      cessful; framework, for success; *and* team's
      success

successful failure(s)   *See* **failure(s), successful**

successful project(s)   **10, 65, 119, 121, 131,
   142–43, 148, 150, 203, 210, 283, 368–69, 379**
   See also project management, successful *and*
      successful project manager(s)

successful project manager(s)   **12, 22, 32, 132**

sunk cost(s)   *See* **cost(s), sunk**

supplier(s)   **63–64, 69, 76, 101, 114, 119, 143,
   145, 169, 187, 189, 207, 222, 226–27, 229,
   231–32, 234, 237–39, 249, 257, 273, 284,
   293, 327, 339, 343–44, 346, 348–49, 351,
   374, 382, 385, 388**

T

tangible conventional risk(s)   *See* **risk(s),
   tangible conventional**

target(s)   **46, 84, 96, 113–16, 122, 152, 156–57,
   168, 173, 179, 182–83, 200–01, 209, 250,
   270, 273, 286–87, 299, 301, 306, 316–17,
   320, 342–43, 365**
   big   27, 110–12, 200
   cost   29, 110, 207, 245–46
   dates   156, 263
   moving   22, 378
   project   111
   small   27, 111, 200
   organization   *See* organization(s), target

team(s)   **46, 68–71, 75–81, 83, 93–96, 110,
   115, 119–20, 128, 139, 146–48, 194–201,
   205–12, 238, 246, 252, 259–63, 268–73, 304,
   314–15, 317, 319–22, 327–29, 350, 355–58,
   370, 372–74, 378, 380–84, 386, 389**
   building   77–78, 95, 143–44, 196, 259, 276
   burn out   76
   culture   95, 305
   dysfunctional   259
   edge-to-edge   247
   effective   6, 79, 95, 143, 193, 199, 239, 257,
      259–60, 263, 273, 276

forming, storming, norming, and performing
   77
   member(s)   19–20, 24, 60, 67–68, 71, 76, 82,
      84, 97, 107, 113, 124–25, 152, 154, 188, 197,
      200, 202, 211–12, 247, 259–61, 263, 268,
      270, 272, 274, 285, 305, 313, 327, 331, 336,
      341, 349, 351, 381, 387
   regenerative   7, 107, 272
   right   53, 247
   project   9, 49, 55, 60, 64, 69–70, 72, 88, 90,
      111–12, 119, 121, 134–36, 140, 143, 146,
      165, 174, 192–93, 195–96, 199–203, 205,
      207, 211, 246, 251, 259, 261, 271–72, 283,
      288, 304, 369, 373, 385
   See also SMART, team(s) *and* team's success

team's success   **247**

technical expertise   **9, 53**

technology   **4, 7–10, 18, 28, 51, 59, 65, 86,
   99–02, 114, 116, 119, 127, 137, 149, 168,
   171, 179, 189, 199, 224, 226–27, 243–44,
   328, 334, 358**

thesaurus   **203**

tools   **3–6, 14–15, 17, 24, 41, 86, 100, 107,
   111–12, 119–21, 124–26, 129, 161–62, 167,
   171, 184, 193, 210–12, 230, 261, 288, 290,
   299–300, 310, 314, 319, 322–23, 332,
   353–55, 359, 363, 368, 373**
   See also aligned, tools, techniques, and
      processes; *and* planning, tools

traditional contract(s)   *See* **contract(s), types
   of, traditional**

tribal culture(s)   **93–95, 203, 211**

tribalism   **79, 93–94, 193, 196, 199, 209, 271,
   273, 295, 359, 387, 389**

troubleshooting flexibility   **48, 54, 84, 87,
   122, 137, 193, 205–06, 227, 248, 265, 269,
   321**

trust   **63, 77, 81, 93, 95–97, 115, 119, 122, 128,
   199, 203, 227, 244, 247–48, 251–52, 272–76,
   374, 382, 389**
   -based contracts   *See* contract(s), types of,
      trust-based
   types of   95–96, 274, 276
      competence   96, 248, 274–75, 330
      emotional   96, 275
      ethical   96, 274
   See also Hartman-Romahn Trust Color Model

U

uncertainty   7, 9, 11, 13, 23–24, 46, 86–87,
100, 103, 106, 108, 111, 146, 154, 159–60,
176, 184, 206, 321, 341, 355, 358–59, 374,
380, 385
See also risk(s)

uncontrollable risk(s)   *See* **risk(s),
uncontrollable**

unit rate contract(s)   *See* **contract(s), unit
rate**

V

value   6, 27, 37, 39–41, 43–44, 51, 73, 112,
120–22, 124–25, 137–38, 140, 148–49, 171,
176, 185, 187–88, 198–99, 214, 224–25, 229,
244, 246, 270, 285, 290, 302, 320, 325–28,
332, 335, 339, 348, 350, 379, 381, 388–89,
392
best   114, 121, 307, 385, 398
design   248–49
perceived   135, 221
See also earned value, and shareholder value

W

WBS   *See* **work breakdown structure (WBS)**

Wall Street motivation theory   62

work breakdown structure (WBS)   14, 121,
203, 383

work environment   75–77, 79, 87–88, 198,
334, 340, 364
regenerative   6, 92, 97, 259
See also fun, at work *and* fun, in the workplace

work packages   207, 231

Upgrade Your
Project Management
Knowledge with First-Class
Publications from PMI

THE ENTER*PRIZE* ORGANIZATION
ORGANIZING SOFTWARE PROJECTS FOR ACCOUNTABILITY AND SUCCESS

Every day project leaders are approached with haunting questions like: *What is the primary reason why projects fail? How technical should managers be? What are the duties of a project management office?* These haunting questions, along with many more, are just a few of the question and answers Whitten discusses in his latest book, *The Enter*Prize *Organization*. This book is for seasoned employees, as well as for those just entering the workforce. From beginning to end, you will recognize familiar ways to define the key project roles and responsibilities, and discover some new ideas in organizing a software project.

ISBN: 1-880410-79-6 (paperback)

A FRAMEWORK FOR PROJECT MANAGEMENT

This complete project management seminar course provides experienced project managers with an easy-to-use set of educational tools to help them deliver a seminar on basic project management concepts, tools, and techniques. *A Framework for Project Management* was developed and designed for seminar leaders by a team of experts within the PMI® membership, and reviewed extensively during its development and piloting stage by a team of PMPs.

ISBN: 1-880410-82-6 (Facilitator's Manual Set)
ISBN: 1-880410-80-X (Participant's Manual Set)

THE PMI PROJECT MANAGEMENT FACT BOOK

A comprehensive resource of information about PMI and the profession it serves. Professionals working in project management require information and resources to function in today's global business environment. Knowledge along with data collection and interpretation are often key to determining success in the marketplace. The Project Management Institute (PMI®) anticipates the needs of the profession with *The PMI Project Management Fact Book*.

ISBN: 1-880410-62-1 (paperback)

PROJECT MANAGEMENT SOFTWARE SURVEY

The PMI® *Project Management Software Survey* offers an efficient way to compare and contrast the capabilities of a wide variety of project management tools. More than two hundred software tools are listed with comprehensive information on systems features; how they perform time analysis, resource analysis, cost analysis, performance analysis, and cost reporting; and how they handle multiple projects, project tracking, charting, and much more. The survey is a valuable tool to help narrow the field when selecting the best project management tools.

ISBN: 1-880410-52-4 (paperback)
ISBN: 1-880410-59-1 (CD-ROM)

THE JUGGLER'S GUIDE
TO MANAGING MULTIPLE PROJECTS

This comprehensive book introduces and explains task-oriented, independent, and interdependent levels of project portfolios. It says that you must first have a strong foundation in time management and priority setting, then introduces the concept of Portfolio Management to time-line multiple projects, determine their resource requirements, and handle emergencies, putting you in charge for possibly the first time in your life!

ISBN: 1-880410-65-6 (paperback)

RECIPES FOR PROJECT SUCCESS

This book is destined to become "the" reference book for beginning project managers, particularly those who like to cook! Practical, logically developed project management concepts are offered in easily understood terms in a lighthearted manner. They are applied to the everyday task of cooking—from simple, single dishes, such as homemade tomato sauce for pasta, made from the bottom up, to increasingly complex dishes or meals for groups that in turn require an understanding of more complex project management terms and techniques. The transition between cooking and project management discussions is smooth, and tidbits of information provided with the recipes are interesting and humorous.

ISBN: 1-880410-58-3 (paperback)

TOOLS AND TIPS FOR TODAY'S PROJECT MANAGER

This guidebook is valuable for understanding project management and performing to quality standards. Includes project management concepts and terms—old and new—that are not only defined but also are explained in much greater detail than you would find in a typical glossary. Also included are tips on handling such seemingly simple everyday tasks as how to say "No" and how to avoid telephone tag. It's a reference you'll want to keep close at hand.

ISBN: 1-880410-61-3 (paperback)

THE FUTURE OF PROJECT MANAGEMENT

The project management profession is going through tremendous change—both evolutionary and revolutionary. Some of these changes are internally driven, while many are externally driven. Here, for the first time, is a composite view of some major trends occurring throughout the world and the implication of them on the profession of project management and on the Project Management Institute. Read the views of the 1998 PMI Research Program Team, a well-respected futurist firm, and other authors. This book represents the beginning of a journey and, through inputs from readers and others, it will continue as a work in progress.

ISBN: 1-880410-71-0 (paperback)

NEW RESOURCES FOR PMP CANDIDATES

The following publications are resources that certification candidates can use to gain information on project management theory, principles, techniques, and procedures.

PMP RESOURCE PACKAGE

Earned Value Project Management
    by Quentin W. Fleming and Joel M. Koppelman

Effective Project Management: How to Plan, Manage, and Deliver Projects on Time and Within Budget
    by Robert K. Wysocki, et al.

A Guide to the Project Management Body of Knowledge (PMBOK® Guide)
    by the PMI Standards Committee

Human Resource Skills for the Project Manager
    by Vijay K. Verma

The New Project Management
    by J. Davidson Frame

Organizing Projects for Success
    by Vijay K. Verma

Principles of Project Management
    by John Adams, et al.

Project & Program Risk Management
    by R. Max Wideman, Editor

Project Management Casebook
    edited by David I. Cleland, et al.

Project Management: A Managerial Approach, Fourth Edition
    by Jack R. Meredith and Samuel J. Mantel Jr.

Project Management: A Systems Approach to Planning, Scheduling, and Controlling, Sixth Edition
    by Harold Kerzner

A GUIDE TO THE PROJECT MANAGEMENT BODY OF KNOWLEDGE (PMBOK® GUIDE)

The basic management reference for everyone who works on projects. Serves as a tool for learning about the generally accepted knowledge and practices of the profession. As "management by projects" becomes more and more a recommended business practice worldwide, the *PMBOK® Guide* becomes an essential source of information that should be on every manager's bookshelf. Available in hardcover or paperback, the *PMBOK® Guide* is an official standards document of the Project Management Institute.

ISBN: 1-880410-12-5 (paperback)
ISBN: 1-880410-13-3 (hardcover)

INTERACTIVE PMBOK® GUIDE

This CD-ROM makes it easy for you to access the valuable information in PMI's *PMBOK® Guide*. Features hypertext links for easy reference—simply click on underlined words in the text, and the software will take you to that particular section in the *PMBOK® Guide*. Minimum system requirements: 486 PC; 8MB RAM; 10MB free disk space; CD-ROM drive, mouse, or other pointing device; and Windows 3.1 or greater.

MANAGING PROJECTS STEP-BY-STEP™

Follow the steps, standards, and procedures used and proven by thousands of professional project managers and leading corporations. This interactive multimedia CD-ROM, based on PMI's *PMBOK® Guide*, will enable you to customize, standardize, and distribute your project plan standards, procedures, and methodology across your entire organization. Multimedia illustrations using 3-D animations and audio make this perfect for both self-paced training or for use by a facilitator.

PMBOK® Q&A

Use this handy pocket-sized question-and-answer study guide to learn more about the key themes and concepts presented in PMI's international standard, *PMBOK® Guide*. More than 160 multiple-choice questions with answers (referenced to the *PMBOK® Guide*) help you with the breadth of knowledge needed to understand key project management concepts.

ISBN: 1-880410-21-4 (paperback)

PMI Proceedings Library CD-ROM

This interactive guide to PMI's annual Seminars & Symposium proceedings offers a powerful new option to the traditional methods of document storage and retrieval, research, training, and technical writing. Contains complete paper presentations from PMI '92–PMI '97 with full-text search capability, convenient onscreen readability, and PC/Mac compatibility.

PMI Publications Library CD-ROM

Using state-of-the-art technology, PMI offers complete articles and information from its major publications on one CD-ROM, including *PM Network* (1990–97), *Project Management Journal* (1990–97), and *A Guide to the Project Management Body of Knowledge*. Offers full-text search capability and indexing by *PMBOK® Guide* knowledge areas. Electronic indexing schemes and sophisticated search engines help to quickly find and retrieve articles that are relevant to your topic or research area.

Also Available from PMI

Project Management for Managers
Mihály Görög, Nigel J. Smith
ISBN: 1-880410-54-0 (paperback)

Project Leadership: From Theory to Practice
Jeffery K. Pinto, Peg Thoms, Jeffrey Trailer, Todd Palmer, Michele Govekar
ISBN: 1-880410-10-9 (paperback)

Annotated Bibliography of Project and Team Management
David I. Cleland, Gary Rafe, Jeffrey Mosher
ISBN: 1-880410-47-8 (paperback)
ISBN: 1-880410-57-5 (CD-ROM)

How to Turn Computer Problems into Competitive Advantage
Tom Ingram
ISBN: 1-880410-08-7 (paperback)

Achieving the Promise of Information Technology
Ralph B. Sackman
ISBN: 1-880410-03-6 (paperback)

Leadership Skills for Project Managers
Editors' Choice Series
Edited by Jeffrey K. Pinto, Jeffrey W. Trailer
ISBN: 1-880410-49-4 (paperback)

The Virtual Edge
Margery Mayer
ISBN: 1-880410-16-8 (paperback)

The ABCs of DPC
Edited by PMI's Design-Procurement-Construction Specific Interest Group
ISBN: 1-880410-07-9 (paperback)

Project Management Casebook
Edited by David I. Cleland, Karen M. Bursic, Richard Puerzer, A. Yaroslav Vlasak
ISBN: 1-880410-45-1 (paperback)

Project Management Casebook Instructor's Manual
Edited by David I. Cleland, Karen M. Bursic, Richard Puerzer, A. Yaroslav Vlasak
ISBN: 1-880410-18-4 (paperback)

The PMI Book of Project Management Forms
ISBN: 1-880410-31-1 (paperback)
ISBN: 1-880410-50-8 (diskette version)

Principles of Project Management
John Adams et al.
ISBN: 1-880410-30-3 (paperback)

Organizing Projects for Success
Human Aspects of Project Management Series, Volume 1
Vijay K. Verma
ISBN: 1-880410-40-0 (paperback)

Human Resource Skills for the Project Manager
Human Aspects of Project Management Series, Volume 2
Vijay K. Verma
ISBN: 1-880410-41-9 (paperback)

Managing the Project Team
Human Aspects of Project Management Series, Volume 3
Vijay K. Verma
ISBN: 1-880410-42-7 (paperback)

Earned Value Project Management
Quentin W. Fleming, Joel M. Koppelman
ISBN: 1-880410-38-9 (paperback)

Value Management Practice
Michel Thiry
ISBN: 1-880410-14-1 (paperback)

Decision Analysis in Projects
John R. Schuyler
ISBN: 1-880410-39-7 (paperback)

The World's Greatest Project
Russell W. Darnall
ISBN: 1-880410-46-X (paperback)

Power & Politics in Project Management
Jeffrey K. Pinto
ISBN: 1-880410-43-5 (paperback)

Best Practices of Project Management Groups in Large Functional Organizations
Frank Toney, Ray Powers
ISBN: 1-880410-05-2 (paperback)

Project Management in Russia
Vladimir I. Voropajev
ISBN: 1-880410-02-8 (paperback)

A Framework for Project and Program Management Integration
R. Max Wideman
ISBN: 1-880410-01-X (paperback)

Quality Management for Projects & Programs
Lewis R. Ireland
ISBN: 1-880410-11-7 (paperback)

Project & Program Risk Management
Edited by R. Max Wideman
ISBN: 1-880410-06-0 (paperback)

Order online at www.pmibookstore.org

Book Ordering Information

Phone: 412.741.6206
Fax: 412.741.0609
Email: pmiorders@abdintl.com

Mail: PMI Publications Fulfillment Center
 PO Box 1020
 Sewickley, Pennsylvania 15143-1020 USA